WHERE

BEAUTY

SURVIVED

Portrait of George Elliott Clarke, October 1965, by William L. Clarke.

WHERE

BEAUTY

SURVIVED

An Africadian Memoir

GEORGE ELLIOTT CLARKE

ALFRED A. KNOPF CANADA

PUBLISHED BY ALFRED A. KNOPF CANADA

Copyright © 2021 George Elliott Clarke

www.penguinrandomhouse.ca

The author has changed the names of some of the individuals in this book, and in some cases modified identifying details to try to preserve anonymity.

Library and Archives Canada Cataloguing in Publication
Title: Where beauty survived : an Africadian memoir / George Elliott Clarke.
Names: Clarke, George Elliott, author.
Identifiers: Canadiana (print) 20210143843 | Canadiana (ebook) 20210149949
| ISBN 9780345812285 (hardcover) | ISBN 9780345812308 (EPUB)
Subjects: LCSH: Clarke, George Elliott—Childhood and youth. | LCSH: Authors, Canadian—Nova Scotia—Halifax—Biography. | LCSH: Authors, Black—Nova Scotia—Halifax—Biography. | CSH: Authors, Canadian (English)—Nova Scotia—Halifax—Biography. | CSH: Black Canadian authors—Nova Scotia—Halifax—Biography. | LCSH: Halifax (N.S.)—Biography. | LCGFT: Autobiographies.
Classification: LCC PS8555.L3748 Z46 2021 | DDC C818/.5409—dc23

Text design: Kate Sinclair
Jacket design: Kate Sinclair
Jacket image: Nettie & Portia White, circa 1930. Courtesy of Sheila White
Map of Nova Scotia © Black Cultural Centre for Nova Scotia
Interior photo of Portia White © Yousuf Karsh
All other interior photos courtesy of the author.

Printed in Canada

10 9 8 7 6 5 4 3 2 1

Penguin
Random House
KNOPF CANADA

For Geraldine Elizabeth Clarke (1939-2000)
& William Lloyd Clarke (1935-2005):
Adepts, Believers, African Baptists.

I want to know how I can bring Beauty.

LOUISE BERNICE HALFE
Burning in This Midnight Dream

But enough. What is all Beauty?

WILLIAM FAULKNER
"Vision in Spring"

Social phenomena are sometimes like the harnessed waters of a mighty river kept in check by the dam of history. When the dam bursts suddenly, it is not history that crumbles into oblivion. No. To the contrary, every drop of that mighty flow resulting from the radical rupture nurtures the soil from which history bursts forth. . . . [The] outcome . . . depends on how far [the people] see and grasp the necessity for change, the necessity to bring about the deep-going transformations demanded by history.

HARDIAL BAINS
Thinking About the Sixties: 1960–1967

CONTENTS

Historic African Nova Scotian Communities

Cape Breton Island

New WaterFord
North Sydney
Whitney Pier
Sydney
Glace Bay

Amherst

Springhill

Trenton
New Glasgow
Antigonish
Monastery
Mulgrave
Upper Big Tracadie
Lincolnville
Sunnyville

Truro

Nova Scotia

Aldershot

Kentville

Middleton
Gibson Woods
Three Miles Plains
ns

Inglewood (Bridgetown)
Cambridge

Delap's Cove
Granville Ferry
Conway
LeQuille
Digby

Jordantown

Weymouth Falls
Acaciaville

Danvers

Southville
Hassett

Greenville
Yarmouth

Birchtown
Shelburne

Liverpool

Halifax

Maroon Hill
Cobequid Road
Cherry Brook
Lake Loon
North Preston
East Preston

Lucasville
Hammonds Plains
Dartmouth

Africville
Beechville
Halifax

Halifax Region

a note on nomenclature

When I was a boy in Nova Scotia, in the early 1960s, the acceptable terms my community used to describe ourselves were either "Negro"—with a majuscule *N*, befitting our dignity, or "Coloured," also oft-capitalized—and for the same reason. By the later 1960s, however, "Black" became the more fashionable and politically advanced descriptor, which caused some conniption, especially for those "Black Nova Scotians" who were part-Caucasian or part-Indigenous (or both), and who deemed themselves "Coloured." Nevertheless, "Black" became *de rigueur*, and it has retained its significance. (However, capitalization of "black" as either noun or adjective is a matter best left, I think, to poetic "feel" rather than political manifesto. I have let my conscience—and the context—determine my inclination.)

By the 1990s, "African-Nova Scotian" began to become the popular denomination, and governments have consecrated it as such. In 1991, I advanced the term "Africadian"—to designate black people arising from the historical communities of Nova Scotia, New Brunswick, and Prince Edward Island, to distinguish our culture and our three-century-long presence from the originally offshore histories and cultures of Black Newcomers. Governments and universities also utilize the term "Indigenous Black" to achieve the same distinction: to recognize that the historical, Africadian population has endured aeons of slavery first and segregation later that merit current attempts at uplift, programs not necessarily required by African-heritage Newcomers.

Untold thousands of Africadians have Indigenous (Cherokee and Mi'kmaq, in my instance) and/or African-American and/or West Indian roots. But what do Africadians call themselves as a down-home slangy dubbing? Simple: "Scotians." (Sometimes written—pronounced—fully as "Nofaskoshans.") And the term may be accidentally more correct than its inventors realize: *Scotia* is Latinized Greek (*skotos*) for *darkness*.

I employ all of the aforementioned epithets at different times throughout the memoir. (The context determines the usage.) But I am, at last, myself: Africadian—and Afro-Métis.* Period.

P.S. I sometimes do not bother with standard, British orthography or grammar. When you happen upon such moments, the apparent "typo" may, in fact, constitute deliberate "error."

---

* Thousands of Africadians are also Afro-Métis—a term that foregrounds our Indigenous heritage. It is not to be confused with the mainly European/Caucasian-derived Métis Nation of Ontario, the Prairies, and British Columbia. We possess our own culture, of which we are—at long last—*proud.*

impetus

Where to begin to chronicle my beginnings? It has to be here—in this dream—from October 2020, which I experienced as I was editing this memoir. I recognized the truth of the dream immediately, and that is why I narrate it here.

In the dream, I'm my current age—sixty, and my father, William Lloyd Clarke, is likely seventy, the age at which he passed away in 2005. I'm standing in the bedroom that he shares with his second wife—I'll call her "Pammy," who is likely sixty-something, and whom I never accepted, liked, or loved, but only tolerated (for I could not see how she could replace my mother, Geraldine). Though Pammy is also deceased, she is alive in my dream, but leaves the marital bedroom so that my father and I can speak. I am standing, waiting for him to apologize, to say that he is sorry for his role in the splitting up of his first—and my birth—family. He is dressed conservatively as usual—a shirt and tie under a V-neck sweater, and he does begin to apologize, saying, "Son"—just as I've wished (forever); and as he relates his regret, I cannot restrain the dam-burst of tears that erupts from my eyes, and I collapse—over the heap of my books, all spread about me, which I know, suddenly, have all been written in yearning for his apology and his acceptance.

nature boy

I was born in the country—in the town of Windsor, Nova Scotia, just a few miles northerly and westerly, of the historical, Africadian (African-Nova Scotian) settlements of Newport Station, Three Mile Plains, and Five Mile Plains, all dubbed collectively Windsor Plains. However, I grew up in the local big city and provincial capital that was Halifax, the unstated capital of all Atlantic Canada.

My parents, William (Bill) and Geraldine (Gerry) Clarke, took my two younger brothers and me for frequent visits to our maternal grandparents in Newport Station—but I was the only sibling with the distinction of being born there. I thought it made me special—in relation to my Halifax-born brethren, namely Bryant (b. 1961) and Billy (b. 1962), for I possessed—in my fairy-tale logic—a princely right to the countryside, while also having a citizen's claim on the city. I felt, as a boy, that I had one foot in Oz, so to speak, and one foot in Batman's Gotham City (if not yet Malcolm X's Harlem), but both locales were mine by practical birthright.

My nanny's pear tree (which seemed always transfigured by lightning) loomed like a lone and stern prophet beside the driveway and in front of the hayfield next door to her home, which was always an oasis of pound cake and bologna and honey-flavoured well water. Raised on margarine in Halifax, I still remember the day that I first tasted butter—in a chicken sandwich—that my granny made for my brothers and me.

Indeed, the word *pantry*, all by itself, brings my granny's kitchen before me, and that table which was always a bounty of plenty good eatin: bread and molasses, salted and vinegar'd, sliced cucumbers from the garden, plus bowls of raspberries, blueberries, blackberries, strawberries, ice creams on occasion, and popcorn and nuts and potato chips; not to mention hash browns and fried bacon, often slathered with green-tomato chow-chow. Even porridge or cold cereal gained from spoonsful of sugar shovelled in or bottles of honey or molasses inverted to release pleasing syrups upon otherwise wan, dull, bland bowls.

Going "up home" to Windsor—to Three Mile Plains and Newport Station—from Halifax, whether by car, train, or bus, was like having Christmas cornucopia visited upon my brothers and me. The "country" really did mean bounty and blessing—even in terms of toys, for our cousin Scoop (whose mother, my Aunt Joan, had moved to Montréal to work) lived with my grandparents, and was always loaded down with games and the like. So, Bryant, Billy, and I loved to "borrow" his boxes of manufactured soldiers and spacecraft, his plastic cowboys and rubber Indians, his bouncing this and peculiar that, to while away the hours while our parents visited, in that—to my child's mind—big house full of knick-knacks and treasures—including a verandah that was always thick with angry, buzzing flies that we three Clarke boys relished killing. How satisfying to smack the plastic-paddle swatter against those insane busybodies and smush those little bugs against the windowpanes!

Having access to that country place made our standard Ginn & Company grade-school readers, depicting Tom, Betty, and Susan (and Flip the dog), seem comfortably real for me, for the characters lived either on a farm or in a partially rural suburb, which resembled the first city residence that I remember: a St. Margaret's Bay Road house with a swamp and shale cliffs and railway tracks behind us, an open field flanking us on one side and a lake on the other, and a stubby, pebbly front yard. I knew of a world, my own home and one not too far from me, where there were horses and cowboys (who flaunted the same tint as orange-pineapple ice cream), chickens scurrying about, hogs snorting and knocking about their pens.

Even though the readers, distributed by a Toronto company, featured blond-and-blonde children, their illustrations of white-picket fences and golden haystacks were not unknown to me. I could see my world as normal, I mean, magical, as following what was laid out in Grimms' Fairy Tales and the Tom/Betty/Susan stories, because the rural was not only imagination for me, but a set of real people and practices.

Furthermore, the painterly images of those early-grade readers, evoking an inviting rural-suburban world, could not seem alien to me because my father conjured up similar scenes in the paintings that he produced on a card table in our dining room. One such work featured an autumn tree, most of its leaves still cladding its limbs, but all blazing daubs of copper, crimson, gold, orange, and ochre. Another piece, *Moonscape*, an oil painting on glass, featuring a yellow-sun-coloured moon, in an indigo sky, overlooking a river streaked—or streaming— white, green, blue, yellow—with black hills in the distance. Central to my childhood imagination was the truth that my father's art—produced at home—hung on a wall in my grandparents' storage room, where they kept items like a baby carriage and which also housed their organ. To see Bill Clarke's art on the Johnson walls (right alongside Warner Sallman's image of a Germanic, blue-eyed Christ) was a ratification of the idea that we—Africadians—could do art—pastoral art—no different than what appeared in the kindergarten-level texts.

My rural-emphasis childhood does not resemble perhaps the usual— if such a thing exists—for Black children cooped up in North American cities and their rental or public housing units. But Africadians differ in this regard, for our ancestors, arriving in Nova Scotia in 1760, 1783, 1796, and during the War of 1812—amounting to some four thousand persons at least—were consigned, as a matter of colonial government policy, the poorest land-allotments possible, so that we would become a low-wage, unskilled lumpenproletariat. And that's exactly what happened. But the unintended result was that our ancestors formed dozens of rural com-munities, anchored by a church, sometimes a school, which became the grounds for our "Scotian" identity. So, even though our families may have been officially—in bureaucratic parlance—"poor," they owned countryside houses and land, and so had access to slaughtered hog and bountiful pears, maybe mackerel and apples, or corn and veal, and so could feel—as I did—wealthy.

I don't know how many of my citified, "Coloured" peers in Halifax had that same sense, and I do know that many were have-nots. However, some of us were blessed with—laid claim to—an alternative measure of *Beauty*. That's why Rocky Jones—Canada's great black radical of the 1960s—loved to hunt deer and fish salmon: He'd grown up on the East Coast with such doings. And my mom's brother, Angus, whom my brothers and I favoured partly because he goes by the name of "Sock"— our Uncle Sock—was a teacher and also a hunter. He became renowned, years later, for his annual "lobster feeds"—where the fine, spooky, marine creature would end up boiled, buttered, and broken open so that we could plane the verdigris "tamale" onto buttered toast: a seri-ous delicacy! (I'm not sure how my uncle came by his—to our children's minds—humorous cognomen. As a boy, I connected Angus to *argyle*, as in argyle-patterned socks, which I believe my uncle favoured back-in-the-day. No matter: nicknames—often richly bizarre—abounded in our Africadian community in my childhood, and they were most often viewed positively—as saying something more pertinent about an individual than the generic, Christian name could.)

To be Africadian is to be—for some of us—partly countrified—right down to wearing plaid jackets and preparing—as my mom's sister, my Aunt Joan, would do—great, big-pot, communal stews of roast beef and boiled cabbage, turnip, carrots, *et cetera*, available to anyone stopping in her doors in Halifax. It also meant—and means—that the map of Nova Scotia can be overlaid with a map of what were once forty-three Black communities, all around the mainland and extending to Cape Breton Island (where West Indian immigrants settled in the early 1900s, arriving there as steel workers and coal miners). This also means that Africadian—or Scotian—identity is partly rooted in the space of one's "homestead" (as opposed to the African-American slang term, "crib"). So, I'm from Three Mile Plains, but someone else is from Weymouth Falls, and another is from North Preston (the largest all-Black community in Canada), and still another is from Gibson Woods or New Glasgow.

Moreover, families are connected with specific locales. The Cromwells and Clements come from Weymouth Falls, just as the Johnsons and the States (short for "from the United States") populate Windsor Plains. How powerful is this sense of rootedness, of landholding, for an otherwise economically marginalized and socially maligned community! We were and are "somebodies" because we had (and have) a homestead and associated church and a "family seat" somewhere in the backs of our minds, no matter what our lived conditions and bitter experiences could be (or often are) among our Euro-Caucasian Nova Scotian neighbours, teachers, bosses, and cops. This fact gives Scotians—Africadians— a firm cultural sensibility and sense of home and belonging.

(I live in Toronto, Canada's largest city, but I'm still the august owner of ¾ of an acre of ant hills, spruce, pine, crab-apple trees, blackberry bushes, on a lot, inherited from my mother, at Three Mile Plains. That fact helps keep me grounded, literally, in my homeland, Nova Scotia, and where I expect to be buried—right beside my mother—when that day arrives.)

The trains streaming by Green Street at Newport Station, making the Railway/Crossing signs clink and blink red; the crab-apples all green and russet (blotchy) easily pulled from trees, the haul of carrots and cucumbers right out the ground, the fearful idea of chickens running around minus their heads: all these facts of country life were my truths, that we could have golden corn, buttered yellow, straight outta my nanny's vegetable garden, was not a preposterous television ad, but constituted real meals.

(There was even a—so we children prayed—haunted house across the road from my mom's parents' house: Pastor Morgan—from Bermuda—had died, and his daughters had gone to the US, so the elements and thieves had broken into the vacant dwelling. I gathered my courage to enter there once, and found a pear tree sprouting through a piano, plus sheet music and broken china scattered across a parlour floor.)

I remember my mom's father, Bob Johnson—a broad-shouldered, exactly chestnut-coloured man, with slick black hair—weighing and slicing bologna in his pantry (which he also operated as the neighbourhood store). A circular saw squealed and screeched as it rounded off whatever number of bologna slices a customer desired, and he'd haul on string descending from a spindle to secure the butcher paper trussing the meat. He had an old-time, Victorian-era cash register, painted silver. You'd press a key and an Old West–style, thick-painted black numeral against a white background would pop up behind a glass enclosure. Who knows when the thing had ceased to have a function? He let us, his daughter Gerry's boys, plunk its keys as if it were a piano. When he needed to figure something out, grandpa would slip a pencil from behind his ear and use as notepaper the cardboard inserts from six-packs or twelve-packs of beer.

If we stayed with him for a week or so in the summer, there was always the excitement of various delivery trucks showing up—such as the ice cream truck, or the fellow bringing chocolate bars and potato chips and candies. A miniature, yellow-coloured banana (sometimes also pink) was always nice to chew—as were the red or black licorice ropes. My mother favoured mint chewing gum and my father liked Bridge Mixture chocolates and Turtles and Turkish Delight and butterscotch-flavoured Life Savers. But such treats were rarities for us kids, for they were reserved for him (likely due to price).

Somewhere around 1967 or so, Bob Johnson set up a roadside canteen, on Highway 1, just down the road—and downhill—from his home. It was really a covered-over roadside stall that he likely constructed himself. Still, it did have working, swivelling barstools—upholstered in red—that I would sit and spin upon, as sophisticated as I could be as a seven-year-old, sucking up Sussex ginger ale or the orange-flavoured soda, Fanta. After the canteen trade folded—due to either lack of business or the onset of senior-level weariness, my grampy—only in his mid-fifties—hauled the whole building (which was only about seven feet high and fourteen feet long and likely ten feet deep)—up Green Street and parked it where it still is—right across the road from his house. Soon, a lady I knew as Aunt Vy moved in, making of the ex-canteen a home, where she stayed for at least two decades. (After she left, the ex-canteen then became a miniature barn for cattle and pigs. Now, the structure is overgrown, and nearer to being a horizontal, rectangular tree or trellis than it is to being a wood-fashioned dwelling.)

Bob Johnson had some letters, and he was very keen, very sharp, and knew how to increase—shrewdly—his capital. The son of George Johnson (a military policeman who was also a church deacon), he was a savvy entrepreneur as well as being a non-stop gypsum quarry miner. That he had cash enough to see his eldest child and daughter and then his youngest son through high school and then into teachers' college says much about his own smarts and pluck in positioning them for future success. (His middle children weren't so immediately lucky. His second daughter, my Aunt Joan, left home as a teen and had a son with a fellow who hobnobbed fatally with mobsters. My grandfather's first-born son, my Uncle David, also left home as a teen, and joined the army. However, my Aunt Joan later became a pioneer—celebrated—social worker in Halifax; my Uncle David became Head of Security at the University of Winnipeg.)

Bob Johnson raised, then sold vegetables and fruits in Halifax; but also spent—fatally for his lungs—too much time under St. Croix's white cliffs of gypsum. Despite his eventual ill-health, he'd walk several miles down to the Newport Station post office to pick up his mail and then return. He could have driven, but I believe that walking was his weekly—if not daily—exercise. My maternal grandfather was scrupulous with money, and so built his own house (still standing), owned the first cars—plural—in his Black community, namely Newport Station, and owned the first TV set in the vicinity, so everyone would have to crowd into his living room to witness the boxing matches and hockey games. And "rassling"!

Throughout Windsor Plains, folks took rassling as a true-to-life battle between Good and Evil, televised straight into their parlours. Viewers wept if the Beast won, if Sweet Daddy Siki lost, if any of that stable went up against a tag team like Danny Kaye and Leo Burke. Next to the African Baptist preachers and NHL hockey legends, the gents who got lionized, who could do no wrong (even if they fought "dirty"), who could walk on water while dancing, skipping, running across the black-and-white, twenty-four-inch-wide TV ring, were the rasslers. When one dude would leap off the rings and belly flop (or pile drive) onto the body of another, my grandmother would clap her hands to her cheeks, and yell, "Oh, how could he do that?!! Why is he poundin on him like that?!!" However, fans loved to see a hero break free of a hammer-lock around his head, a scissor-lock around his head or chest, and then pummel the thuggish lout opposing into Kingdom Come or just out the ring, while parlour viewers or the ring-side audience cheered, jeered, hooted, stamped feet, whistled, clapped, or hurled insults (much as the rasslers would snarl at each other). They weren't mere entertainers; they were deities: Samson and Hercules and Atlas, all sporting trunks and/or leotards rather than togas.

Bob Johnson wasn't—as I recall—attuned to rassling. No: my grand-father preferred films bout cattle rustlin to shows bout futile acrobatics.

He wore overalls or jeans with a wallet in his back pocket that was always chained, I guess, to his belt. He didn't talk very much to my brothers and me; he spat a lot of black phlegm—the result of his gyp-sum quarrying—into the orange-yellow-red leaping flames of his iron wood stove, into which he was always also pushing sticks of kindling. He'd also hum or whistle and, in that, would be joined by his boarder, whom we always knew as old and as the closest being to an African that we'd ever encounter until our teenage years.

The boarder's name was Dickie, which we thought was funny because, as boys, we associated his name with the slang for penis. Yet, we did respect him simply because he was older than ourselves, and was always seemingly happy, an idea that sprang up because he would never speak in complete phrases—let alone sentences: he'd say a couple of words, cackle, slide his eyes from side to side, pick up his pipe and stick some tobacco in it, or just sit in his chair in the kitchen, near the back door, whistling, blowing harmonica, or warbling some old shanty. He resembled the Buddha, but black, and with much less of a belly, but just as stolid, except for his staccato cackling which, for all I knew, bespoke a wisdom that only he could ascertain.

Dickie was a mysterious figure, and never threatening. He was likely mentally slow, and he seemed never to change: a licorice-coloured man, he had a grey moustache and hair (but no beard), big hands, big feet locked in work-boots, and was always decked in denim overalls or jeans. If he didn't have his pipe in his mouth, it was his harmonica. He caused a commotion one day when he led my brothers and I on a foray into the woods, down paths perhaps known only to him, with his strange, ear-scratching cackle and one alder-wood cane from among the many he was always whittling.

When we got back, an hour or so later, the adults—my parents included—were all alarmed. They seemed to know about scary possibilities attending to our lark in the woods that were utterly unguessable for my brothers and me. (Maybe they feared that Dickie would do something to us? Or that he'd get us lost?) Anyway, we were sorry that Dickie got scolded, for we'd simply had a lot of fun, and a bit of a wilderness adventure, and I'd enjoyed finding out more about the forest, since I prided myself on being a Junior Know-It-All. Even though, beyond the very superficial guide of skin colour, I could not have distinguished an Angolan from an Albanian in those days, there was something not-of-this-place about Dickie, something that seemed—at least to three Negro boys—ancient and from overseas.

We were not allowed to enter Dickie's room which was, of course, *his*—that he paid for. But a couple of times, because the door was open, I wandered inside, and noticed that his bedside table was a museum of harmonicas and pipes and tobacco, which was always his scent. But as generally uncommunicative as Dickie was, he was still part and parcel of my maternal relatives' rural scene. A backwoods philosopher in a stocking-cap and a plaid jacket or dungarees, and whose blackness was as natural a presence as was the night and its stars.

Back then, my world was half-imaginary, and that imagination half-peopled by white superheroes and Greco-Roman and Norse gods, their "reality" reinforced by the films I watched, the cartoons and comic books that I consumed, and the children's books that I read. So, though the adults in my life were a palette of colours, Dickie's harmonica-playing, self-directed monologues, and indecipherable stutter, set him apart as practically a wizard. If he'd suddenly sprouted wings and said, "Come on, we's a-gonna fly off somewhere right now," I'd've not been surprised in the slightest.

I need to say more about the rainbow of incarnate hues that I encountered as a boy in that magical space of Windsor Plains. My mom, Gerry, looked white (more about that later) as did her mother, born Jean Croxen. Yet, my mom's sister, my startlingly beautiful and elegant Aunt Joan, is copper-skinned, with wavy black hair. Her first-born son, Scoop, looked white, as did his father. My mom's youngest brother, my Uncle Sock, looks tan-complected, while her other brother, my Uncle Dave, was closer to beige in complexion.

The reason for this array of tints among all Africadians is that we intermixed, not only with European Caucasians, but with Indigenous peoples, namely the Mi'kmaq of Nova Scotia and the American Cherokee who, during the War of 1812, sided with Great Britain and got removed to Nova Scotia, along with Blacks, once they made their way to Royal Navy vessels. Furthermore, because the colonial authorities placed Africadians alongside Mi'kmaq reserves (because we were both refuse peoples as far as the Yankee-and-Dixie-descended slaveholders' government was concerned), there was lots of exchange, of skills and goods and cultural practices (including drumming and basket-weaving), and, naturally, of DNA.

So, my child eyes and mind did not find an automatic discrepancy between the white characters on screens or in schoolbooks and the brown, red, golden, black, and ivory relatives who were all around me and present in any Black community household into which I wandered or chanced to visit. I'll mention here, too, that my dad, Bill, was mahogany in complexion, while his mother, Nettie, was molasses-coloured, and one of his brothers, Gerald, boasts a creamy buff tint.

ii.

I cannot be too nostalgically romantic, however. In that other childhood country place that I inhabited, on the outskirts of Halifax, I was shortly reminded that I could think I was "raceless," but others could disagree. My tutelage in this regard was my introduction to "race"—or, more precisely, racism. That poignant May day—if May it was—likely fell in 1964. The temperature was genteel, the weather gracious, the sunlight gay. On the small plot of a front yard in front of our house, #117 St. Margaret's Bay Road, at Halifax, my two brothers, both only slightly younger than me, were playing at—God knows what, maybe incinerating ants with a magnifying glass or a piece of pop-bottle glass—when our doppelgängers came up the hill towards our home. (It was a two-storey house, fronting on the road and built on a hillside, so that the lower level had a separate apartment and was somewhat smaller than our upper level. My Uncle Sock stayed there at one point, but may have moved after marrying his first wife, a bubbly, gregarious redhead, my Aunt Judy.)

I'd likely seen them before—these three, older white boys—but I'd paid them little heed, except for according them due respect as schoolboys. They were *older*: to my child's mind they were naturally superior to my brothers and me; Bill was still a toddler and Bryant was barely *kindergarten* age.

I can still see those three boys approaching us—coming up the slight hill toward our home—like wraiths. They were, really, spectres of our future—representatives of the white people who would antagonize us—either directly or indirectly—once we were older and bereft of the protections of childhood myths that Good must always triumph over Evil.

So, as the schoolboys came abreast of us, our home, our driveway, they bent and picked up rocks—pebbles, principally—and fired them at our direction. They yelled "Niggers!" as they found the stones and threw them at our trio. I don't think I'd ever heard the word before, though I had a vague sense that it was negative, an "ethnic slur." However, I'd seen enough Saturday morning *Looney Tunes* to know that, when attacked, one must defend oneself. I stooped and picked up stones and flung them back, yelling "Niggers!" too. My use of "niggers" stunned—perplexed—confused the white boys, for I'm pretty sure their fusillade began to wane as they considered the possibility that they also were "niggers." Meanwhile, my brothers now joined in the answering bombardment and a kiddy-level race riot was on.

While my mother taught at one of the still-segregated schools in North Preston, Nova Scotia, Bill Clarke, who worked nights at the train station, loading and unloading sleeping-car train linens and luggage, either en route to Montréal or just arrived therefrom, was at home. He heard the commotion and strode to the front door of our house and shoo'd the projectile-launching yahoos away. When I turned and saw him, looming dark as a thundercloud in our doorway, I sensed that I was in trouble: I knew then that *nigger* was a "bad" word, and I felt I could be smacked about for the infraction. (I deplore corporal punishment; my father did not.) He called us indoors, and I was nervous, thinking that I would be whipped with a belt for having let a word—that I somehow knew instantly was foul—slip my lips. Being the oldest, I could not escape censure, though—*maybe*—my brothers could.

However, in a complete reversal of my fears, our father called my brothers and I together and sat us before a mirror. I can still see our three brown faces looking into the glass. He also un-cupboarded two bowls of sugar—one brown, the other white. He told us to look into the mirror and to take a look at the brown sugar bowl. He explained, "You see that you boys are coloured brown like the brown sugar?" "Yes, Daddy," was our singsong answer. He then went on to say, "Those boys who were throwing rocks at you were coloured white like the white sugar." Three heads nodded in unison; three serious, burnt-sienna faces ogled the mirror. Bill Clarke then intoned, "Some white-sugar people don't like brown-sugar people like us. But don't use that bad word they use."

Thus ended his impromptu, schoolmarm-like, storybook-*sorta* lesson. Did he serve us ice cream afterward—to take the sharp edge off his blunt assertion? Strangely—or not—his favourite dessert was Oreo cookies slathered with vanilla ice cream. He also liked ice cream floats—ginger ale and Neapolitan. (My mom was a devotee of Coca-Cola.) I can't recall such a mollifying gesture. In any event, the stinging, pricking truth of that moment stayed with me—has endured—and rightly so, for the truth of my father's words—his warning—has coloured my life in every way, from choice of books to read to choice of women to love (and be loved by).

Of course, that Mayday was also confusing: my bitter learning about *race* arrived with a sweet, sugar-coating.

Was I four years old? If so, my brothers—Bryant and Billy—were three and two years old respectively. But maybe we were all old enough to register what happened. That we were blackened.

iii.

From my boyhood right up to today, my closest relative has been my Aunt Joan. She is, like my Uncle Sock, the family member who best exemplifies in her looks our normally unspoken, only partly visible, Indigenous heritage. Also, she was very beautiful in her definite copper colour and black curly hair. Due perhaps to "shadeism," i.e. the prejudicial preference, among black and brown people, for a Caucasian appearance rather than a Negro or Indigenous one, my aunt was treated less well by her birth parents than was my light-complected mother. My mom, Gerry, also received special treatment because her right leg was half an inch shorter than her left, resulting in a limp, and so she got chauffeured to school, the tony Windsor Academy. In contrast, I've seen a photo of my aunt, barefoot, standing in the doorway of the local Windsor Plains school, which was segregated at the time. No deluxe treatment for her. She gave birth to her first-born while still unmarried, but realized that she had to leave Nova Scotia for better job possibilities in Montréal, and so left her son with her own parents.

When I was four, I was selected to be the ring bearer for my Aunt Joan's wedding. I did badly want to conduct the role, but I came down with the flu and was thus housebound. How grief-stricken I was. I still remember mourning—maybe in December 1964—that sad sidelining in performing this majestic chore. Instead of quaffing ginger ale and eating cake as if a cartoon blue-blood, I was bed-ridden on a rainy night, taking spoonfuls of Benylin which always—*always*—sent my brothers and me into spasms of upchucking, thus contributing to our misery. (Worse, no matter how much we lobbied our parents that Benylin made us sick—literally—they still spooned it down our throats, with inevitable, reactionary results!)

What I most admired about my Aunt Joan was her great strength, fortitude, smarts, and her refusal to be intimidated by anyone. In her forties, she gained finally a degree in sociology, but she had always been performing the teachings, intuitively, in raising her own children, and assisting other Black and Afro-Métis women. She was that rare combo: a big heart—preparing open-door celebrations for everyone of all backgrounds—but also very tough-minded, able to chastise scoundrels and upbraid rascals, and to scold Caucasian officials—bankers and bureaucrats—into doing the right thing—*or else*. Like my mother and her brother, my Uncle Sock, my aunt champions African-American—Black—culture above all comers.

On a trip to Charlottetown in 1973 or so, my Aunt Joan and my mother stopped in a shopping mall to buy some clothing, and I accompanied. When the white shop clerk tried to follow them around, implying that, along with their Coloured children, they were devious thieves, Joan-and-Gerry became a sisterly tag team that politely, but firmly, urged the clerk to wonder why she should have been born to meet two Black women who would not accept being stereotyped as criminals. Well, that young sales clerk was so flummoxed and ashamed that she turned cherry-pie-pink and then erupted into a geyser of tears. I felt sorry for her, but my aunt and my mom were irrepressibly right when they were right, and possessed so much dignity and hauteur that it's a wonder the Queen never did call them in to take some first-hand and first-class lessons for herself on the etiquette of being indomitable.

For years—annually, on New Year's Day—I had one prayer: "Please, God, make me more like Aunt Joan!" Able to stand ground and talk back; able to be assertive and not care about who says I'm wrong. She'd say "Hot damn!" to affirm a positive, and "Shit damn!" to denounce a negative. Or she'd exclaim, about some misbehaviour or some misdemeanour, "Now, ain't that hellish!" Never would you want to be on the receiving end of her ire. Lawdy, Lawd, no!

Uncle Sock was schooled profoundly in country ways, but also exuded panache, sophistication, suavité. If he wasn't back of the woods hunting, all plaid-jacketed and booted, he was at a soirée, bow-tied, white-ruffle-shirted, black-suited, his shoes way too slick for his feet. He and Gerry both attended teachers' college, but he was the one who emerged with a line for every situation, a limerick for every salon. His library (which he stored at his parents' home) consisted of risqué novels plus Milton's *Paradise Lost*, burlesque "science" jests (one explored metallurgy by fusing a platinum blonde and a copper-haired lady) and Bob Dylan 45s ("Subterranean Homesick Blues" b/w "She Belongs to Me"). Like his father, Bob, Uncle Sock was a natchal-bo'n entrepreneur and builder; like Gerry, he was a teacher; like both his sisters, he esteemed Black culture supremely; yet, he seems to have been the one to whom his father conveyed Indigenous lore about herbs, tree bark, hunting, and trapping. He is one-part Renaissance Man (he built his own house, just like his dad)—carpenter, outdoorsman, Search-and-Rescue volunteer, teacher (retired now), but also one-part Sam & Dave "Soul Man"—a Motown aficionado, stylish, tuxedo'd when needed, helming a Cadillac wherever he's goin ...

At Christmastime, 1965, when I was about to turn six, Uncle Sock loaded up his yellow VW Beetle with gifts intended for the Johnson Xmas tree from the Clarke household. How proud I was to be chosen— or permitted—to accompany my debonair and comical uncle from Halifax up to Newport Station to deliver these goodies. (And maybe pick up an early Xmas gift of my own from my beloved grandparents.) Well, we set out westbound on Highway 1—the Evangeline Trail— put-putting along speedily enough. The engine thrummed and hummed, the exhaust pipe-organ-noised along, and I soon found myself, in the back seat, lulled into a doze. Suddenly, bumped awake, I saw, through the window, as if it were a spacecraft port, the adjacent fir trees revolving, somersaulting: the yellow bug had hit a slick of black ice and my uncle had lost control, and we were tumbling into a ditch. When I regained consciousness, the car was on its curved roof and my uncle was pulling me out from a window. I had only mild cuts and bruises, but it was sad to see that car flipped over, wheels spinning, so reminiscent of a real beetle's legs flailing.

Fortunately, this accident occurred right across the road, in Upper Sackville, from an auto-repair shop. Briskly, a tow was arranged, the car righted, and ourselves put back on the road. Even so, the damage was great enough that we never did make it all the way to Green Street, Newport Station. The engine conked out, in a field, only about a mile or so away, and my grandfather arrived with his big truck to rescue his first-born grandson, his youngest son, and a back seat full of gifts.

That car accident was scary, of course, but it also made me feel kinda hallowed, again, to be connected to the country. Originally, my uncle and I were supposed to return to Halifax. Instead, we had to stay over with his parents, and I enjoyed the sound of wood crackling in the iron stove, the smell of that pine-scent tree all lit up with a fiesta of blue-green-red-yellow-white-purple lights, the colourful bandoliers of paper rings or strings of popcorn, and the drizzly—no, grisly—drapery of tinsel icicles that made the tree hoary with gleam and splash. I now had a story to tell, where I was the "Junior Achiever" of something, which was, well, being tossed about like a garment in a dryer, but emerging none the worse for wear.

When my brothers and I would visit our grandparents, we preferred to play indoors with our cousin Scoop's bottomless inventory of toys, or to sit around comfortably reading comic books and eating nuts, chips, and lapping ice cream, and drinking pop; but Uncle Sock would rouse us up and drive us out into the great outdoors, which I detested for it was a tyranny of bugs. Nor did I welcome inhaling the outhouse reek. (The indoor plumbing seemed reserved for the adults.) So, as much as I liked my humorously nicknamed uncle, he loved to hijack our playtime by getting us to go outside to romp—within the DDT insecticide fog preserving his mother's giant, Leaning Tower sunflow-ers, the dust or hard mud (albeit perfect for dirt "hand-grenades"), the bullish horseflies and the dogfighting mosquitoes, the chickens run-ning crazy—headless or not—and foamy, soapy water gurgling down the ditches running beside the then-unpaved, pothole-acne'd street. There was also the outside chance—literally—of being pummelled by whole-milk-nursed, beefy, wiry but muscular local boys in raggedy shirts and patched pants who didn't need to "like" Haligonian Negroes just because our colorations were similar. No way!

I don't know whether my Uncle Sock was aware of how, by forcing me outdoors, he was exposing my boyhood self to becoming a poor-black-boy's punching bag. But he may have thought—rightly—that my brothers and I needed toughening, and rough-and-tumble sport with dudes whose baseball bats were sawed-off hockey sticks could be just what any doctor would order. Yes, I admit I was fearful of the true-blue Black country kids—the boys—those big bruisers—for I knew that my book smarts and supposedly disarming smile would not get me very far if one or two of them decided to make hash—mincemeat—of me, way too much a "brain" for my own good.

But there was one excellent result bout havin to get my "brown behind" (as my mom would say) outside: I scouted out a bull-run that led from way back behind my grandparents' house down to the Windsor-Halifax-Windsor railway tracks. (I praise God that they still exist, though they're no longer in use). Luckily, I never did encounter any bulls on that path, but it was also a trail of magic—through appled this and hazelnutted that, leading downhill through dew and over spruce needles and anthills, and relatively quick to traverse while also being blessedly hidden. Some older guys—under the low-hanging branches of a pine tree—had set up a scrounged-up car-seat, blankets, and a few pots and dishes, so that they could have a free hangout. I never did lounge in that somewhat secreted camp. But as a teen, it was joyous to sit at the railway track terminus—on a hillside—and scribble verses among the buttercups and wild roses, the tall grass and the humming bees, or to lead a young lady down and along that primrose—or, rather, mayflower—path. Ahem!

Later on, in my teens, Uncle Sock took me along with him into the backwoods of Green Street to chop down right-sized pines to sell at Christmas. I was most definitely an amateur at wielding the axe, but it was fun to be a woodsman for a day (morn to late afternoon), to wander through that already deeply snowed-upon field and woodlot, to yell "Timber!" and step out of the path of a tumbling- down tree, to enjoy a Thermos of coffee and cold sandwiches for lunch, and also to pluck "tea leaves" right out the soil, after clearing away the snow, to suck on for some Red Rose tea-calibre saliva. If I can call myself a backwoods or street-corner intellectual, Uncle Sock is responsible for the first adjective and Bill and Geraldine Clarke for the second.

(Always somewhat a rogue, a roustabout, and a Romeo, Uncle Sock told me, decades later, that he used to go on double dates with Eric "Rick" Trethewey, a Caucasian Windsor Plainsman, then courting a local Africadian woman. Well, after relocating to the US and marrying an African-American bride from Mississippi, Trethewey, himself a poet, sired Natasha, a future Poet Laureate of the United States. I'll speculate that Windsor Plains is a rare principality given that it is the family seat, as it were, of two national [and black] poets laureate for two different countries!)

iv.

Back in those days, one of the most popular television shows in the Maritimes (alongside *Hockey Night in Canada* and Saturday afternoon rassling matches) was *Don Messer's Jubilee.* As a boy who'd twisted to the Beatles' "I Want to Hold Your Hand" at age four, I was no fan of Don Messer and His (Prince Edward) Islanders. City life seemed to demand raucous jive and jumpy rhythms, whereas country music required nasal whining and dreary guitars or annoying yodelling. But my mother's parents loved the music that seemed to represent their workaday lives and the broken hearts born of hard work, hard drink, and hard luck. Their radio was always tuned to AVR—Annapolis Valley Radio—and that meant that Nashville, Tennessee, was kissin cousin to Windsor, Nova Scotia. For sure, the Coloured folks of Hants County, Kings County, Annapolis County, Digby County, Yarmouth County, well, they also liked Patsy Cline, Hank Williams, Jr., and George Jones; and Hank Snow was rumoured to have fathered a Coloured child or two, so closely involved was he with the South Shore Scotian Black community (those descendants of Black Loyalists of 1783 or the Black Refugees of 1812, who made livings as maids and unskilled labourers around Yarmouth, Shelburne, and Liverpool, because they were forbidden the right to fish commercially).

Nanny would sometimes do a little jig in her living room when a particularly winsome song reeled out the radio or the TV. Her brother— my (Great) Uncle Charlie Croxen—had made a living playing fiddle and guitar at shindigs all up and down the Annapolis Valley. His wife, my (Great) Aunt Mousie, sported the satin and spangled shirts of the

Nashville lady stars, and was fully and only a devotee of Country-n-Western. Later on, she led her own bands. (Play one of her songs with an intoxicant in your hand, and tell me that you don't break out in the heartiest, most cathartic tears!) Charley Pride and Ray Charles were big African-American Country stars, but there were a bunch of Scotians—Africadians—for whom Nashville was their go-to music too, either rivalling Motown, Manhattan, and Memphis or displacing em altogether. I can't recall whether Bob Johnson ever blew on a harmonica or played the spoons; but he did like Country-n-Western, of that I'm sure. For one thing, his home was full of calendar pictures that featured a) darling, blonde cowgirls in satin and rhinestone outfits; b) white-painted, wooden churches mirrored in nearby streams; or c) a 100-kilowatt-smile cowboy—or a blond-maned horse (sometimes both)—in the precincts of a chapel.

Africadian culture was never only one type of specifically (stereo-typically) Black cultural interests or practices. Rather, our "blackness" could slide toward Nashville by way of Charlottetown, P.E.I., or tap the Metropolitan Opera by way of Truro, Nova Scotia.

v.

On country weekends, Grampy Bob would have fellas over for cards and beer. The kitchen table would suddenly sprout a Stonehenge of tall beer bottles (no stubbies back then), and the card players and drinking pals would talk up their various antics or buddies' fiascos, all chugging ale, puffing at cigarettes or pipes, and eyeing, poker-faced, a hand of cards. He would sit in his suspenders, gazing at his lot, and always ruled the party from the head of the table.

The left-overs of these conclaves would be hand-drawn playing cards, utilizing the grey cardboard dividers found in twelve-beer cartons. The players' voices were gruff, huffing or literally puffing. I don't recall seeing anyone ever lurch away—sick—from the table, or stagger out the door. Whatever the gravitas of a loss or the glee of triumph, the games were played with cards taut to the chest, lips only pursed for whistling and grunts and smoking nicotine.

Yet, as pleasurably garrulous as the guys' gatherings could be, all of Creation would have to stop in its tracks when my mom, her mom, my Aunt Joan, and other countrified ladies would get together to gossip and sip tea—maybe a little beer too. Then, they'd occupy the kitchen table, and the adult males would be gone—likely banished from the premises. Lemme tell ya, when those three or four or five women got to laughin, their voices were obnoxious screeches, side-splitting hollers, guttural hee-haws, white-noise-scratchy-soundin cackles, just unadulterated, in-yo-eardrums pandemonium. I used to eavesdrop on the women by sitting, out of sight, at the top of the stairs. I had absolutely no idea what they were discussing, but their laughter was full-bodied, awesome, thunderous, even scary. Their tee-hees sounded like tom-toms and their guffaws were kettledrums. What entertainment they gave each other— and what men's and women's reputations were chewed up and spat out, chortled over, rapturously, or spitefully but delightfully degraded. One would have to resurrect Dante and revisit a corner of his Inferno to ever ascertain the comprehensiveness of their damnations. The world was divvied into "bastoods" and "bitches." When they let down their hair, so to speak, well, the gloves came off too, and no adult miscreant escaped their scorn and derision. When nanny laughed, her tongue would slip slightly past her closed lips as she vented rib-shaking, earthy mirth.

One present-participle verb that would come up again and again was the very strange word "runnin." I became an adult before I knew that it meant "sleeping with" or "having sex with." So, Gerry, her sis Joan, and their mother Jean, would expose the secret shenanigans (whether merely suspected or not) of various couples whose official mates were "runnin" other persons, male or female. I don't think it really mattered how careful, circumspect, sly, and/or devious the alleged lovers and philanderers could attempt to be. Once that trio (or more) got hold of a shred of evidence against the purported lovers, well, the suspects got transformed into committed fornicators, and the joy over the ribald tales of their (mis)adventures had all the ladies laughing so hard that tears dissolved into their tea or beer. Not only that, but they were all privy to a community catalogue of definite and likely paternities that had nothing to do with official registers of marriages or births. Of course, all such edification was kept mentally and remembered in communal tales of who was (or had been) "runnin'" whom, with appended lists of real daddies and false daddies, with the children almost never being allowed to know who their actual daddy (or mommy, sometimes) was.

I look back at those moments now, or recall those episodes, as my having been privy to the tales—true, but gossip-gone-epic—that Africadians tell each other. My truest—soundest—poetry still takes inspiration from eavesdropping, from transferring to paper the revelations of womanish griots tellin the real, no matter who be irritated, upset, revolted, dissed. But the best part of such experiences—for me as a boy—was registering that rollicking, hard-core laughter. And the worst part—for me now—is to know that those moments of gossip-sharing might have been the very happiest of my mother's adult life.

vi.

In our father's boyhood in Halifax, how stark things must have seemed. To be off-colour, by being Coloured; and then off-the-radar, by being poor—and thus "invisible" as a citizen, but too "visible" as a Negro.[*] Born in 1935, Bill Clarke had the double-whammy of being born underclass in an underprivileged neighbourhood, during a time of widespread dearth, Depression, hunger, homelessness, and joblessness—"the Dirty Thirties." Although he never spoke about his missing father, his mother's absent husband (and our disappeared, paternal grandfather), Bill Clarke told us often about how he and his siblings had to sleep like playing-card

---

[*] The official, Canuck bureaucratese to designate "People of Colour" is "visible minorities." It's meant to be a neutral descriptor, but what it means truly is that the more melanin that one possesses, the less one "counts"—or matters—as a citizen or voter.

figures, so that one boy's feet were always in the face of his brother; in this fashion, they were able to sleep three to a bed. They would have to hunt down rats—in the barn where he was raised—before being able to go to sleep. He told us about bedding down on straw, on newspapers, about having to make do with soup and gruel. We knew he spent his boyhood on Belle Aire Terrace, an address as far away from Bel Air (Hollywood) as grit is from glitz. (In sorting through Bill's papers after his decease in 2005, I found a photo of a fancy Chevy Bel Air—a 1950s model—parked on Belle Aire Terrace. I think his artist's eye appreciated the poetic incongruity.)

He didn't tell us about having to quit school when he was fifteen; but he did tell us about working as a sign painter's apprentice at that age. Over and over again, he preached the necessity of making an honest living, the honour of labour—at whatever wage. He lectured us about the immorality of criminality (stealing, robbing, thieving, fighting, and fibbing—lying); but he also hated "foul language" and "bad English," which were, for him, all akin to delinquency, or possessing a stunted character.

My father was, in fact, the *Work Ethic* made flesh. Whatever his flaws, he was always a faithful labourer, a trustworthy employee, a polite helper, and his modelling of these behaviours (plus his prayerful attitude as a young man) was meant to impress upon us, his sons— along with the very real threat of his belt coming out of his pants' belt loops to impress its leather against our tan skins—that we must not envy the rich, or crave their bounty, but work hard, obey laws, and strive to improve our lot.

These are perfectly fine civics lessons, of sorts, and they stood him— my father—in good stead. But they were little help to him in appreciating the proclivities of my mother, who grew up in circumstances almost a total opposite to those of the man she'd marry. Far from being poor, Gerry Johnson was born at the end of the Depression, in 1939. She could talk about deprivation too—but only in terms of the World War II rationing of sugar and butter and flour and paper and silk. Otherwise, as a country girl, she enjoyed a cornucopia of fruit, vegetables, poultry, beef-and-milk-and-cream-and-butter (and ice cream), pork, berries and nuts (hazelnuts), all pretty much at her doorstep. And she grew up in a house with a porch and a verandah; nor did she have to share a bed with a sibling.

Thus, my father came from definite poverty, but my mom came from relative prosperity. It's likely hard to reconcile tarpaper shack and silver spoon—even when my mom had relatives who lived in precisely such abodes (with newspapers serving as window coverings) and my father had relatives who boasted silver spoons (and trophies to boot).

But there were other differences too. Gerry was a teacher, specializing in Early Childhood Development. She was always chuffed by her education—I mean, the fact that she was a college graduate, and a trained professional. Indeed, she was one of the few African-Nova Scotian women to have a high-school diploma back then, and, in our minds, that fact granted her distinction. Her Cherokee ancestry (both her parents were descendants of exiles of the War of 1812) gave her black, curly—and sometimes straight—hair, brown eyes, and creamy white skin. Some folks compared her to Elizabeth Taylor, and she thought they were right. She looked white—could pass for white—and, as a boy, I used to think that she was white, but she grew up—and identified and socialized as cheerfully, indelibly, and purely *black*. (My mother's girl role-model was Shirley Temple, and she too was outspokenly preening of her "naturally curly hair." But, in every other way, by every other measure, Gerry was righteously *black*.)

Still, Gerry was part-country: she liked buttered, raisin-bread toast peppered with cinnamon, plus Red Rose orange pekoe tea browned by thick cream; and she loved strawberry shortcake; and strawberries and cream; and pansies—the flowers beloved by farmers' wives.

I reiterate: Gerry was Caucasian in look, but profoundly Coloured in taste: food, fashion, dance moves, speech (when she chose to be funky)— and she liked dark-complected men. (After she divorced my father, her lovers and common-law hubbies were all definitely black—Jamaican,

Nigerian, and Africadian men. Once, one of my junior high teachers, white, asked me to tell Gerry that he'd like her to go out with him for coffee. When I passed along the message to my mother, she put both hands up to her face and hooted and guffawed: "Me and So-and-So?" she laughed raucously—and with a bawdy and satirical undertone.) She rued my teen interest in white girlfriends; she preferred that my dates and love-mates be black, and tried to coax or finagle me into several relationships. She was also ecumenical in reading: she knew her T. S. Eliot and her William Shakespeare, but she delighted in her "Bee-Line" adult novels, so full of sass and free-spirited, "no-holes-barred" fooping (to employ Austin Clarke's euphemism).

My mom had a chum, a woman who worked at a nearby dry cleaner's, who was white—and a brunette—just like Gerry. I don't know why I still remember us chatting with that lady except that her pale skin and dark hair served as a mirror image of my mother's. Maybe I was intrigued by Mary's scent, so redolent of dry-cleaning fluid (ironically, a process invented by an African-American, Thomas L. Jennings, and patented by him in 1821)—which got associated in my mind with Mary's proffered tin of Peek Freans cookies (which possessed a similar sweet-sickly scent), and that made her seem potentially physically sugary—vanilla ice cream in-the-flesh. To top all off, Mary and Gerry both wore bonnets—to ward off rain, I suppose—which added to their resemblance and confirmed for me my mother's equivalent—if not unequivocal—whiteness due to her reflection of Mary's complexion, though Mary was truly white and my mother not (however, I could see no difference then).

My mother was a bourgeois professional by training, and yet, didn't put on airs. She was Windsor Plains in her roots and Windsor Castle in her elegance, but being chic did not contradict being ribald. After her divorce from Bill in 1974, she bought black satin sheets and pillow-cases for her bed, and arranged a helpful mirror overhead (though, as a teen, I couldn't fathom why). She drove a luxury Ford, would sport furs, and a rakish hat. She liked creature comforts, and could be earthy—when she deemed it proper—in her speech. And so, like my Uncle Sock, she modelled for me the joint possibility of intellectual— airy-fairy—engagement, but also taking delight in the salt of the earth and the straight-forward, pungent vinegar of honest lingo.

My father, though he was, for thirty years (1955-85), a railway worker (first toting luggage, next issuing tickets, then selling vacation packages), was also an autodidact, cinephile, painter (artist), racing-car aficionado, and speed-reader of Great Books. Before marrying Gerry in June 1960, he was a motorcyclist (never "biker")—well-acquainted with Times Square, Broadway, Forty-Second Street, Harlem, and Greenwich Village, New York, New York. He liked Puccini, *Playboy*, and Plato—not necessarily in that order. (In his hierarchy, nudes could trump neo-realism, anytime.) My dad was a mahogany-dark man who preferred classical music, spoke polished English, and eschewed the typical, Africadian male stride, which was part-dip, part-glide. He was most directly a fast walker—almost a *race* walker (excuse the pun)—and my brothers and I had no choice but to *run* to keep up with him as he strode purposefully along. (Indeed, his casually capacious stride equalled that of any top-hatted plutocrat twirling jauntily a cane.) He was a black man who grandly refuted every single black-male stereotype but one: he did like white women (which helped trigger his split from my mother).

However, as a boy, I admired greatly this black man who seemed to fearlessly stride into the world, to work unshirkingly at usually two or even three jobs, to be able to joke with bons-vivants and bandy puns and wit with lawyers (who were my father's best friends in later life), to be able to hold forth on likely any entry in the *Encyclopaedia Britannica* (which he also sold), and to show up on the job with a Strauss melody on his lips and a poetry anthology in his lunch-pail. (But he, too, pored over his Bee-Line-brand and other risqué sex-books.) During my 1960s boyhood, Bill also invested in subscriptions to *Popular Science* and *Popular Mechanics* magazines, for he was fascinated by inventions and experiments, including in child-raising (more on that later). And he was an avid punster. (I remember fondly a pun-trading match he had with the novelist Alistair MacLeod, in 2002, for they knew each other and liked each other well.)

My mother was dainty in manner, gracious in style. These attributes were polished and magnified by her because of her locomotive disability: she wore special shoes, pumps with a lift on the right heel, to even out her gait, but never did she have an ordinary step.

To compensate for her ambulatory challenge, she found it helpful to dress extra nice, to be a capital-L Lady, and even to act as if she really did need the charity of others (*à la* Blanche DuBois in Tennessee Williams's *A Streetcar Named Desire*)—especially men. Moreover, she enjoyed being *that* fair-skinned black woman who could walk—no, jiggle (one effect of her step was to set all of her curves in motion)—into a room and make every other woman jealous and turn their men and husbands into fawning swains. She'd wear lace gloves; fascinator hats; black-lace hosiery with floral patterns; and when she had a cane, it was deluxe in make and loud in approach. When she took up smoking, in her mid-thirties, she had an Audrey Hepburn, *Breakfast at Tiffany's* pose, and a cigarette holder that seemed as well poised to spout Latinisms as it did humdrum smoke. She even boasted a beauty spot on her right cheek.

My parents seemed types of the Gershwin line (somewhat amended): "Your daddy's *smart*, and your mama's good-lookin." Except that my mother was her sons' stay-at-home educator through most of the 1960s; *she* was the one with the communicated *smarts*. Also, my father perceived himself as attractive—suave—mocha-chocolate in appearance and silver-tongued in eloquence. (In a photo taken in 1970 or '71, when he was thirty-five or thirty-six, at a Black community picnic, he's descending a hillside in shorts, a tight shirt, and dark sunglasses, and seems to be announcing that he's *way sexy* for all those women with eyes to see.)

Although I was impressed by Bill Clarke's gravitas—his intellect—as a boy, I also saw him as a storybook, stereotypical father: he smelled of Old Spice cologne and would shave with a tub of cream, a brush, and a steel safety razor, and then slap the aftershave on his face when he was done. His shoes were always leather, brogues, I think, and always brown or oxblood in tint. His closet was jammed with suits—seemingly—and his ties were always Windsor-knotted. He was always dapper, and my Uncle Sock says that Bill Clarke taught him how to dress, showed him how to shine his shoes so he could see his face in them, and expounded other haberdashery. How much of this classiness was left over from his motorcyclist-bachelor days, I can't say. But he did sport the 1950s *Father Knows Best* accoutrements: the fedora, the overcoat draped over an arm, the shirt-and-tie, spic-and-span, Civil-Rights-Era Negro male look: JFK lookin like MLK (not the other way around). Never for him the afro: sideburns and an orange-brown-leather coat (which I now own) were his concession to '60s black-radical chic: Le Château, not Harry Rosen. But he was, really, a Tip Top Tailor kind of guy—for the most part: adequately dashing, bourgeois-basic . . .

Bill Clarke was apt to—not grease—but "grit" his palms with Snap Hand Cleaner—a conglomeration of glycerin, lanolin, pumice stone bits, and soap—intended to clear oil and gunk from hard-workin, rough-to-the-touch hands. How beautifully contradictory that his worker hands—*proletarian* mandibles—were also able to wield paint brushes delicately and consummately. I never saw, as a boy, any insurmountable opposition, *per se*, between his being a toiler—a wage-slave, said Marxism—and an artist. He had a copy of a book by Eric Hoffer—the US stevedore-philosopher—in his personal library. (One of my joys, though it occurred a few years after his death in 2005, was my receipt of the Eric Hoffer Book Award for my collection *Blues and Bliss*, a book that also saw my father's art nominated as best cover for a small press poetry book, some fifty-five years after he had painted the surreal pattern at the age of eighteen.)

My father's life suggested that one could be a worker and an artist. That the labour of one's calloused hands and the sweat of one's brow did not rule out access to *Philosophy* and *Beauty*. Moreover, given his humble job of moving linens and luggage from train to train at the

Halifax Canadian National Railway station, I little doubted that he cherished those moments when some white passenger would look at him, incredulously, and say to his "Negro porter," "How is it that you're whistling the Kreutzer Sonata?"

vii.

As a country hick, but city-slicker boy, I believed myself rich. If the statisticians wanted to declare my family "lower-middle-class," they'd be right. But I can tell you that I felt wealthy—maybe like the "Beverly Hillbillies"—because I could go to that "second home" in the country, and have all the apples and roast ham and fried sausages and fresh milk in the world, but could also walk fifteen minutes from my second downtown Halifax home (on Maynard Street) to peep at two movie theatres, both playing two full features, plus cartoons and documentaries, in between, every Saturday, for only 50¢.

Our original city home was a Haligonian country place, west of downtown Halifax, on St. Margaret's Bay Road. It was far enough from the Central Business District that it had a suburban, rural feel. Our house was two storeys, but set on a slope.

Across the street from us, the hill continued to rise toward the sky. The houses located there had wooden stairs or concrete steps that had to make their way to the roadway down some twenty-five or thirty-four feet or more. One of our babysitters lived across the street, in one of those high hillside houses that were lofty enough up to allow one to look over, miles away, to Bedford Basin and Africville, if not upwards at the North Star.

Surely, we were a rare black family in a majority white space, as the accosting of me and my brothers by older white boys will attest. But it was generally pacific and utopic—the autumn trees were floral bouquets; the winter brought clean snow, never dog-dumped-upon; the spring was pussy willows and a molten spring suddenly on Fenerty Road; the summer was a field of spurting grass en route to being hay and

Scotian-gold-and-Ethiopian-black bees hopscotching among dandelion, daisy, and wildflowers. One spring, when I had the mumps, my mother tied a handkerchief around my head—with the bow on top—to hold my cheeks in place. (That was okay by me: I was happy to resemble Bugs Bunny and/or the Easter Bunny.) I was delighted to see my head's rabbit-like shadow bobbing over weeds and pebbles as I wandered, bouncing an India rubber ball, on the path through flowers adjacent to our house.

Due to our near-country position, we could enjoy the overpass of RCAF jets from Shearwater Air Force base, come Dominion Day (July 1). Those roaring engines shook our house and are probably the reason why one of my boyhood heroes ended up being Manfred von Richthofen, the bloody "Red Baron," chief ace of the Great War.

For sure, there was something paradisal about living out on the Bay Road—close to the historical Africadian community of Beechville, but also *not in it*—not "ghettoized" (as my father would have thought, considering that the lack of municipal services was somehow the fault of black residents, rather than a deliberate act of white discounting)—and living among more-or-less, white-collar white folk—with shale and blueberries and a home garden (boasting lettuce heads, cucumbers, and tomatoes) adjacent to our house, along with a field, but also, to the rear, a sewer swamp disguised by bulrushes—like some sluice outta Alice Munro's *Lives of Girls and Women*.

(I once, Pied-Piper-like, led my two brothers into that stinking slough of sludge, and we sloshed some distance away, until my father, who'd fallen asleep—because he worked nights—awoke, came looking for us, swooped us up in his arms and on his shoulders, trudged us back home, and then very royally paddled our behinds—mine above all, for having marched my brothers astray.)

From our countrified space, we could hear the rumble of trains passing on the tracks that ran atop and between the nearby shale cliffs, and it was satisfying to pick bowls of blueberries (so piquant, acerbically sweet, with sugar and milk) and then perch and watch the trains grumble by, or hooting their horns, trundle down to the Halifax South End terminus. The trains were romantic to me because my father worked at the Halifax Canadian National Railway station, a white-painted or white-stone or white-plastered Beaux Arts-style building of Greek columns and Britannia-Rules-the-Waves masthead. So, I believed his job to be heroic, and my first choice of a dream job would have been to be a train engineer. Soon, I became enamoured with the American folk legend Casey Jones and the African-American folk hero John Henry, "born with a hammer in his hand." (Hear Trini Lopez here: "If I Had a Hammer.") Both railroad (or railway in Canuck) heroes were images of my father for me, and the railway connected me as well to Newport Station, Green Street (where my maternal grandparents lived), Windsor, and, the blue-gold-grey shale cliffs of Armdale and Rockingham, Halifax, all the way from Bedford Basin to the South End train terminal. As an older boy, learning of the Underground Railroad escape route for Blacks fleeing enslavement, I really did want to imagine a subterranean train chugging folks from Dixie plantations to North Star–illuminated stations . . . *

The first school that I attended was Clarence A. Beckett Elementary, which, as I recall, had two rooms: the ground floor was Primary; the other class—for grade one—occupied the upper floor. I recall walking to school, sometimes, on my own, aged four to five, going downhill on the slope beside a nearby corner store; but I also recall making the trek sometimes with my Aunt Joan, one hand in hers, the other holding a bookbag (which I considered to be as grown-up and mysterious as a briefcase), and her making sure that I got to school safely and then home again. (School ended at twelve noon). But I loved that walk to the little school (since demolished), which seemed so gigantic to my child

---

* (I'm still ga-ga about trains, and would, if so empowered, restore passenger rail throughout Nova Scotia: Halifax-Yarmouth-Halifax and Halifax-Sydney/Glace Bay-Halifax. I'd do it in a jiffy—and tear out the Windsor Causeway too, to replace it with a bridge, to restore the natural tides of the Avon River at Windsor.)

eyes and legs. In autumn, leaves daubed the brook's surface; in winter, the water gurgled under a see-through (or frosted) ice surface. The lanes near the school smelled robustly of muck in the spring and woodsmoke in the fall and winter. The school and the treed lands around it did seem extensions of Newport Station and the Johnson homestead.

Being the first-born child, I was the first to go to school and the first to do homework, aided by my parents. School attendance was helped along by the fact that my father was painting and drawing, sometimes on weekends, and there was a ready supply of Eberhard-Faber pencils; a fountain pen (that I still own) with an ink-pump lever on the side; a rainbow set of pastels unintended for children, but which became toys, anyway; and even paint brushes and oil paints. I viewed these arty implements as manifest school supplies, right alongside the paperback *Roget's Thesaurus* (which I also still own), not to mention the painter's papers that could also be pressed into service as emergency notepads.

Also, suspended on ledges about the living-room wall at 117 Bay Road were model aircraft (WWII fighters), a motorcycle, and 1930s-style convertibles, the tops down. Each had been meticulously detailed and painted so that plastic looked like metal, and each object looked like it could roar to life in a nanosecond, with chrome wheel-spokes glinting and engines percolating immaculately, no oil or grease to spoil the perfection of the highlighted parts. (It was only after his death in 2005 that I learned, *via* his 1959 *Diary*, that Bill Clarke was so savvy a model-kit builder and finisher that he was hired, as a twenty-four-year-old, to put together some pieces for collectors.) We three boys were forbidden— on pain of death (practically)—to play with those carefully wrought crafts of art.

Anyway, the fact of watching that stern man concentrate on painting a model plane like the Lockheed P-38 Lightning, and then set it upon its mount so that it seemed prepared to go on a Dinky Toy bombing run out to Shearwater Base, encouraged a similar studiousness—or discipline—in myself. Brushes, pens, pastels, pencils, became noble tools, expressive of thought, no less than chalk and blackboard or the alphabet itself, so radically cannibalized anew with each word one reads, a process both festive and violent. To view my father rendering our pet cat and puppy into a painted reality was as magic for me as were the shapes of letters and numbers, the fantasies conjured by reading and the construction and/or demolition logic of arithmetic.

Having a father who seemed committed to making art—for himself, on his own terms, and thus to meticulously articulating the marvel of illustrated observation, it arrived as an unpleasant jolt to me to discover that the school system abided mechanistic restrictions. I recall a Valentine's Day assignment from this era where the teacher bade us five-to-six-year-olds (maybe twenty-five of us) to colour the surface of a cut-out white cardboard heart. We must have had our own coloured pencils as part of our school supplies, for I decided that a red-coloured heart was a tad boring: Why not a pink heart? I scribbled away, feeling very pleased and excited to be drafting a heart different from those of my peers, a pink heart! My pencil laid down the pink field, producing a rosé or blushing—as opposed to bleeding—heart. Devastated was I when the teacher held up my drawing at class's end and lectured my classmates, "This is NOT how one should colour a heart!" I was brain-smote, agonizingly, resolutely dissed. My pink-pencilling had been about expressing my connection to Bill Clarke's seemingly intuitive, spontaneous, and organic painting, but here was an art teacher announcing that strict rules apply; that personal imagination is rebellious.

(I experienced a like comeuppance—even trauma—in a grade 1 art class. The teacher held up—for class ridicule—my elephant cut-out, for it was saddled with a radar dish on its forehead, rockets on its feet, laser beams at its tusks, and an anti-gravity belt. That teacher belonged in a Soviet gulag!)

Xmas 1965 (the Xmas of my car accident with Uncle Sock) is likely the first that I remember. Excited by the approaching flying-reindeer-piloted arrival of Santa Claus to 117 St. Margaret's Bay Road, I wrapped up a toy car (that I'd already received) and set it under our tree, which was already replete with presents. Yessum! But being eager to experience the kaleidoscopic shock of the Xmas tree lights, I got up in the middle of the night, crept out to the living room where the tree was standing dark and majestic, festooned with its tinsel icicles and coloured bulbs, and decided that the best way to engineer the flash and twinkle of lights was to take a kitchen knife and slide it into an outlet. I do truly remember the hum of electricity thrilling through the steel knife, and how I managed to let go of it without being blasted by Reddy Kilowatt (a lightning-bolt-shaped cartoon figure representing Nova Scotia Light and Power), I really can't say. However, the whole moment was entirely surreptitious, and no one awoke to present me with unforgiving corporal punishment (I mean, a thrashing), for having done such a stupid and dangerous thing. It was surely a second sideswipe with potential, horrid injury (to say the least), but inflicted this time by myself, not sleazy highway ice conditions.

(A less dangerous caper resulted from my exercise of my secret power to grab a chair and clamber onto a ledge and then open up the cupboards. One afternoon, desirous of sugar, I made my way into the kitchen treasury and stealthily removed a jar. I then spooned the white sweetness over two slices of margarine-gilded bread to compose what I thought would be a humdinger of a dessert. Once I bit into my confection, I learned that it is possible to have too much of a good thing. Thus, to keep my escapade undiscovered, I had to chomp the whole sandwich, the sugar gritting in my mouth like sand, the bread seeming as dry as sandpaper.)

The Bay Road, that bucolic space where I first learned about "race," is also where I confronted the potential bleakness of the world beyond our front yard: certainly, one of my earliest childhood memories is of the assassination of President John Fitzgerald Kennedy, though I was only 3 and ¾ years old when the event occurred. I'd been napping that Friday, November 22, 1963, when, at 3 p.m. AST, a neighbour woman who sometimes babysat my brothers and me came running up the slope of St. Margaret's Bay Road, screaming, yelling, crying. The commotion woke me. I went to the open front door of our house, where my mother was standing, and I held on to her skirt or dress. I had no idea what our sometime babysitter was shouting, but it was likely something akin to "Kennedy's been shot" or "the president's dead." I recall the scene vividly because it was the first time in my life I saw an adult who was distressed (excepting, of course, on a TV melodrama). The air was gold with the gold of late afternoon and the late-autumn leaves that still clung to the trees across the way or which were falling, winking gold, in the light. Later that day, my father took me in his dark-blue pickup, the radio spitting blue sparks, to the train station.

Along the way, the radio played sombre—CBC-serious—music, with reportage bracketing the classical melodies (which now seemed connected to death, I'm sorry to say). The afternoon remained golden, but with a dark undertone, and, somehow, while the radio imported concerted gloom and imparted acoustic sobriety, Bill Clarke explained the fact of Death to my child self. I don't recall exactly what he said, but he may have referred to the falling leaves as examples of the life cycle and mortality. Whatever his metaphors or allegories, they made sense to my child's mind. There were shadows mingled with the august gold of that late afternoon, and somehow the bright sunlight seemed sombre then. Death became something like gold flaking off of bone. Something like that.

about the "north ender":

a draconian and/or apollonian haligonian

i.

In spring 1966, my parents moved us from 117 St. Margaret's Bay Road to 5847 Cunard Street, close to downtown Halifax. I'm not sure why they decided to leave that comfortable little house on the Bay Road, but maybe it was because the two-room Clarence A. Beckett school could not long suffice educationally. Perhaps, too, my parents were investing in real estate in a neighbourhood that they could afford.

In any event, I recall my father painting our new house number, vertically, on the outside, front-door frame. That house (long replaced by an apartment building) was intended for roomers. Indeed, my parents rented out two or three rooms upstairs and they lived downstairs, with my brothers and I installed in the basement. There was a black payphone in the front hallway—intended for the boarders or renters, who could drop nickels, dimes, quarters, in the proper slots to get an outside line or make a long-distance call. The day that we moved in, I found a hacksaw blade left behind in a bureau; and there was a package of Warfarin rat poison in the bathroom.

Perhaps the dwelling had two bathrooms, one for ourselves and one for the boarders, but I can't say for sure. I do recall that one of the boarders, a young woman, had rented the small, front, upstairs room, which seemed to have just enough space for a single bed, and a TV, and suitcases (I guess) out of which sprawled a profusion of chiffon and cosmetics. I remember only that she was blonde, took a liking to me, and let me watch a TV show in her room, and gave me a hug, and may have called me "Georgy Girl," because it was summer '66, and the Seekers' hit was chart-climbing. I was confused and angry about the song's use of my boy's name, but I was also chuffed to have it hurled, whistling from radios. Our roomer's hug mollified me somewhat—as did the follow-up milkshake she took me to a nearby restaurant to savour.

Another set of boarders represented an introduction to urban destitution—though I didn't know that then. My parents rented one room—maybe two—to a family (just like ours) of five. They were white, working-class, but I remember nothing more about their features or names, only that they smelled of wheat (perhaps porridge). They lived with us some months, and Bryant and Bill and I did play with those of their children who were old enough to chum about with us.

Cunard Street was definitely a rougher neighbourhood than the Bay Road. A beloved tabby cat—a pet given me out there and immortalized in one of my dad's paintings—straggled home mewling, one Saturday morn, its mouth kicked in, teeth kicked out, drooling dismally. Bill Clarke took it to the SPCA—which was just a few doors away from us—to have my pet gassed—"put to sleep." I couldn't believe that someone could be so cruel as to assault my cat so lethally, but the truth was undeniable.

I also received a bitter comeuppance in play. I had a bag of marbles that two older boys on my block coveted. They talked me into shooting marbles, but I was a novice at the game, and had no beginner's luck. Shortly, I was skunked, beaten in the match, and all my marbles dribbled into the older guys' pockets. I whined; I was loudly upset; I felt cheated. My father emerged from our home's back door, researched the commotion, and stated clearly, "You have lost the game, and so you have forfeited the marbles, and there is nothing you can do about it.

You were beaten, fair and square." The older boys sauntered off with the spoils, and I retreated indoors, feeling that I had been tricked, and could not trust any of the local lads, still mainly strangers to me.

I feared that, in moving from the Bay Road to Cunard Street, I'd left behind an Apollonian realm of order and decency (more or less), and now was plunked among draconian Haligonians, these windbreaker-jacketed thugs, kitten-clobberers, and marble-muggers. My best defence was my smile; my next-best defence was my speed-walker's gait; my third-best defence was ensuring that I had elders around—teachers, please—who could help keep me safe—at least in school and on the school grounds. And then I thought to stave off bullies by scribbling short stories in which they starred.

Such was the North End. *Hub of Crime and Home to Deviance*, clucked the newspapers. Assuredly, North End crime stories decorated sensational broadsheets, the scarlet headlines bludgeoning the black newsprint. You could take your pick of horrors . . . A black woman sex- worker would be stabbed—umpteen times—by her white john and left to perish like a dog in the streets. (Her assailant would be convicted of manslaughter and pull a sentence of three years.) Or some stooge of hooch would have his face punched in, the shit beaten outta him. Or some black husband would level a black shotgun at the belly of his black wife and pull the trigger: soon came the crude sloshing and squishing and squelching of blood as cops' sinister, black shoes traipsed up and down a fire-escape. Or two best friends bickering over the favours of a devil-may-care, chain-smoking trollop (on Trollope Street) would duel with meat cleavers until one managed to wallop off the other's head, let dogs snarl and growl over and bite at the pate, roll the body into bushes, and then stroll off with the untroubled lady for a delicious screw.

Given the frequency of such stories, we were all—from the standpoint of the reporters—adult gargoyles and juvenile pickaninnies—delinquents—the vulgar, properly damned—the builders of personal sarcophagi—unless we excelled in sports. And such ingenuity was explained as the result of our terribly primeval flesh, our too-loud, unwheezing churches, our brutal guffaws at altars, our signal, rat-infested shadows. As impossible to titivate as it would be to cleanse the harbour—itself a frank sewer, accepting bouquets of effluvia browning the turquoise tides, so as to turn em streaks and blobs of black.

ii.

Certainly, the immediate consequence of relocating from near-country and near-Northwest Arm West End Halifax Armdale to North End plateau Halifax was the shift in schools. No longer was I the sole Coloured kid among fifty or so pupils at Clarence A. Beckett Elementary in a pocket-forest setting. Now, in spring '66, I was ensconced in a working-class, welfare-income, Warfarin-rat-poison-household-garnish, neighbourhood primary school: Alexandra, namesake of the Princess of Wales, Alexandra of Denmark, whose husband became Edward VII, who was the father of George V and great-grandfather of Elizabeth II. Despite the school's royal cognomen, it was intended to serve the offspring of waged workers, blue-collar and pink-collar, sailors (white-collar or indigo-collar), Blacks (unskilled labour and menial labour), Mi'kmaq, immigrants (Greek, Italian, Finns, Lebanese, a few Indian, a few West Indian), and those considered riffraff, the mob (minuscule-initial *m*), the low-wage, high-crime scum of the gutter rather than the salt of the earth. Indeed, whatever the civic duty of the school in drilling we North Enders in letters and numbers and British history (none other mattered), its socio-economic purpose was to reproduce our class status as dirt-cheap workers and as easy pickings for cadets first and the Navy soon after. (Some lads could end up as grunts and flyboys, but most would become Jack Tars.)

My parents were a constant presence at the school, above and beyond any parent-teacher association meetings, and so the school administration could not ignore the Clarke boys—George, Bryant, and Billy—in terms of making sure that our parents were always aware of how we were doing—or of any *faux pas* of which we were guilty. Certainly, if Bryant or Billy received a strap across their palms in school, dad would be ready to strap them a little extra at home. I never misbehaved, never questioned authority, so I never got strapped. Indeed, my report cards were always gold-star—Apollonian—which meant that Bill Clarke would give me a quarter and a pat on the head, which was a terrific boon because I was elsewise uncertain utterly about his love. Even so, my paternal-approval-seeking scholastic triumphs didn't score me many points with my peers, who dissed me as a nerd, an Oreo ("black" in colour, but "white"-identified internally), a teacher's pet, and/or a lapdog of school authority.

One summer day, I was gifted a quarter—a whole quarter—from a white older man who liked my smile—or something like that. Unfortunately for me, the gift was given in full sight of some three or four other Coloured kids, who insisted that I pass on to them the coveted coin. I refused. Next thing I knew, each of my bare arms (I was wearing a T-shirt) was yanked wide from my body; two kids stripped fallen branches of their bark, and then whipped my arms with the thin, biting, green-core sting of their weapons, raising bright red whelps and stripes and licks. I cried, but I did not relinquish my death grip on the quarter—no finger could be pried loose. No adult appeared to save me from further drubbing; instead, the whipper-snapper kids just got tired of slashing my arms. Soon enough—or not quite soon enough—faced with my implacable will to hold that coin at all costs, they gave up, relinquished my arms, and lurched, dejected, away. But I raced to the corner store with my treasure, to salve my hurts and wounds with various, sugary treats, all just for me.

Being in the North End, attending a rough-and-tumble, workin-class and po-boy school, I had to expect bullying, and it was soon manifest. I did my best to schmooze my way around conflicts and contests and fisticuffs. I wasn't a coward; I just didn't fancy getting smashed to mush by amateur but gifted pugilists. My solution to harassment was to scrawl—in pencil—four-page foolscap tales about the lugs in my classes, transforming em into temporary heroes, even if I let a Tyrannosaurus rex gobble em up or a Martian ray-gun em into puddles. Well, the juvenile ogres loved being celebrated (even if dinosaur-decapitated), and their teasing and threats against me changed to begging for mentions in my stories, which teachers would let me recite to the rapt classroom.

Although fisticuffs were pandemic among our underclass cohort, I think that my brother Billy was the only one of our Clarke trio to throw punches in a scuffle. Maybe I was in grade four by this point. But I do remember that the circle of white and brown faces who gathered around my brother, on this after-school but schoolyard battle, were chanting—strangely, "Get him, Uncle Bill! Get him, Uncle Bill!" I'm ashamed to say that I did not intervene in the fight, not even to ensure that my brother had a "fair" tussle. But I thought that I had to be aloof to any imbroglio—following my father's dicta against "getting into trouble." I think Billy won his grudge-match, but why he acquired the avuncular nickname—one both endearing and disturbing, as if he were an adoptive family member—as a prelude to bloodying the opponent's nose or blacking his eye or puffing his lips, remains very much a mystery.

At 5847 Cunard Street, because the upstairs was reserved for roomers, Bryant and Bill and me kept to the basement. I think we had bunk beds, and we'd make tents out of em by dropping the covers of the upper bed over the side to shroud the lower bunk, which was a great way to turn a drab basement into an otherworldly space. We'd be sent to bed by seven and then be up by seven, to be prepared for school, which meant porridge and oatmeal and porridge and oatmeal, again and again; or, there'd be the surprise luxury of pancakes and bacon and eggs and toast (weekends, most likely), and then we'd be dispatched to Alexandra, all trusted to traverse, without adults, the fifteen-to-twenty minutes needed to get there by 9 a.m.

However, sometime in grade one, when I was seven, our trio kept arriving late to school, no matter how early we left home. I was the leader, so it must have been my fault. Maybe we lollygagged, enjoying the sights and sounds and aromas of our trek. For instance, there was the tang of ale out of the almost-next-door-to-our-home Royal Canadian Legion hall (where ex-soldiers, pensioned, drank themselves into oblivion, while, at the SPCA nearby, unwanted dogs and homeless cats got gassed into offal); the smell of beer out of the Nova Scotia Liquor Commission outlet almost cornering Maynard and Cornwallis (and sometimes we could stop our progress to watch the beer bottle boxes trundle—clinking and clanking—down a gangway of steel rollers into the bowels of the building); a musty smell wafted from the Armoury (due to the mustering of soldiery and their dull, olive-drab, field artillery, oily, greasy, and itchin to make someone bloody); but there was also the window shopping we could do along Gottingen ("Got-a-gun") Street, where we found the pawn shop windows, always curiously boasting instruments—bright brass, shimmering silver—always a cornucopia, a Utopia, of musical pretzels. We'd also ogle the windows of a French pastry shop, whose advertising mascot was the Eiffel Tower, and whose eyeful of sweets promised rapturously humdinger harmonies for the tongue. We'd sidle into the Metropolitan or Woolworth's department stores to study the toys and sports gear, dreaming about what Santa might deliver at Xmas, the Easter Bunny at Easter, or the end-of-school deliver us for summer. (Floorwalkers or managers would sometimes chase us out of their stores because they classed all us Coloured kids as sneakered thieves.) We'd pass trolley buses whose long, upraised-tail-like poles and contact-shoe caps had lost touch with the overhead wires, freezing the vehicle in its tracks and spitting a shower of sparks until the operator would emerge from the cabin and, using another pole, nudge the contact pole back into place.

We'd walk by a legless veteran (of World War II vintage, most likely), who, perched in a wheelchair with a blanket hiding his stumped appendages, would sell pencils from one cup and collect coins in the other. We found mannequins astonishing because the poses and the fashions were—to our boys' eyes—patently comic; but we also discovered, in window-box store displays, that we could stand at the corner where two windows met and create a kaleidoscopic effect for our eyes, arms, and legs, by pressing our faces into that corner, so each eye looked in a different direction simultaneously. Of course, winter gave us snowbanks—skyscraper-high—to tramp among, to jump into and climb upon, to make forts and tunnels and snowballs. Autumn brought leaves to kick or scuff through; rainy weather gave our black raincoats and hoods and boots a wonderful rinsing or dousing, while we could splatter puddles (maybe muddy) over each other or an unsuspecting buddy.

After a spell of these tardy arrivals at school, my father called us together and asked us for an explanation. He couldn't understand why it was that we could be up at seven, but not reach Alexandra until 9 a.m. I gave a lawyerly rationale about not understanding the operation of clock hands. This mealy-mouthed argument prompted Bill Clarke to instruct us all on the meaning of the little hand and the big hand. After that lesson, we knew we could not be late again. Next time, our butts would face corporeal pain unless there was a real reason for our meandering or delayed progress. (I think I received my first wristwatch right about then.)

I don't say we kids were angels; yes, we were mischievous. Without our parents knowing, we'd do things like grab a ride from a bread truck by sitting on its back step, just above the fender. As soon as the driver completed the delivery to a nearby corner store and went round to his van cabin, we'd run and jump and sit on that back step, our little legs swaying as the truck would jerk and swerve. We'd leap off before it could get up to any real speed, but I was likely only six when leading my brothers on this little adventure, and that none of us was grievously hurt was truly a miracle.

However, when I was around the same age, an uncle needed cigarettes, and I was commissioned to run to a drug store—at Cunard and Robie Streets—to pick up the smokes. I know I felt proud to have that responsibility, but I didn't understand car turn signals. So, when I was set to cross Robie Street with the green light, I was either unaware that a car to my left wanted to make a right turn or I presumed blithely that I had the uncontested right-of-way. Well, whatever the cause, I know I started across the street, but didn't make it. I got knocked down by the turning car—and I hit the blacktop hard enough that I blacked out. Next thing I knew, an ambulance had arrived, and two attendants were dragging out a stretcher and asking me to lie on it. But I refused! I wanted to sit up front with them as they turned on the siren and carted me to the hospital Emergency. My request was permitted, and I had the gaiety of arriving at Emergency, truly under my own power, while watching other vehicles pull over to let us go by, our roof-light swirling cherry-red and our siren blasting earth-shatteringly loud.

At the hospital, I simply sat in the visitor's room—after X-rays had been done—to await my father's arrival. Later that day, the woman who'd hit me came to our house to apologize, and explained that she hadn't seen me. My parents murmured that all was fine, and I remember lamenting her mournful guilt I had occasioned—truly accidentally—all this fuss. But maybe I'd also learned something about the power of words: that my boyish interest in sitting almost in the driver's seat of the ambulance—as opposed to being stretched out in the back—had been agreed to by two adult professionals who'd decided that an articulate Coloured boy—despite bumps and cuts to his noggin—should command their acquiescence.

At 5847 Cunard Street, we lived directly opposite the Commons, a public green space that we witnessed being refurbished, in '67, with shrubs, several baseball diamonds (with bleachers), and a central fountain, girded by coloured lights, that shifted the central plume of water all the prismatic shades at night, thus imitating the natural rainbow we could observe during the day, when sunbeams arcing through the spray and mist etched a spectrum against the sky. The Commons was a perfect place for us three boys to play, being so close to home (though we had to cross a boulevard and several lanes of traffic to gambol the sports field and playground). Also, it had two distinct parts: the North Commons was the site of the fountain and the baseball diamonds; the South Commons presented us with public swings, two pools (a shallow one for wading kids, and one for older kids and adult swimmers), an "Egg Pond" (named for its oval shape) which was really a swamp—or slough—out of which Dracula mosquitoes arose in sweeping, Genghis-Khan formations, to spread misery upon any lost souls who lingered there. (In winter, it became a decent public skating rink, and our father would lace up our skates, set us on the ice, and then, on his portable Coleman stove, heat up chocolate for us to slurp.)

From time to time, I'd stand on a slip of stone or concrete that led from the surrounding ground into that smelly, stagnant, oasis of dragonflies and skeeters (and maybe tadpoles), and if I fixed my eyes on one spot on wind-rippled water, I'd have that Einsteinian sensation of moving—*Relativity* in action—as if I were captaining a boat or ship.

Also in '67, a half-dozen or so upright, concrete slabs, resembling figure eights, were installed on the South Commons, and we somehow found ways to clamber atop em, stand on each summit and pretend to be Everest conquerors or dictators. If one happened to fall off one of those Haligonian Stonehenge (or Dr. Seuss-weird) structures, you'd drop six feet down to a concrete surface. If you were wearing T-shirt and shorts, expect bruises and scrapes and cuts and gouges. If no one suffered brain damage or death as a result of leaping from monolith to monolith, then God was looking out for em—and for the City of Halifax (in terms of preventing a blood-transfusing lawsuit).

In our current era of over-protective and over-prescriptive parenting, it is amazing to me that we school kids were permitted so much freedom to run the streets, firing off our cap guns in backwardly racist games of Cowboys and Indians or Yanks vs. Japs, and building forts out of cardboard boxes in vacant lots (being careful to avoid cutting open our knees on the shards of broken glass or planting our feet on the rusty nails poking up everywhere, or encountering outraged canines, baring teeth, growling, racing down a length of leash to try to sink fangs in a juicy leg. We were street-proofed to avoid talking to adult strangers and certainly not to accept candy from them, and to call on other adults or the police if we were suspicious about anyone's intent. But we were not made fearful of others, just careful.

We were cognizant of colour, but I don't remember any nasty instances of name-calling. Maybe because the older Coloured boys could make mincemeat readily of any stupidly braying Caucasian kid. No matter how "prejudiced" (that was the term used; "racist" was a later epithet) a white chum's parents could be, they all knew better than to employ the n-word or anything like it around most of us Negroes. Then again, Bill Clarke gave his trio of boys this piece of redoubtable advice: the best way to deal with a bully is to hit him unexpectedly. To that end, he'd tell us his anecdote of having been badgered and razzed and picked on when he was a boy. He explained to us that, after figuring out the bully's pathway home from school, he grabbed a two-by-four piece of wood, hid behind a corner, and when the bad lad came abreast with him, whacked and walloped the mean kid so sufficiently that his target melted mushily into tears, and that was the end of our father's travails.

Perhaps I adopted my father's slyness—though, as usual, in a less, physically direct manner. In junior high-school, I was plagued by a white youth—twelve or thirteen years old, brawny and big-voiced, who had decided that, being a black nerd, I'd be an easy guy to pick on, and he did make my passage to and from school an ordeal. After several weeks of fear and torment, I prepared a bottle of blue food colouring, and when he stalked me on the school ground one Friday afternoon, I threw it at him, staining half his jacket and half his face blue— much to his blue-mouthed, blue-language astonishment. The following Monday, he threw some vegetable oil at me, but it landed on my wet-look jacket, whose polyurethane coating made the oil easy to wipe off. The tit-for-tat volleys of non-vitriolic "vitriol" concluded, he called a truce which I upheld. Possibly, he had fewer clothes that he could afford to see ruined . . .

iii.

Although my brothers and I were close in age, and although our parents dressed us, from time to time, in identical beanie caps and blazers and pants and shoes (or sneakers), we were not raised to look out for each other; not really. There seemed to be a premium on individualism, which I valued, for I considered it my birthright to be "the first" or "the (favoured) one," and my excelling at school helped to make me (feel) "more deserving" of reward. Moreover, our talents and tastes were different. Bryant and Billy seemed to be closer—though they fought inexorably—to each other than I was to either brother. I wanted my father's regard; that's where my effort went; and sibling unity—or rivalry—didn't enter into that emotional picture. Yet, I was jealous of Bryant because he was genuinely handsome, had athletic prowess (particularly in basketball), was talented in music (taking lessons in drum and recorder, violin and ukulele) and voice, could dance supremely (he modelled himself on Michael Jackson), and seemed very sure of himself. He was even adept at checkers, astute at chess. Though I teased him for being "fat"—or chubby—he was the single one of us to achieve true cool, to know how to talk to gals, to strut, and to dress with charismatic appeal. He also came first to realize himself as a Black youth, to style his afro correctly, to know that he would be treated unfairly, and that his gifts didn't really matter in the eyes of white supremacists. I deluded myself into thinking that, if I were an A-student, I would not face any real repercussions for being Black, despite my brown complexion. Bryant could not accept any such delusion: He was one of the young Africadian guys that Caucasian hooligans, wielding baseball bats, chased away from a dance at the Waegwoltic Club, a South End hangout of the ritzy rednecks and their fair, tartan-skirted maidens.

As the youngest of us, Billy seemed to model himself on either Bryant or me before establishing his own separate personality. When I was a stamp collector, so was he. When I became a grocery store clerk, so did he. When Bryant would chum around with one of our black friends, so would Billy. Yet, as much as I valued and prided my

favoured position as first-born—and born in Windsor, not Halifax—
Billy bore my father's name, and he was, if I recall right, treated by
him somewhat more favourably than Bryant and I. So, I was eleven
when I received a bicycle, which I'd been hankering after for a couple
of years. But how unfair I thought it was that Bryant and Billy got their
bikes at the same time! (One side effect of our mutual receipt of separate, brand-new bikes was that we did cycle all over Halifax together,
and sometimes with other friends.) Furthermore, Billy Clarke and Bill
Clarke had one feature in common: both could be ferociously moody,
and those moods altered quickly, like sun pursuing clouds (or vice
versa) across a lake.

My brothers and I also differed in our choices of "best friends."
Throughout grade school, mine were always Caucasian lads, who were
rivals for good marks in our classes—Robbie, Victor, and Wayne. What
all three had in common was that they were either poor, or much less
provided for than was my family. When I visited the homes of Robbie
and Victor, their digs seemed to exude an earthy smell, suggestive
of a dusty miasma, and then their furniture and possessions seemed
rickety, patchwork, rigged up, and/or second-hand. Yet, I liked them
and their families greatly, though I was more comfortable having them
visit me than the alternative. (So, though the stereotype has Negroes
"poor and struggling" and Caucasians "comfortable and privileged,"
almost all my white friends had less means than I, and were less provi-
sioned than was my family. I grew up quite sensitive to my class
position because I was "better off," and I knew it, and I felt awkward:
Should I share with friends or ignore the financial differences? I could
never arrive at an adequate answer to the question, and swung between
shame at "having more" and exhibiting pretentious nonchalance at the
fact. I did tend to avoid exercising what might have seemed rank—or
rank-pulling—charity.

My friendship with Wayne was a little different for, at one point, his
mother and grandmother—who could emit the word "niggers," not
at all endearingly—were paid a weekly sum by my mother to fix my

brothers and me an after-school lunch, almost always of tepid spa-ghetti topped by tomato sauce that tasted more like flour than anything that could be confused with a condiment. This arrangement, which may have lasted for a fall and winter in 1973-74, always seemed a bit tense because Wayne's grandmother was not at all happy about having "niggers" at their dining table, but her daughter—Wayne's mother—needed the money, having been deserted, years before, by her sailor-husband. The other curiosity about Wayne's abode was seeing all these *True Crime* and *True Detective* magazines that were household reading fare, displaying white women in bra-and-panties, white men with a knife or gun, and everybody's eyes blacked out with a rectangular bar.)

Bryant's best friends were resolutely black kids who shared his inter-est in basketball and then music and girls (once we were all a touch older). What I mean is, Bryant's buddies never succumbed to the schoolhouse propaganda that we would win admission to the rich, white world *if* we could bleach ourselves Caucasian. Bryant and his sidekicks knew that obsequious behaviour to try to secure white approval was pointless; that they—we—should revel in our black selves—our handsome looks and sleek bodies—because the white folk would never accept us, anyway.

We all chummed around together, but I was never as close to Bryant's friends Tony and Martino as I was to Wayne—or Ronnie and Victor. Tony and Martino were also have-nots—financially—in com-parison to ourselves, but they also came from intriguing—funky—households. Tony's father liked to rouse his children every morn by bugling "Taps" out a dented horn, while Martino was from a family who monopolized the black jazz scene in Halifax—grandfather, father, and sons—all of em profusely wicked on trumpet, piano, saxo-phone, and drums. (In the mid-1970s, come summer, horn-players seemed always roaming the streets, brown chests bare save for leather vests, in bell-bottom denims and platform shoes, with trumpets ready for tooting or snorting, lookin like castaways from the Isley Brothers.) Martino and Tony also had a yen for storytelling. Tony regaled us with one gag about an Italian girl who twice tells her mother, "*Mamma mia!"* The punchline was the girl telling her mother, on the third go-round, *"Me a mamma!"*

Bryant's friends were all black boys helping each other mature to become well-groomed, sharp-dressing, debonair young black men, all handy at basketball and gifted at chatting up "young ladies." But I was on my own, thinking I could get there by following Caucasian heroes and reading manuals and novels. Either I never quite got it right, or I evolved an independent sensibility.

I think that Billy's friends were a mix—both Black and Caucasian. Although we were close in age, we were worlds apart too. He became a Trekkie, but I could never muster similar enthusiasm for Spock, Bones, and Kirk (though I could admire Uhura). Also, when Bryant and I left our father's house as older teens, Billy remained. Though Bill Clarke had told our trio—as mere boys—that we'd have to leave his home by the time we were eighteen, and Bryant and I did so, Billy stayed, into his early twenties, with our father. (Now, Bill—no longer Billy—is the glue that keeps our atomized trio together.)

iv.

In the summer of '67, our family took the train to Montréal to visit my Aunt Joan, and to stay with her while checking out Expo 67. Because Bill Clarke worked for the CNR (the "Canadian Negro Railway," according to the jocular opinion of railway porters), we were all accorded a free pass on the rails. We all had berths in the sleeper car, which meant that our parents had one to themselves, and we three boys had to share one overhead. It was fun to sleep on the train, to write our menu choices in pencil on a slip, and then to have waiters bring us mashed potatoes, boiled green peas, and roast beef, floating these steaming plates absolutely smoothly to our hungering knives and forks, despite the bobbing and weaving locomotion of the dining car.

To get to the observation car at the rear of the train, we'd have to pass through car after car of sleeping quarters, traversing the clickety-clackety vestibule between each. If we made that trek with our dad, he'd stop sometimes in a vestibule, and let us feel the open air rushing past, gushing into nostrils and eardrums. As I passed through one sleeper car of olive-drab-curtained berths, ready for lights out, a blonde Hippy pulled me into her arms as she sat on her bed. I suppose the gesture was intended as expressing personal solidarity with the Civil Rights Movement, but still I squirmed to get away because I thought it was ignoble for a boy to accept hugs and caresses from anyone but a mother or aunt.

At 5 or 6 a.m., the train paused at Lévis, opposite Québec City, and I had my first eyeful of the Château Frontenac hotel, which appeared to me like a fairy-tale castle overlooking the Saint Lawrence River. (Years later, I fell in love with Julie, the mother of our daughter, Aurélia, partly because of my romantic childhood memory of that great hotel, in Julie's natal city, looming gothically over a fabled waterway.) Simultaneously, now having left behind Anglophone Nova Scotia and bilingual Nouveau-Brunswick, my ears encountered French—Québécois French—as these passengers boarded our train. Maybe I thought I was hearing gibberish. But I must have known that I was also being re-educated, in real-time, about the truth of Canada, its being a miscellany of cultures and lingos and practices, and all are possible (with agreeable, mutual tolerance of our stimulating differences).

Back home in Halifax, likely in the spring of '67, Bill Clarke took up an entire living-room wall of our house at 5847 Cunard Street, to paste together his personal homage to Canada's Centennial: cut-up CN tourism brochures (slashing and suturing images of Peggy's Cove lighthouse and Vancouver mountains, Toronto City Hall and Québec City's Château Frontenac), newspaper pages, railway magazines, and pieces of paste-backed string thrown—randomly—upon the clashing assembly of multicoloured images. (Perhaps the string was meant to represent railway tracks?) These elements all got slathered across this three-foot-tall, six-foot-long sheet of plywood, stuck down by glue paste and glossed over by shellac. It was an awesome—if unholy—work of art, *bric-à-brac*, with Klondike cancan gals shellacked into Cubist positions, cheek-by-jowl with Nova Scotia Government-built, *Playboy*-praised Clairtone (hi-fi) stereo ads, or with *Herald* headlines about PM Lester Bowles Pearson, ex-PM John George Diefenbaker, or N.S. premier Robert Lorne Stanfield (whose name now graces YHZ airport). That piece of working-class, newsprint-based, magazine-glossy, and epic collage was Bill's largest artistic statement in our home, for a chunk of my childhood, and it made me believe—wrongly or not—that the arts were potential avenues even for me.

Assuredly, he was proud of it, and I was proud of his art for him, and it did grace that living-room wall powerfully, perhaps with the pizzazz of a Picasso piece. (Years later, it was replaced—displaced—by some ersatz burgundy ink-wash—against white paper—of a man's hand rising, from behind and between her legs, to cover a bare-breasted woman's crotch. I do think Bill Clarke's art hands-down superior to that framed poster which was, despite its naked eroticism, irrefutably bland.) That dazzling display of my father's talent, so tactile and glistening and jarring and eye-dancing and surreal, had to have made me open-minded about putting together poems out of shards of this and bits of that, a technique of *bricolage*.

Then again, Bill was a bit of an *artiste-manqué*. He loved the editorial cartoons of Bob Chambers in the *Chronicle-Herald*, and, as a MOMA-touring motorcyclist on his Gotham City jaunts, had picked up enough Duchamp and Picasso and Warhol to want to experiment with collage. (His own style—as a cartoonist—recalled Montmartre's Francisque Poulbot and his tenderly rendered ragamuffins.)

v.

From 1966 until 1978, we lived in the North End—the proletarian, soldier-and-sailor, petty-hoodlum, immigrant, Black, and Mi'kmaq quarter of Halifax that made the city a just-as-dirty, just-as-scandalous warren as similar sites like Marseilles, the Bronx, East London, and so forth: all locales of tolerated vice, chest-thumping illiteracy, and heightened vagrancy. The North End was not disreputable because of us citizenry, but because of the prejudices of the South End elite, who awarded themselves statues and trees, but gave us cops to fear and troops to emulate.

Now, my father was a North Ender through-and-through, which meant that he liked his suds, his pin-ups, saluted the Queen, and honoured black boxers (alongside Caucasian racing car drivers and some hockey players, for he viewed *Hockey Night in Canada* every seasonal Saturday).

For working-class Negro men, whatever their fealties to white lovers or wives, or their enforced truckling to white bosses and cops, there was one category of heroes that they all admired: the pugilists, whether local or African-American. Even if my dad saw himself as, ideally, "raceless," I mean, that he expected to be treated as an equal by everyone, without regard to his "colour," he had a strong affinity for black boxers—as did all my Africadian uncles. Whenever a fight was on, black men dropped all other pursuits and congregated around black-and-white TV sets in barbershops or in someone's living room, hoping that Sugar Ray or Cassius Clay or Joe Louis or some other Great-Black-Hope would demolish the Great-White-Hope by turning boxing into a version of pyrotechnics, gloved-fists striking some puffy, pasty chops like fireworks splintering nightfall with a thousand, flailing sparks. Bill Clarke might not have been much of a fighter himself, but he surely appreciated the allegorical significance of the Coloured practitioners of the "sweet science."

True: Cassius Clay—as he was then—was disliked by my father, who saw the boxer as being too much "a loud-mouth" (translation: too radical). Still, Bill Clarke followed boxing—because that was one of the awesome passions of African-Nova Scotian men—for the same reason that it was a passion for African-American men: to see "whitey" left broken and bloodied by the powerful fists of a black man, permitted, in this one arena, to lay "white boys" low—publicly, in plain view and with unquestionable proof of who was *really* inferior and who superior. And the boxing gloves—or dukes—doubled as a symbol of whose manhood was most erect, most sterling.

(The racial allegory of boxing is still prominent—in Nova Scotia at least. I remember driving through Windsor, in summer 2012, stopping at a four-way stop, and glancing over at a lamppost on the passenger side of my car. It featured a grainy, cheap, tacked-up photocopy of an Africadian and a Caucasian man, both with their dukes up. The poster headline was blood-simple: "Fight Tonight!" I guessed that the advertisement would attract a standing-room-only crowd, and that a lot of dudes would be happy to shell out some bucks in hopes that the "symbol" of either "race" would prevail over that of the other.)

For many Africadian men, then and now, a fistfight—or a pro boxing match—was a clear demarcation of who was really more powerful—physically—in stark black-and-white terms. There could also be an understanding—as Muhammad Ali proved—that a champion boxer was not only fast on his feet, and fast on the draw, but also mentally fast, intellectually quick, to be able to beat up—most spectacularly—a white man—and walk away with the belt, the trophy, the purse, and even the opponent's "woman" (if he wanted her and she him). However, as potent as that pride in black boxers—and in black athletes generally—was, there could also be an anti-intellectual component, an anti-smarty-pants bias, that had something to do with white authority—teachers, bankers, cops, politicians—using their book-learning and highfalutin vocabularies to t'ief (to spell a Jamaican pronunciation) from black people and increase our economic exploitation and thus impoverishment.

Thus, even among us schoolkids, if there was any black classmate who sought to excel in study, he (and sometimes she) would soon hear the slurs of being a "teacher's pet" or "stuck up" ("big feeling") or—even worse—an Oreo, or an Uncle Tom or Aunt Jemima—a "traitor to the race." So, school—schooling—got dissed, slammed, got the bad rap about being about brainwashing black people to hate themselves, hate other black people, and yearn to be white. But white working-class schoolkids could also be berated for being nerdy, for being hoity-toity, for wanting to join the middle-class and forget about their buddies in the "hood." So, the price of venerating boxers and other athletes was a concomitant devaluation of the urgent necessity for literacy. Worse, educational aspiration was seen as a "sissy" orientation. To be buff was classy; to be brainy was wimpy, about as bad as being a snitch or a goody-two-shoes.

The sole reading considered appropriate among us working-class boys was the comic book. A corner store near our home, namely Mrs. Petrie's—operated a much-loved exchange, which meant that you could rummage through piles of used comics, buy one for 10¢ and return it for 5¢. It was standard practice for us kids to walk up to Mrs. Petrie's, each buy a comic, take it home and read it, exchange with each other, and then all go back to use the returned nickles to buy another couple. It was not uncommon for the underprivileged kids to lounge about the store, leafing through or reading the used comics, but not purchasing any.

But comic-book reading was an exception. Too often, in my community, reading and writing were not only belittled, but considered futile, piffle, and even treasonous. (In my twenties, one of my uncles threatened to throw my books in a stove, to burn em up as fuel, because, being temporarily unemployed, I had proven that education for a young black man was pointless, and yet, there I was, sitting at his kitchen table, eating his wife's cooking. It was a searing experience that was repaired, only years later, when the same uncle attended the ceremony wherein I received my doctorate.)

But these destructive attitudes even got reinforced by the school system. I recall how, in grade school, for at least two years in a row, at the June ceremony wherein high-achieving pupils were awarded scrolls and books gifted by the Imperial Order Daughters of the Empire, our guest speaker was a Haligonian—and draconian—cop. The constable stressed—to all of us five-to-ten-year-olds—how useless study was, how worthless reading was, and how irrelevant academics were. He lectured us that we'd be, all of us—boys most of all—better off to rank boxing and fighting and sports over readin, writin, rithmetic. This constable—his firearm holstered—brought this questionable message—with unquestionable authority—to the ears of working-class kids and parents, who were now told, *within the school itself,* that our scholastic excellence was of no avail. Red-leather boxing gloves—not gold stars—were supposed to be our "silver bullets" for life success. That *zwieback* (cracker) cop warned us that, if we encountered a bully in an alleyway, all our textbook study and exam cramming would prove inadequate. Athletics over mathematics, the boxing ring over the class ring, the basketball over the book . . . not that I knew it then, but such is the messaging of Fascism: the strong-man is the smartest man because he can, with brute force, demolish the scholar, who has no equivalent brawn. So, what was the point of a working-class school to invite a cop to tell a bunch of junior eggheads that they were—at the very moment of their accomplishment— examples of "survival-of-the-fittest" failures?

As disgraceful—and as off-putting—as those would-be hold-your-head-high graduating moments were, the point that we working-class, North End kids had no business contemplating going on to high school and university, was brought home viscerally to me in my grade seven math class. Indeed, in early 1973, a Canada Manpower (now Employment) worker invited our body of twelve-to-fifteen-year-olds to sign up for Social Insurance Numbers so we could join the work-force as soon as possible (i.e. "drop out" of school once we reached age sixteen). Here again, as with the case of the Halifax city cop, a representative of the State—this time the Government of Canada— was discouraging destitute and/or proletarian pupils from trying to ascend the class ladder by expanding their educational attainments. Instead, we would "benefit" by being able to earn our own money— yes, by being waitresses and cleaners.

There is nothing wrong with doing any sort of honest work. However, there is something not just wrong, but *diabolical,* when the

State—through its officials—attempts to coerce the children of the welfare recipient and of low-waged and military workers ("army brats") to accept limited, occupational options by bidding them choose immediate, minimum-wage employment over achieving—at least—a high-school diploma. Given that black pupils, notably, have been subjected to "streaming" (whereby teachers and school administrators push them into less-challenging courses which will, when completed, only grant them skills for entry-level work), for generations, one has to recognize that the suppression of their *Intelligence* is an evil act of government-sanctioned *Sabotage* of their life opportunities.

When I was twelve, in civics class, at the beginning of grade seven, the teacher asked us (some thirty pupils, most likely), the meaning of the abbreviation "MP." Every single one of us—tutored by comic books and the naval base CFB Stadacona (situated in North End Halifax)—insisted, "Military Policeman." I remember how floored I was when, after at least five minutes of classroom clamour that the teacher must be stupid to not know the meaning of "MP," she revealed the answer: "Member of Parliament." Shortly thereafter, I led a few classmates over to the committee room of the Hon. Robert L. Stanfield, the Tory leader who was contesting the riding of Halifax in the federal election that fall. I thought we'd be welcomed with open arms as youth volunteers, though we were all but twelve and thirteen years old. Well, when I opened the Almon Street door of the Progressive Conservative office, my little group of would-be Tory comrades was met by a dozen surprised and stony faced—pale-faced—Tory operatives, who classed us instantly as rabble and Negro riffraff. No one told us to leave; no one welcomed us. Alert to the cold-eyed silence, my passion to assist in the election diminished immediately to my save-face request for some "Elect Stanfield" stickers. These got quickly disseminated to my troupe; quickly we were dismissed to the autumnal gloom. Despite that chilly reception from the Stanfield committee room, I was—like most Nova Scotians—thrilled that the underpants king almost unseated Trudeau on E-Night, which fell fittingly on Halloween Eve.

(In truth, I did prefer Trudeau, and, around age nineteen, I savoured his savvy and snappy, even humorous essays in *Approaches to Politics* [1970], and his witty and insightful travelogue [with Jacques Hébert], *Two Innocents in Red China* [English editon, 1968]. But I also admire the Red Toryism so poignantly put by George Grant in *Lament for a Nation* [1965]*.)

Earlier that year, riding my bike about, I got into a debate with an adult selling a Communist newspaper in front of the local branch of the Royal Bank (when it was more than just an acronym). I didn't know anything about it except the crimson hammer-and-sickle which meant all manners of sins to my African Baptist (though unbaptized) and royalist (thanks to grade-school propaganda) self. The pedlar was very patient in trying to educate me—a smart-alecky, snot-nosed brat—about his views, but I reacted—I'm ashamed to say—rudely because I thought I had all righteousness on my side, when all I had, in truth, was the educated—I mean, instilled—political faith of most of the struggling class. (However, we could have kept in mind that good ol Maritime proverb: "Tory times are hard times," eh?)

vi.

Though he loved black-vs.-white boxing matches, Bill Clarke was publicly committed, really, to "gradualism," to non-violence, to "turning the other cheek," to presuming the best of others as opposed to assuming the worst. He valued bourgeois politesse, assumed a bearing of good breeding and civil behaviour, of a gentleman-scholar (inveterate-newspaper-clipper) and whistling raconteur, a hail-fellow-well-met most def comfy with soup-kitchen inmates right alongside with royalty.

Yet, Bill Clarke's sons, all three of us, were, like him, North Enders. Which meant that we came from a neighbourhood of booze and

---

* Unfortunately, social-spending-supportive Red Tories tend to morph into blue-blood Scrooges as soon as they take office.

boxing, of sailors and cigarettes, of "sluts" and "cocksuckers" (a term almost always applied to males), of "buggers" and "grog," of tattoos and cops, of garbage strewn everywhere and of porn cartoons sold at kiddie-eye-level in the corner stores. Furthermore, other big-bust- and big-butt-targeted fare, often lampooning men's lusts as much as ladies' intellects, usually of British origin (think of *Benny Hill* and the "Carry On Gang"), abounded on our store shelves. The reason? Sailors—"Jack Tars"—who were libertine, sybarite, rummies, winos, drunks, Cockney and Liverpudlian, Cuban and Soviet and Yankee, West Injun and Afro-Am—swarmed North End Halifax between sailing off to fish—or war—or deliver containers and oil. (The scuzzy "Tijuana bibles" and other newsprint porn were first meant for them, and only as secondary, customer merchandise for us chillun—the sly smokers, the precocious crooks, the secret, drunken vomiteers, confusing *methadone* for *Me-That-Had-One* in our illiterate graffiti-ing of grocery-store walls.)

Our streets were shiny, not due to gold bricks, or piss, but broken glass—busted bottles of all types—ground into asphalt or concrete or left to compete with the sparkle of dew—or frost—in grass. Maybe because we were all considered cast-offs—as labourers, as cannon fodder, as bastards, as welfare bums, as addicts, as drunks, as dastards, we treated all goods as litter: Chip bags, candy bar wrappers, cigarette tinfoil, cardboard boxes of all shapes and sizes, condoms, cigarette lighters, playing cards, newspapers, porno pages, everything was torn out, squashed, crumpled up, allowed to blow every which way, to be thrown to the winds—literally—to settle wherever it happened to fly.

It was clear that we people—North Enders—were disposable. Too many days did my brothers and I, in walking to school, scrubbed and preppy in blazers and beanie caps, see ourselves have to sidestep the corpse-like stiff of a redneck drunk, lying out in broad daylight on our sidewalk, with blood still pulsing from where his forehead had struck the pavement.

When I was twelve, there was a proper fuss—with ambulances, police cars, and fire trucks—because a man had taken a shotgun and blown away his wife: both were Black—or Coloured or Negro. I remember joining other neighbourhood kids as we buzzed our bikes in and out among the ranks of the cops and white-uniformed docs and the firefighters. It was more like a holiday for everyone than a case of vicious manslaughter. Yes, the husband and murderer went to prison and his infant daughter went to the Nova Scotia Home for Coloured Children orphanage, but there was no hue and cry over injustice or poverty or racism or sexism, because the perpetrator and victim(s) were Negro North Enders. We were the part of Halifax from which the obvious criminals emerged, those usually having "No Fixed Address."

In contrast, the South End was the Shangri-La of mansions and demi-castles and banks of flowers sloping from some muckamuck's address to the sidewalk, sort of demarcating the cut-off between private grandeur and public spending. The boys and men of the South End didn't walk; they promenaded. They weren't in prison stripes, but pin-stripes. (They didn't have jailors; they had tailors.) They were upper-crust, not bottom-of-the-barrel. They were talking heads on TV, not heads busted open by cops' batons. They always felt like a million bucks, not bad pennies or funny money. Due to their Midas touch, they could afford to be touchy-feely; to do high-profile charity events as opposed to having to fall down on their knees and kiss the rings of whoever was handing out this second-hand toy, this crummy garment, this rusty lettuce. Now, the girls and women from the South End of Halifax could never be confused with streetwalkers; their perfume was Chanel No. 5, not cigarette smoke; their rumps were silk-clad, linen-clad, wool-clad; not "roast," not "toast." They didn't come through back doors with an apron on; they had front doors opened for them and they had the latest fashions on. Their *heels* were lofty—and were shoes, rather than the low-down back-ends of bread loaves.

If our side of town—the North—was smokestacks (still) and rats and cockroaches and "cocksuckers"; the South End was the Public Gardens and Point Pleasant Park and cock-robins on front lawns and steamed cockles and mussels served on fine china with silverware settings. Even though what we knew of the world—my bros and I—was mainly a set of Disney cartoon and comic-book images, we knew that our Haligonian turf was defined by the gutter, not by gardens, and that we were the ones to be fingerprinted and handcuffed, not to finger pianos or hand-paint masterpieces.

(Intriguingly, Halifax's university-dubbed streets—Oxford, Cambridge, and Harvard—all run north-south, but are, except for the main thoroughfare of Oxford, principally located in the South End. The anomaly is Yale Street, which runs east-west, but is adjacent to the well-off—if not well-to-do—West End. Even the placement of ivy-league-named city streets tell North-Enders that we are not likely candidates for university degrees.)

Even so, our North End boyhoods were—to my mind—cheerful, partly because we never knew need. Never did I go to bed hungry; never was our house cold. We had well-stocked cupboards, stoves always topped with kerosene, oil-rich furnaces, glasses brimming with milk or Kool-Aid (if not fresh-squeezed, home-made orange juice). And clean sheets and plenty of blankets and quilts. Our clothes were never patches of rags; we always had polished shoes for church and sneakers for scuffing about and horseplay.

Our parents were respected and our teachers knew who we were: we were the Clarkes—good kids, good boys, from a good home, who spoke good English, got good grades, and seldom required, at school, the corrective slap of a strap across our palms. We were well-turned-out and well-groomed; spiffy, with short haircuts and a "part" sawn into our scalps by a barber (black) who hated afros. Moreover, our Christmas tree always presided over plenty: toys and fresh clothes, hockey sticks and skates. Our eats composed a feast: ham with pineapple rings (sometimes a cherry) and cinnamon-soaked—not to mention all the walnuts and cashews and oranges that almost made our socks drop from the nails affixed to the living-room mantelpiece. Tinsel festooned everything and the smell of the pine, plus the turkey and/or ham basting, was itself juicy, not merely nostril-quivering.

My family's fine diet of mackerel was often bought from black men, who'd walk behind slow-moving pick-up trucks, hollering, "MAAAAACKERREL! Fresh MAAAAACKERREL!" As they proceeded like motorized snails through North End streets, pacing themselves as deliberately as New Orleans jazz-band mourners, housewives would run out their doors, in slippers and housecoats, curlers in—or bandanas over—their hair, to press coins into those big, rough hands, and then withdraw into their houses with a nice, sharp-tailed mackerel or two, and then reach for a newspaper to begin the supper-preparation work.

In our household, it was Bill who performed the mackerel taxidermy, so to speak. The process required decapitation. I can still hear the sawing sound of the knife grinding through the skin and bone; I can still smell the wet, ozone odour of Halifax-area Atlantic saltwater and fish-flesh and guts, as my father scraped his knife down the middle of the headless fish, eliminating the fin-borne tripe. I disliked the obnoxious aroma, the dead, staring eye of the fish, the gaping mouth, the mess of innards—that slop—all plopped onto newspaper pages that were then wrapped up tight about the remains, to keep down the smell, to ward off ferreting vermin.

(Yet another brush with death as a boy, following the near-electrocution and the two auto accidents: a fish bone caught in my throat when we still lived on the Bay Road. I remember my terror at choking and then my father grabbing me, swinging me upside-down by the heels, and then beating my spine until I gasped out the offending—likely mackerel—bone and now-spit-gunked flesh. I remain fastidious—finicky—about eating fish for that very reason.)

Only a block away—west of us—was a fish-n-chip shop that was heavy on grease and batter and heat: to bite into one of those greasy blobs of cod was always to risk a singed mouth. You had to knife it open and let the steam rise up and then make the grease palatable by assaulting the fish bits and fries with salt, with vinegar, or ketchup, or tartar sauce. It was always a terrific Friday night treat for my brothers and I.

Or, our parents would order the sinfully tasty fried clams, but that was usually for them alone, while we had to content ourselves with the fish-n-chips—snowed over with salt and rained upon by vinegar—and all powered down thanks to ginger ale.

vii.

Although my mom's parents were very much together, very much present in our lives, my father's father was missing. I don't remember ever questioning or pondering that absence as a boy. My paternal grandmother, Nettie Clarke, deigned to welcome us, but was never as warm to my brothers and I as were our maternal grandparents. They doted on us; but when we visited Nanny Clarke, it was as if we were being received, being granted an audience. She always seemed a Victorian figure, very severe, austere, seldom smiling, never offering us candies or cake. She wasn't dour, just stand-offish, or maybe a bit remote because, after all, we were only children, and not princes or the sons of plutocrats or potentates, of whose satisfaction, I believe, she would've been far more solicitous.

In visiting her far-North, North End home, we had to be virtuous scions, and never could there be play or tomfoolery. We sat still, hands clasped on our laps. She wasn't "Nanny," she was "Nanny Clarke." Her posture was always domineering; and though her voice was as rich as hot-chocolate froth, it velvetized an iron tongue. I could not imagine anyone—ever—saying *nyet* to her. Also, like our father, Nettie was devoted to classical music; likely because her sister, Portia May White, had achieved renown throughout all the Americas as a supremely—and superbly—gifted contralto, and my paternal grandmother and my father were insistent that my brothers and I adore Portia as our first-stop, full-stop role-model.

Yes, my father and his mother made sure that my brothers and I knew all about his aunt, our great-aunt, namely, Portia. Born in 1911, she was only fifty-six when she died in Toronto, due to throat cancer, the day after my eighth birthday, on February 13, 1968. I recall the moment well, for Portia was not just a diva, but a deity in Halifax, and her death was reported with almost Soviet-style, black-crepe, sombre-music gravitas. Memorials and testimonials, eulogies and obituaries abounded in the Haligonian press. Referred to in hushed, reverential terms by our grandmother and father, Great-Aunt Portia, my brothers and I were taught, had come to international prominence—if not quite world-wide fame—as a once-in-a-century voice, in coloratura registers, of a repertoire of bel canto, operatic arias, Broadway show tunes, and Negro spirituals. She was one of the truly Apollonian once-North-Enders.

Our connection to the fabled Miss White was cemented *via* our childhood stops at Nanny Clarke's home. She would pour tap water for my brothers and I, but something more flavourful for my parents. Then, in magisterial tones, a photo album would be produced, demonstrating Portia's posh pix, maybe from her life in New York City or Toronto, or depicting her tour to Latin and South America, where she became the first ever classically trained singer to perform a concert at ten thousand feet above sea level—in Quito, Ecuador, among the Andes. (For an African Baptist Church-raised woman, it must have been stirring to sing above the clouds—just a smidgen closer to Heaven.) Or there were snaps of her in Panama City, Panama, where the Isthmian Negro Youth Congress presented her with a gold medal. We also had to know that Portia travelled—to Curaçao and Grenada, to Bogotá (Colombia), and to Barbados and Jamaica; that she was a kind of roving, African-Canadian ambassador of song. Pride of place was the snap of her 1964 "Command Performance" before the Queen in Charlottetown, PEI.

The respectful turning of those photo-album pages energized my psyche—and, I think, *our* psyches as boys. Whatever slights, insults, or barriers that we confronted as black boys, as Negroes, as Coloured squirts, all were somehow lessened because we could say, "My great-aunt sang before the Queen." There we were, bratty, snotty (at times), but we could still say, to better-off white kids in our schools, "My great-aunt sang before the Queen." It suggested that we were nigh *Royalty*, that our dungarees and sneakers and corduroy pants and blue jeans and penny loafers did not separate us inapproachably from Canada's ruling family. We could play street hockey and swing from monkey bars, but still feel equal to classmates who arrived at school, in mid-winter, sporting Florida tans: "My great-aunt sang before the Queen!" We figured that none of our classmates—of whatever background—were but two degrees of separation from the Crown, Hollywood, and Broadway. We also knew that, among Africadians, whatever our class or status shortcomings, we were still the great nephews of the grand, Africadian songstress who answered thrillingly the Queen's command that she perform. We were whip-keen Bill Clarke's boys, and we occupied, neatly, an antechamber to stage-and-screen- and sceptred aristocracy.

Likewise, knowing that Lorne Greene, star of the popular TV show *Gunsmoke*, who'd also scored a pop-song hit with "Ringo" (1964), was a voice pupil of Great-Aunt Portia—along with singers Dinah Christie and Robert Goulet,* all household names in Halifax and Toronto and New York City, also meant we could walk to school with our heads craned high. Indeed, the Portia-connected figures who emanated from radios and television screens were dining-room eminences for us. Our awareness of our relative proximity to stars of action, dance, and voice and, for that matter, to veritable palace owners, reinforced for us the notion that were not to be discarded in—or dissuaded from—our search for a profitable education, though such was the doom of too many black and brown pupils.

Portia was a crucial talisman—even though we could not play any of her records because she did not record any (despite being under

---

* That Goulet originated the role of Lancelot in the Broadway musical that defined the JFK administration suggests that Portia was, again, only two degrees of separation from Washington power, and so we—three Coloured lads—were but three degrees removed.

contract to Columbia Records management in NYC). I never heard her voice—so that it resonated—until I was twenty-one when, on a visit to Toronto, I dined with her brother, Great-Uncle Jack (a leader of the Canadian Union of Public Employees and the Ontario Federation of Labour). He gave me a copy of the LP—*Portia White: Think On Me*—that her siblings had assembled, recording scattered reel-to-reel tapes of her 1940s-era concert performances. I remember my Aunt Wendy, Nanny Clarke's youngest child, playing one of the tapes that ended up on the record—with a jacket cover photo by celebrity photographer Yousuf Karsh*. Still, I was more impressed by the reel-to-reel tape player than I was by my great-aunt's voice. Really, hearing her voice felt anticlimactic because she had already been established as the transcendent symbol—in our household, in our clan, in our culture—of Black excellence.

Before Nettie moved to Rector Street (almost half-the-city-away from our Maynard Street address), we'd all have to cross the Halifax Commons to get to her then-place, and we always had to be the acme of blackish, boyish perfection: a part seared into our scalps, a bow tie at each neck, pants pressed to a razor-sharp crease, polished shoes properly laced. We'd need to line up and sit—silent unless spoken to—on her carefully tended furniture. We resembled Alvin and the Chipmunks or Disney's Huey, Dewey, and Louie or the Three Stooges (pint-size, tanned)—a trio of taciturn, well-scrubbed and "well-behaved" poster-boys: *Brylcreem* in our hair (it had a quasi-toothpaste smell, just sharper—as if cut with *Tang*); yes-suh, no-ma'am on our lips. (In truth, our father would have had us say, "No, sir" and "Yes, madam" because he was a stickler for enunciation and resolute *Courtesy*. When

---

* Portia is—as is usual for Karsh—backlit, and is gazing up at the camera, with an aspiring glance, an ingénue expression, with whiteness reserved for a slight halo effect about her head, the toothy smile, and stereotypical glittering eyes. Her look says she yearns for our notice. Yet, Karsh's portrait suggests that Portia had earned a place in his pantheon of global personalities and/or celebrities.

we were old enough to address cards to relatives and/or friends, the instruction was intoned: boys were to be addressed as "Master" plus surname, and girls as "Mistress" plus surname. I'm not sure whether Bill Clarke intended the echo of slavery in those locutions, but my chums and classmates received from me birthday cards addressed to Master X or Valentines addressed to Mistress X.)

Yet, there was a flaw in this familial program of instilling self-confidence in us boys by limning our relationship to the acclaim gracing our great-aunt. For one thing, she was a contralto, a classically trained vocalist, a high-note art that seemed precious—if not pseudo-ridiculous and quasi-pretentious—and medievally remote in the Age of the Beatles. As boys, my brothers and I lauded the songs issuing from our transistor radios and hi-fi-spun 45s, *not* the opera arias and the Broadway show tunes that our father adored. So Great-Aunt Portia's fame—beyond Halifax, beyond Nova Scotia—registered a cloistered transcendence. She had aficionados whereas James Brown had fans. There's a difference.

Though Portia was an icon and magic shield for us, especially in Halifax, where the mention of her name would make white folks sit up and take notice of our brown selves, she remained yet as distant from us as the Good Witch of the *Wizard of Oz*. A resident of the Big Crab Apple, Toronto, whose then-brand-new city hall resembled a kind of spaceship or UFO, thus establishing the metropolis as other-worldly, Portia seemed equally alien—at a remove. Did she ever telephone her nephew, Bill, or ever dispatch a Xmas card our way? I do know that she was not averse to tossing a mink coat, one she'd tired of, to her sister, Nettie; that she'd touch down at hardscrabble Belle Aire Terrace and float pizzazz up and down the poverty-stricken and rickety-fenced street of my father's boyhood, thus ameliorating, briefly, its run-down aura.

Nevertheless, that name "Portia"—with its suggestion of the pricey sports car, Porsche, and its Shakespearean resonances—was also a portal to another, better world. But the surname "White" communicated pixie dust too. For Portia White was Negro, but had a silvery voice; she was black, but she could sport pearls and diamonds; she was dark, but she was brilliant. In a sense, she was the embodiment of the most famous line in Hebrew scripture for black people: "I am black, but comely" (Solomon 1:5).

Bill and Nanny Clarke underlined the importance of Portia by noting that the Nova Scotia Talent Trust—a provincial-government, classical-musician-and-singer-supporting fund—had been founded, initially, to back Miss White's career. My brothers and I were asked to appreciate that the very state—I mean, the *province* of Nova Scotia—had invested in a black woman's vocal chords and had, simultaneously, decades before our birth, granted special approval of the White clan. What we couldn't have known, back then, was that the government of Nova Scotia was fostering tourism-related symbols, "brands" that would attract US visitors to "the Land of Evangeline" (to reference the Acadian heroine imagined and popularized by the "Song of Hiawatha" author, Hank—"Get out your hanky"—Longfellow). The government's strategy resulted in the racing schooner *Bluenose* finding a permanent home on the Canadian dime, while Portia was wowing the concert stage in Manhattan. But the bottom line for us boys was Portia's star gleamed bright enough that we could bask in the afterglow.

One oddity about the veneration of Great-Aunt Portia during my boyhood: her own illustrious father was seldom mentioned, either by Nanny Clarke or by our father. However, just as I never questioned the absence of Mr. Clarke—Nettie's husband and Bill Clarke's dad—from her household, nor did I wonder about the omission of Portia's and Nettie's father, my great-grandfather. I think we were told that he was a great preacher and had served in World War I, but these successes were not ballyhooed. Rev. Capt. Dr. William Andrew White was definitely, in our household, second-fiddle to his celebrity daughter.

Long before I began to ponder the possibility of being a poet, and amidst the reverence for my laudable great-aunt, I had my own chosen boyhood heroes: I imagined my unkempt afro could mimic Einstein's tousled hair; my long, lean legs could catch up to and surpass track star Roger Bannister; I could flaunt and vaunt a scarf like the fleet, sleek Red Baron. But Great-Aunt Portia's star was literally closer to home (though not at all down-to-earth), and I also had the in-house example of my father—her nephew—whistling along to Richard Strauss while bent over a card-table, painting a credible landscape using little jars of oil paint.

If Great-Aunt Portia was a long-distance Muse, the diva of the Whites and the African Baptist Church, my father was Portia domesticated— and male-gendered—and turned to canvas and oils, cut-up images and paste and shellac. I found it easy to juxtapose the aunt and the nephew. She'd been the toast of Town Hall; he'd been an unusual visitor to NYC—a dashing young black man helming a purple BMW. She'd met the Queen; he'd tried to make the Queen notice him by straddling and walking his "machine" (dubbed "Elizabeth II") through the crowds gathered for Her Majesty's Halifax stop in the summer of 1959. She'd played Tituba in Miller's *The Crucible* for CBC-TV (in 1959); he'd played a cop in Dürrenmatt's *The Physicists* for Halifax's Neptune Theatre in 1966; the Nova Scotia government had supported her; but he supported the Nova Scotia government by purchasing a Clairtone stereo . . .

(Throughout our childhoods, Bill was always chuffed about his Clairtone stereo. It was a maple-wood-coloured floor-model, a nifty cabinet, and I think that Bill savoured the idea of local socialism. The Clairtone became a Government of Nova Scotia-bankrolled hi-fi system 1966-79, in the name of economic "diversification.")

viii.

Because my father had been an *artiste*—a painter—throughout my childhood, and had decorated our Maynard Street home with Old Master reproductions, he was the in-house epitome of a people's artist. Indeed, dad took us all on family visits to the public art galleries in universities, or—socialistically—to the democratic (amateur) art displays slap-dashed on construction-site hoardings. I didn't know, until after his death, that my father hadn't finished high school, but had taken one course in art at Queen Elizabeth High School, Halifax, executing a number of pieces (in crayon, charcoal, pastel, and watercolour). I believe that he attended grade ten—at age seventeen to eighteen (1952-53)—just so he could take that single art course at taxpayers' expense. However, before then, he'd spent two years as a sign-painter's apprentice (ages fifteen to seventeen), becoming an expert in a merchandising craft that would soon be well-nigh supplanted by neon lights and plastic signs fluorescent-lit from within. Still, Bill's lettering was always expressive and clear; and he had drawers full of pastels (often crumbled into stubs), Eberhard-Faber pencils (grey, red, brown, or blue), and a compass. He gave my brothers and I fistfuls of pencils and pastels to scribble and scrawl with, and "Santa" delivered paint-by-number oil-paint sets when we were seven, eight, and nine years old. (I graduated from paint sets to chemistry sets—and a microscope—by the time I was ten, thus planning surrealistically noxious combos and toxic, psychedelic gumbos. My microscope slides also vaunted oily, garish smears.)

Only Bryant developed any finesse for painting inside the pale blue lines of the outlined figures. For me, those Sundays when my father sat with us and tried to teach us to paint were taxing, for his pedagogy was to hector and shame, bully and snort: you either had talent, or you didn't. (I didn't because I could never make those ornery plumes of paintbrush hair sop up and drop down the oils within those fine blue lines. My horse heads, for instance, just hosted freaky blobs and gobs and streaks. I could've called myself an Expressionist, if I hadn't just been shaky with the brush and clumsy with the paints!) So, Bill Clarke's cheesed-off looks and put-downs of amateurish oil painting were more damaging to my ego than they were support for my striving. But his tempestuous teaching didn't matter; that he was an artist, that's what influenced me.

Bill's art experience—the once-application of his aptitude to acquire income—was not unique among African North American men. Bob Beatty's *Florida's Highwaymen: Legendary Landscapes* (2005) documents a school of African-American artists (1950s-80s), all self-taught, who abandoned menial labour in favour of painting, not as dilettantes, but as guys who wanted dollars without having to do joe-jobs, slave in sugarcane fields, or turn to fast-buck, penny-ante crime (and end up in chain-gangs or on Death Row).

Again, respecting his exemplary Aunt Portia, Bill understood that *Art* could free him from the customary humiliations visited upon Africadian men. To be able to devote himself to painting while whis-tling along to classical music, either spun off the big Clairtone stereo cabinet or out of the kitchen-based portable radio, likely helped him transcend whatever shames or slights he'd experienced during the work week.

But Bill's most successful outing as a truly commercial artist was also short-lived. On Friday, October 30, 1959, he lost his linen-checker and luggage-carrier job at CN Halifax. Though his railway employ had always been precarious, my father loathed the prospect of unemployment. After a desultory motorcycle trip to Newport Station and Three Mile Plains—not to see my mother, who was visibly pregnant (with me)—but to take sundry gals for spins on "Liz II," his big purple BMW motorcycle, Bill resolved to entrepreneur—in art. So, within forty-eight hours of being laid off from the Canadian National Railway, my father was painting picture after picture in his apartment living room, suddenly a minuscule prototype of Warhol's Factory.

Next, he went running about town—by foot, trolley, and by taxi—to sell this art—for $5, $10, $15, depending on size. He'd drop in on or telephone friends, relatives, acquaintances, to flaunt his "samples" and collect orders, and let word-of-mouth bring purchasers flocking. At the end of his first weekend as a commercial artist, he'd earned more than he had working for his weekly wage at CN. Better yet, he was his own boss; and he soon had orders for more paintings. Finding that he had a knack for assembly-line-produced art and/or *Commerce*, he continued to bang out his pix, on glass, backed with tinfoil, right up to his wedding in 1960 to Gerry.

Bill's 1959 *Diary* reveals his plans to utilize the mainly black Brotherhood of Sleeping Car Porters to carry his art (samples-as-advertisements) everywhere the night trains whistled: Toronto, Montréal, Halifax, and south to New York and Boston. Poignantly, in his teens and early twenties, my dad had yearned to go to New York and/or Paris, to live an artist's life, and, frankly, to "audition" ladies as nude models. His decision to marry Gerry (and her acceptance of his proposal) in June 1960 saw him put away his youthful ambition to pursue art in favour of becoming the head-of-a-household and a provider of wherewithal.

To serve as a husband and dad, he sidelined his art and mainlined his railway employ. True: Great-Aunt Portia was able to live as a classical concert contralto and music teacher and voice coach. However, after her initial struggles to both teach grade school and sing part-time, and thanks to winning local and then national adulation, Portia acquired Government of Nova Scotia backing. Later in her career, there was often a mink stole and a bouquet of roses awaiting her back-stage. Being a family man, and the breadwinner, Bill abandoned dreams of artistic fame and resultant luxuries—all that his Aunt Portia epitomized. Instead, he had to ensure our bellies could be stuffed with bologna and macaroni, not filet mignon and caviar.

(Intriguingly, his Aunt Portia had written my father to advise that he come to New York, in 1960, for she was sure that she could find him a job painting Broadway sets. How different my life would have been had he taken her up on that offer!)

Although Bill was a workday railwayman, he was still, throughout my childhood, a weekend artist. So, he filled our hallways with his art, or with purchased reproductions of classical works bought from the local, ghetto-quality grocery store (tainted meats, rotten fruit, and cheapo, dented tins). His Rembrandts were glued onto inch-thick Styrofoam and then stuck on nails, so that the "gallery'd" paintings appeared floating projections. A one-dollar-tea-towel, rectangular illustration of a clipper ship received a Styrofoam frame whose four sides were then covered with black construction paper; next, this frame was cross-hatched with three horizontal strips and two vertical strips of black construction paper, to create the effect that, from a window—or prison bars—one was watching the vessel skip upon waves.

In his drawings, Bill toyed with perspectives and geometric shapes—of men, machines, and letters (the Roman alphabet). A font that he drew with pencil, ink, and ruler, in 1969, is a rough-hewn but elegant, mainly majuscule typeface that testifies to the nature of Africadian culture: our art is *crafty*. (I do remember him drawing the font, when I was but nine, what Andrew Steeves of Gaspereau Press digitized—in 2011—as "Bill Clarke Caps.") It is impossible to delimit any culture, but, to me, Africadian culture is raw heart, raunchy eyes, earthy tongues, bluesy filth, raucous gospel, beautiful mourning, gutbucket preachifying, the sensual always more sexual than sensuous, the weird combo of grit and glitz, banjo and violin, saxophone and spittoon, piano and pigfeet. In our culture, *Hamlet* is best staged in a hamlet, to make the tragedy feel real down-home, and starring not the Prince of Denmark, but a pauper, lollygagging in the express commission to stab-to-death his motherfucking, adulterous, two-faced uncle . . .

ix.

I didn't recognize the irony, as a black boy, of descending from an illustrious clan branded with the surname of the "enemy," I mean, of the slave-master(s) of Virginia who'd owned our ancestors. Yet, the black Whites of Virginia were as much a deliberate, ironic refutation of racial segregation and its fantasies of black inferiority and inequality as were all those African-American slaves stuck with presidential (slaveholder) surnames: Washington, Jefferson, Madison, Monroe, Jackson, Tyler, Polk, and Taylor. (Lookit! Twenty-five percent of US presidents owned slaves.)

Thus, George Washington himself was only the white-faced precursor of all the black Washingtons, his namesakes if not heirs. Every time a black Washington was humiliated, denied service, refused a job, falsely arrested, beaten up, and/or lynched, his (or her) surname proved American pretensions to *Liberty* to be a damned lie.

Just as assuredly, every time a black Washington excelled and/or won plaudits and prizes, it served to prove that the arguments for black incapacity were vicious, hatemongering propaganda, for the black Washington could assert a claim to a seat beside the white Founding Father of the Republic. This argument also suits the black Whites: whatever the white Whites achieve, there may be a black White who outdoes em. Lookit! This was the special burden of the black Whites: to establish—to seize—for themselves whatever lustre and prestige that pertained originally to the white Whites: To prove ourselves as good—if not better.

The black Whites accepted that pressure. The son of ex-slaves, William Andrew White (WAW), of Virginia, at first planned to become the first black millionaire in postbellum, robber-baron America. However, a chance meeting with a white Baptist from Nova Scotia careened WAW (as I like to dub him) to that province, into Acadia University, and then into the African Baptist ministry. His children—not only Portia—became remarkable: a gold-medal, blue-ribbon, red-letter crew. Eventually enrolled in the Order of Canada, Bill White (William Andrew White III) was a composer and the first African-Canadian to seek federal political office (in 1949)—as a Democratic Socialist candidate for the Co-operative Commonwealth Federation; he also found time to help found Don Heights Unitarian Congregation in Toronto. Jack White was a charismatic union leader in Ontario and a historic champion of Workmen's Compensation; Lorne White starred with singer Anne Murray on CBC-TV's *Singalong Jubilee* (1961-74); George White became—likely—the first black pharmacist in Nova Scotia. They were (are) a family of strivers and achievers, on the American side of the border as well as on the Canadian. William Andrew White was grandfather to the second Black Canadian senator, Don Oliver, Q.C., but also grandfather to Anthony Sherwood, the filmmaker and a star of CBC-TV's *Street Legal* (1987-94). And grandfather to the co-founder of the Ottawa Folk Festival, Chris White. And grandfather to Chris's sister, NDP strategist Sheila White. The black Whites are folks whose ancestors toiled in Dixie dirt so that their progeny could navigate toward the North Star.

It is unlikely that many Canadian families have produced as many persons of such prominence—across music, the arts, religious devotion, and socio-political leadership, and always with a progressive or socialist bias.* (Notably, WAW himself preached a sermon on "Race Consciousness" in Toronto in 1922; so, the black Whites have always situated themselves as a vanguard lot, always aiming for a humanitarian, just, and egalitarian society.)

Yet, there's a downside to the requirement to excel. In striving for Caucasian acknowledgement of our equality and/or excellence, did we also shun the people—our people—who were strugglers (rather than strivers)? Did we act snooty? Were we too dismissive of those whose morals left space for pleasure and expediency, rather than a policy of puritanical rigour (whether or not it was sustainable)? Were we aware that *zwieback* adulation could be hypocritical, self-interested, and exploitative? Didn't we feel alone, isolated, lonesome, depressed, to be too often solitary in walking out on stage, in delivering that spiritual, in reciting that sermon, in performing that song, in acting that part, in teaching that class, in "representing" in union hall or senate chamber? Were we aware of how other family and community members could feel sidelined by our ascension, even if we felt we were forwarding—audaciously—the best of our people, so that when we stood on podiums, as when Portia posed for Karsh, we were saying, "Yes, we are, the descendants of slaves. But note our majesty and beauty! Neither can be further denied!" Sure: striving can end in achieving, but it can

---

* Cf. The Hills and the McCurdys—both of Ontario; *and* the Olivers of Nova Scotia.

also end in a self-sabotaging separation from those who nursed and nurtured, those who taught and trained. That *beau risque* is there, and the striver ignores it at peril of alienation.

Even so, in coming to idolize Portia *White* as a supreme black-woman relative who escaped—partially—the boundaries of race, gender, and class, I glimpsed the possibility of creative contradiction, everywhere resonant in colour imagery. I could peer into the dark heart of whiteness, or note notions of *Black Beauty* as being equivalent to *Snow White*. More yin-and-yang than polar opposites.

x.

But that appreciation was an adult realization. Returning to my North End boyhood, I still say that visiting with Portia's sister, my Nanny Clarke, was about as much fun as sensing a dentist's drill invading a tooth. Indeed, if entering my mom's parents' home in Newport Station was like entering a Disneyland of feast and frolic, going to Nanny Clarke's home was like going to penance—all sombre and shadows. She was, like my father, dark-complected, and, also like him, icily European in attitude. I mean, she seemed to project nat'chal-bo'n hauteur—plus noblesse oblige, but the softening element of charity was inadvertent. With my mom's parents, my brothers and I could be playful, although our maternal grandfather could be gruff when he was not taciturn, or whistling, or spitting black phlegm into the stove. Still he didn't pose as reverential. Yet, we had to approach our dad's mom as if she were regal, even saintly.

I deem our household a blend of European and Black influence, with the general precept being, "Follow Caucasian 'norms' where beneficial; reject em when they seem inhumane." So, dad always had Bach, Beethoven, or Brahms circulating on the turntable, and he'd whistle along while he bent over a painting-in-progress. But when he wasn't hogging the hi-fi or the radio (tuned to CBC when within his earshot), Gerry could throw down the Platters, the Supremes, James

Brown, Aretha Franklin, all the soul and R&B that she loved. Happily, they both agreed on the Beatles and Broadway; so there'd be Belafonte crooning, or Bob Dylan's "Like a Rolling Stone," exploding steely and gnarly outta transistors; or there'd be the Gershwin Bros.' *Porgy & Bess* plus a blast of Bizet's *Carmen* or Puccini's *Madama Butterfly*. Nor can I omit Henry Mancini's *Pink Panther* soundtrack; that was also music to which we could all cha-cha-cha. However, church music was never heard—not at home; not even spirituals got played. But dad's dad—though mysteriously absent—hailed from Jamaica, and so Bill Clarke had a cache of 1930s calypso records. Along with the *Mary Poppins* soundtrack, Duke Ellington's sassy LP *A Drum Is a Woman*, and a 45 of Shirley Bassey belting "Goldfinger," he gave my brothers and me a naughty calypso. Here's the punch line:

> I kissed her lips,
> I kissed her hands,
> And I left her *be-hind*
> For you.

We laughed uproariously at the singer's emphasis on "behind." Though too young to know the phrase *double-entendre*, we did get the sassy, double meaning of that bottom-dollar line.

When Bill helmed the radio, classical music issued. When my mother commandeered the air waves, we got to hear Top 40 pop songs—everything from the itsy-bitsy-teenie-weenie-yellow-polka-dot-bikini to lost-someone-a-million-to-one. Those collisions of tunes—like my father's collages—all suggested that wholeness in art is always a callaloo, a stew, a medley. . . .

xi.

Whatever their different tastes in music, my parents knew that, when hosting friends and relatives for a party, only black music—funky, bluesy, earthy, guttural, sweet, salty, spicy, would suffice. Indeed, the "house party" was an Africadian custom. Until the 1990s, in Halifax, white-owned nightclubs often barred most Negro men (using any pretext), or were expensive (though pouring watered-down, iced-up drinks), and so—weekly (in the 1960s)—select households would lay in a store of booze, a stack of 45s, plus crackers-sardines-olives-potato-chips-beer-nuts, and invite a mix of singles and couples to come and waltz and sing and hum and shindig and grope and drink and smoke until somewhere "round bout three a.m." Whenever my parents hosted a gathering, my brothers and I would be dispatched to our bedrooms—or allowed to watch television in our parents' bedroom—but we definitely had to be shut away from the adults, apart from presenting perfunctory, respectful greetings to any early arrivals. We'd have to disappear by 7 or 8 p.m., and then the party would start hopping, assuredly by 9 p.m.

Naturally, Bryant and Bill and I would make up excuses to slip downstairs because the presence of all these black, brown, white adults—couples, singles, relatives—was strange and exciting. When I'd go downstairs to the kitchen, I'd try to sneak a glimpse of those mysterious, cackling goings-on. I'd see that the living room was opaque—dense—black with multi-coloured people (a few pale girls in the mix). I always wondered, when I'd beg a glass of milk from my tolerant-this-time, smiling parents, how did so many adults compress themselves into those compressing corners of the living room, and what possible *Pleasure* could they gain from the physical pressure of having to dance, stand, sit, almost always tightly intertwined?

Must've been the music—the songs—that let the couples brush against each other, press against each other, melt into each other, to kiss lips, hair, eyelids, cheeks. Laughter was guffaws, roars, bawdy, or folks' voices receded to whispers. Cigarette smoke was an amoeba against the ceiling and then slowly silvered—silted down—saturating every close, clinging body and all the tight, clinging clothes. Pumps would slide off so nylon'd or bare feet could shift and shuffle over the carpet. Men's brogues got untied or their loafers would get kicked off. Somehow, anywhere between a dozen to two dozen adults could clinch and clutch and kiss and "tighten up" in our living-room—the lights off and/or the lamps covered over; the record player spinning the "slow jams"—the waltzes—so that the couples could really feel each other as female hips ground into male groins. These nights were when the serious music got played; the rhythm-n-blues that went well with rum-n-coke or rye-n-ginger. It was all blue light, black light, Millie Jackson and James Brown and Peaches-n-Herb. Nor were the drinks skimpy, i.e., half-water, with ice bulking up the content to dull the ache of absent alcohol.

(I confess that the foregoing portrait is part childhood-memory and part adult-observation. In my late teens, in 1978-79, the "house party" was still a favoured means of entertainment because the Halifax-Dartmouth nightclubs still screened out black men. I imagine that what I enjoyed in the latter 70s, my parents enjoyed the previous decade.)

Sometimes, I'd wonder if my father regretted not playing his Beethoven on such nights. But he knew—as did my mom—that the folks were assembling to hear *their* music—black music—the music of real love, physical love and orgasmic Satisfaction saturatin every corpuscle and follicle and nerve-end and brain cell. The artistry of European classicists? Could it compete with the moans and cries and hollers and howls borne out of plush-lipped Negro mouths and the guttural depths of the tuneful soul and properly tuned heart? Could it make you wanna love and be loved; to get down and get happy? In my dad's 1959 *Diary*, he recounts an incident wherein he invited a black couple to audit his preferred music—either classical or crooners—and became irked when they pooh-poohed it. So irritated was he, he bade em leave his premises.

I'm guessing that he clutched the "Serious Music" LPs to his chest as a means of saying to the world, "I may be a Negro worker, but my tastes are more refined than those of many middle-class Caucasians, and so I am their equal (if not their superior)." But this predilection was also his inheritance—as a matrilineal White, with Portia as his aunt—that he'd see himself as not "just another Coloured guy." Yet, that passive-aggressive attitude can also cut one off from soul-nurturing sources of *Joy* and self-regard. So, certainly, by the early 1960s, my father had learned his lesson. Or maybe my mom had influenced him positively. He now knew he could save Rachmaninoff for cerebral contemplation and Otis Redding for sensual delight.

If a guy got too plastered at one of my parents' parties, he'd stay overnight, snoring on the sofa or the living-room floor, until he became elastic enough to move on. As a boy, it was always disconcerting or disgusting for me to get up from bed and go downstairs into those morning-after situations where cigarette butts would float—with olive pits—in one rum-n-coke tumbler or some almost-emptied glass of ale. There'd be the stink of stale beer, the revolting tang of cigarette-smoke-saturated clothes. But it was also exciting to experience the aftershock of explicitly non-Baptist activities, and then, dressed up, troop off to Sunday school. By the time the regular church service began at 11 a.m., even the hardest-partying, Sat'-nite adult would show, suave and spiffy. Assuredly, God was awfully tolerant of Black Baptist sinners . . .

At a Bay Road house party that my parents hosted in '63, I forged a happy memory of black platters, of sable-vinyl music overturning mores. "Limbo Rock" (1962)—by Chubby Checker—was the rage, and I got to witness my parents, their adult siblings, and black and white friends (*women*), shimmy down as low as they could to bring their chests level with their shins (if not ankles) and pass under a yardstick (my father's humble, handyman instrument) hand-held low, or supported by two stools. I just remember the looks of sheer gaiety on the faces—dark, lovely, pale, lustrous—as the skirts and dresses got hiked, shoes bounced off, and folks "got down." Seven p.m. was beddy-bye time for the kiddies, so I didn't long witness the gymnastic shenanigans, but I was impressed by the hoopla, the whoopee, the cha-cha-cha of those integrated Nova Scotians slinking—yoyoing—their haunches to Carib-backbeat, Afro-Am R-n-B. "Oh, how I long to be in that number . . ."

There was *Salvation*-level ecstasy in such fiestas, and a sense that this was a heaven that only Negroes could enter.

(Not that it was always "fun-n-games." I remember one Sunday morn, when I was older, that a friend of my mom's, I'll call her "Lady," showed up at our door with a black eye. Her "man" had hit her the night before and thrown her out. My parents took her in—at least for the day—without any apparent question or discussion. They'd likely figured that the squabble would blow over and that Lady would go back to her guy. But, it was still sobering for me—as an eight-year-old or so—to see this adult black woman, who I was used to seeing and hearing laughing and drinking and smoking and gossiping—with my mom—now standing on our front doorstep with a bruised eye—and on a Sunday morning at that.)

xii.

Given this laudable auditory background, the mash-up of Mozart and Motown, the classical and calypso, Procol Harum and Peaches & Herb, how could my brothers and I, as older boys, *not* league with other Maynard Street, Creighton Street, Agricola Street, Gerrish Street, "boyz in da hood," to assemble drums, using steel garbage cans and lids, pieces of two-by-four, toy xylophones, kazoos, and a flat stringed instrument—the zither—to pound out and sing (often using our own lyrics) our street-corner versions of the hits? I recall that we—the four, five, six of us—aged seven, eight, nine, ten, eleven—changed at least one line of the notoriously indecipherable "Louie Louie" (by the Kingsmen), namely, "Said we gotta go" to "I said a weiner roast," which is what we heard, though it made no sense. These sessions of spontaneous song-fashioning always involved us black guys improvising rhythms and riffs, as we participated—in our long-distance, Black North Atlantic way—in a song-making custom with deep roots in the Slave Trade. I didn't know, back then, that my father, Bill, had made a small living by touring his gospel-singing quartet about Nova Scotian churches, at least in 1959. So, not only was he briefly a commercial artist in autumn 1959 and winter 1960, he was also a "gospeleer"—a musketeer of song, so to speak, launching hymns and spirituals for uplift of others and the accumulation of tithes for himself and his harmonizing cadres.

To be clear: Bill Clarke may have preferred classical music above all, but his *Great*-Aunt Portia had always numbered spirituals in her repertoire. Too, I think he would have known, thanks to the spilling over into Canadian living rooms of US Civil Rights Movement songs, that Caucasian Christians north of the 49th Parallel would also love to hear local Coloureds singing those soul-stirring songs. He was pro-classical, but not anti-spiritual . . .

(In my mid-teen years, when I began to hanker to be a troubadour, Gerry bought me an acoustic guitar that I never learned to play, and gave me the poetry of T. S. Eliot to read. However, by then, I was studying Bob Dylan, whose voice—that blend of screech and howl—she could never abide, save for the Nashville-professional, plangent tone of "Lay Lady Lay.")

Music was everywhere about the Africadian community. A cousin to my mom, Billy Downey, founded the Arrows Club, which opened not far from our home on Maynard. The Arrows was on the corner of West Street and Agricola Street, an area my brothers and I knew well because there was a field—a vacant lot—on West Street, across from what became a fire station, and which was absurdly richly supplied with four-leaf clovers. (I still have a few—now fifty-plus-years-old—pressed sacredly between the pages of my Scofield Reference Bible.)

Billy Downey brought many African-American acts to Halifax, thus adding Nova Scotia to the "Chitlin Circuit" (an informal chain of US night spots and halls, juke-joints and bars, that featured Negro singers, musicians, comics, and actors during the segregation era). So, Ike and Tina Turner and Teddy Pendergrass delivered real R-n-B to the land of tartan and fiddles. Many less famed acts also took to the Arrows stage, performing on Saturday nights for the adults. But, on Saturday afternoons, the touring singer or group would rehearse, and these sessions were open to chillun. For 50¢ each, we'd get to dance and waltz to the same group—playing the same music—that would later entertain the adults. I remember best Lotsa Poppa being billed as "400 Pounds of Solid Soul." Did he weigh that much? I do remember that, when he moved his feet along the stage (a platform raised only about a foot off the floor), it sagged if it didn't creak, and it creaked where it didn't sag. He should have carried a hanky like Louis Armstrong, for he did sweat an awful lot as he rehearsed his numbers and steps.

I was too shy to ask any of the girls—my school mates—to dance. When the slow jams got tried out, I'd just go and sit on the edge of the stage, trying to look aloof and brainy, when all the time I was both hoping I'd get up the nerve to ask someone to dance, and then feeling very shy all over again because I knew that I didn't know how to dance, anyway.

As a schoolboy, my brother Bryant piped a recorder, beat on a drum pad, and strummed a ukulele. I'm sure that Bill and Gerry saw in him a true instinct for rhythm and melody and voice, unlike me. In fact, I took trombone lessons for two years, age ten to twelve, but found the sliding-valve brass instrument exactingly boring—unless working the slide could help one to learn how to box! I'd lusted for a trumpet, but the Halifax city music program instructor informed me that my buck teeth would never fit the mouthpiece, and so the trombone got palmed off on me instead. I often wonder how differently I'd've made the trumpet sound—if I'd striven to learn to move the air around and through my teeth into the valves and chambers of that elegant, sonorous, tooting, burping, and snorting instrument.

At age twelve, I was commanded, by my parents, to go to the Cornwallis Street Baptist Church and "join the choir"—those voices half molasses-intoxicating and half thunderous-stern. Boy, did I drag my feet on that Friday night on my way to the church! I was not lookin forward to havin to warble hymns and spirituals and other churchy ditties—with an organ pumping breathlessly alongside or a piano tinkling as if chiming jingly bells—while severe elders cupped a hand to an ear, listening intently for every garbled phrase or fluffed note.

(Despite—or because of—slavery and segregation, black folks became master, amateur critics of singin, sermonizin, speechifyin, comic-timin, dancin, boxin, instrumentalizin, and improvising . . . Combine all these skills and you get jazz: somebody punchin a keyboard or thwackin a bass; somebody elongating notes or words or cutting em off sharp—all for the sake of the drama inherent in treating words and notes like putty or rubber, the voice as projectile or boomerang.) So, I was quickly relieved of any fears re: losing Friday nights to choir practice and Sundays to singin along. The choir director, at the audition, proclaimed, "You can't sing," and freed me from any obligation to lisp scripture or mumble hymns. I must've skipped all the way home, sprung so instantly from a sentence of imposed, weekend piety and sobriety; instead, I could boogie; I could woogie; I could rock-n-roll . . .

So what if I couldn't sing? By age twelve and/or thirteen, I joined my brother Bryant in spontaneously composing songs, such as "Little Girl Up in the Window," and crooning these tunes under streetlights and under some mooned-after lil gal's window, somewhere around ½ of 10 p.m., until the gal—such as one Miss Royale—would come to the window or to her front stoop—to humour us—or until the intended gal's parents (or mom) would emerge and snap, "That's enough." At that point, we'd have to repair sheepishly to our beds—just across the street, or down the street, from the serenaded darling's home. Still, wasn't there much intoxicating power in those songs! Our duets taught us that there was a degree of real Black Power—and Black Magic—inherent in our lungs and lips and tongues.

Not only was music always swishing round the turntable in our childhood homes, Bill was a fanatic for CBC news, commentaries, and documentaries. So, gathering for supper, we'd tune into *The World at Six* and hear the latest news about presidents, prime ministers, politicians, and, yes, the Queen, and Martin Luther King, and other potentates and personalities, and Bill would comment on anything that seemed pertinent to our young ears. When the Beatles appeared on Ed Sullivan in 1964, we were permitted to stay up beyond our bedtime and watch the Fab Four seduce America. Our parents made sure that we witnessed Neil Armstrong set booted foot on the moon. Moreover, we had the daily newspaper and weekly receipt of *TIME* and *LIFE* magazines, and we'd have almost daily discussions of unfolding events. Though I was born in 1960 and was only a child through that decade, I experienced all the major events as if I'd been born already aged ten. I was aware of the greater world beyond our home, beyond Halifax, beyond Nova Scotia and Canada, because Bill and Gerry bothered to include their three sons, us boys, in their mulling over contemporary goings-on.

xiii.

During my childhood, my father rarely spoke about "race." His love of Rembrandt and Chagall, Henry Miller and Eldridge Cleaver, Nat King Cole and Frank Sinatra, indicated his lived conception of the natural equality of all people. Except for the sugar-bowl lesson on the reality of race prejudice that we Negro sons would face, seldom did Bill Clarke discourse on the "struggle" for *Equality* or on civil rights. He presumed *Equality*, and that was that. He expected that his sons should be taken at face value as decent and moral, and that we should reciprocate this courtesy to others. He also believed in the find-your-own-level-of-equality *available via* meritocracy; that we should rise as high in prestige and income as our talents and hard work could achieve. Moreover, he felt that aggressive racists should, under most circumstances, be ignored, for they are merely "ignorant" persons. (Once, when I was seven, my father claimed that "Coloured people are smarter than white people." He did not intend the statement as a prejudicial sentiment; rather, he was trying to prepare me to understand that, to survive—let alone succeed—in what was called back then, without irony, "a white man's world," I'd need guile, wit, and smarts.)

Yet, Bill was an independent, inadvertent "civil rights activist." When a white taxi driver smacked my younger brother Billy's fingers for snapping up-and-down the back seat, arm rest, ash-tray lid, our father summoned the hack operator to court, and won the case. However, as would become his pattern, Bill did not want any sanctions applied to the taxi driver—he'd just wanted the man to learn a lesson: that Coloured kids were not to be interfered with by white adults; that they—we—were not white folks' property, at least not anymore.

My mother did not impart any such wisdom. Not then! She simply told my brothers and me, when we asked why we were brown, that "we'd been left a little later in the oven: you're gingerbread boys." Liking ginger snaps as I did, plus the story about the Gingerbread Man, I also favoured her explanation. Besides, we liked cinnamon, which was also brown.

Given his desire for recognized *Equality*, Bill once quipped to a motorcycle buddy that, situated as we once were on the Bay Road on a hilltop, he could see the towers of Dalhousie University, a few miles yonder. That meant he was—we were—"on the same level" as the university profs and students. He would have relished the positioning, being a railway worker who had achieved grade ten—practically an unheard-of accoutrement for a Nova Scotia Negro, but whose reading level—and digested dictionary—were absolutely at a Supreme Court-jurist level, never mind the mere Baccalaureate degree attained by university grads. I assure one and all that the previous statement is not a matter of filial piety or poetic license: Bill Clarke's vocabulary brandished multitudinous polysyllables at instant beck-and-call. I write these words as a Ph.D. who holds eight honorary doctorates as surplus (but very appreciated) endowments, yet I will state that I have never met anyone who has had a higher number of Latinisms dancing attendance on the tongue. When my brothers and I would seek to escape a whuppin by uttering a fib, he would not accuse us of lying, but of "prevarication," which, really, sounded much nerve-rackingly worse because those five syllables fell on our ears like five whacks of a strap.

When I was seventeen, my father came home, fuming, to 2357 Maynard Street, because two Haligonian cops had given him a ticket for driving without his headlights on. It was late autumn or early winter, nightfall came early, and he'd been stopped by the white constables only about two blocks from our home. So, why was he outraged? His headlights were on, but the Ku Klux Klan Koppers laughed in his face and gave him the ticket anyway, because he was a black man, and who would credit his testimony over theirs in traffic court?

Unfortunately for the cops, they'd ticketed the wrong black man. Bill Clarke represented himself in traffic court, cross-examined the peace officers, and so enmeshed them in the illogicality of their "prevarications" (I gotta use *that* word) that the judge halted the case and asked my father if he would like him to charge the constables with perjury. I still regret that my father declined the offer. If he had said, "Yes, charge these two disgraceful and dishonest public servants," perhaps decades would not have had to pass before Halifax Police were finally investigated and called to account for their racist practices. However, Bill likely surmised that if he had called for punishment, he and all of us would have been targeted for reprisal.

So, yes, his intellect—his diction—were impeccable—right along with his pronunciation and enunciation. In the mid-1970s, he was a successful part-time salesman of the *Encyclopaedia Britannica*. I'm pretty sure that if anyone knew those volumes inside and out, it was he. (In the early 1970s, he'd even subscribed to a weekly book series on World War II weaponry, battles, and principal figures—generals, dictators, prime ministers, and presidents.)

After his death in 2005, at age seventy, I found *several* letters addressed to him, by the City of Halifax*, commending him—a taxi driver—for having enlivened the city's history for tourists who happened to have him as an accidental guide, during a run to and from the airport, or Peggy's Cove. He could talk for hours about the *Titanic*

---

* My father was so respected that, in 1971 (I think), Nova Scotia Premier Gerry Regan dispatched an agent to prod Bill to stand as a Liberal Party candidate for city council. He declined. Instead, in 1974, Graham Downey became Halifax's first Black alderman.

Disaster, the Halifax Explosion, and also the crash of Swissair 111 off Peggy's Cove in September 1998. (Thanks to the aid of Alexa McDonough, MP, I had him interred in Halifax's North End-located Fairview Cemetery—near the *Titanic* and Halifax Explosion deceased.) Poignantly too, when I went through his papers in 2005, I found that he had torn out of the local paper every single one of my bi-weekly book-review columns, plus every instance where I had been interviewed or had one of my own books reviewed. That unforgettable progenitor had not forgotten his progeny—not at all—after all.

discord and dissension

I now offer this contradictory comment. I had a happy childhood; I had a hellish childhood. Have I already sketched the cheerful part? Materially, I never had a sense of deprivation.

Apart from the plenty that coddled me as a kid, I knew that my mother loved me—but I could only hope that my father did. I did feel hallowed—as the first-born, as a child born in the country, but also because I did well at school, and my excellent report cards would earn me extra appreciation from my father. In fact, I learned to excel—to strive for good marks—because I craved kind words and that gift of a coin—from him.

I sought Bill Clarke's approval, for I loved and feared him as the stern disciplinarian that he was. To me, he was a figure of rectitude, of courtesy, of almost fetishized enunciation of English. He was also fastidious in dress, handled razor and shaving brush with panache, was proud of both his toolbox and his home library, and seemed as clear about right-and-wrong as is God in laying down the Ten Command-ments in Exodus XX. He was an old-school, retro-*paterfamilias*, despite his bachelor, Bohemian tastes, most of which he'd set aside once wed.

For all my adoration of William Lloyd Clarke, however, I always sensed—always dreaded—his presence as the judge, the meter out of

Punishment (often for minor infractions), and his steady application of his unfurled belt to his boys' backsides: to correct us, to admonish us, to perfect us, maybe, but also to terrorize us and to salve his own chafing frustrations.

I could not know the reasons for his resort to corporal assault, only that I had to do all I could, as a child, to avoid his destabilizing shifts into sudden, violent moodiness. I must have figured out, when I was three or so, that one way to curry his favour was to excel at learning. A good report card would win 25¢—to purchase tuck shop treats—chocolate bars, pop, potato chips, bubble-gum, or maybe to splurge on a picture show. It would also win sparsely provided praise. I sought his delight in my high marks because I was very uncertain about his love.

To prove my devotion to him, I liked what he liked: he liked Ian Fleming's Bond novels and the spin-off movie franchise, so did I; he liked *2001: A Space Odyssey*, so did I; he despised Richard Nixon; I despised Tricky Dick; he liked Turkish delight chocolates, so did I. I even became a teenage Elton John fan in the 1970s because he'd announced that he favoured Elton John's music. That I might now be an intellectual is partly because I wanted to establish myself as being "smart"—to receive his version of a merit badge.

I did appreciate, as a boy, his stand-out differentiations: it meant that I could fashion my own way to be myself, rather than a prisoner of white people's prejudices or some black folks' stereotyped reactions—to drop out, to turn to crime, to adopt and internalize white racism . . .

But none of that changes the truth that Bill Clarke was a hard man; a difficult man; a cold man; a bull-headed Taurus astrologically and a tyrant behind the closed doors of his "castle."

So, my brothers and I were beaten—with a belt—several times a year. I do know that it was frequent, less than daily but definitely more than once annually. We were thrashed for the slightest infraction—or so my slight frame felt. Often, beatings occurred because our father's mood had simply fluctuated, whimsically, toward aggression.

Us boys'd be home with our mom playing or gluing leaves and scrap paper into scribblers or coating autumn leaves with wax or licking the left-over batter or frosting from her Mixmaster blades—just having fun, when we'd hear the thud of Bill Clarke's tread on our front doorstep. Instantly, we had to arrest our entertainments, our frolics; assume a glum face and disposition, and wait, fearfully—*all of us*—to try to suss out his mood.

If he arrived troubled and angry, surly and grumpy, and one of us boys seemed to be acting foolishly or seemed too cheery, he'd snarl and snap at us. Next, if he heard that we were guilty of any booboo, then it could be time for him to release his belt, pull down our pants, and give our behinds a serious whipping. Sometimes, his assault would be so harsh, so relentless, that my mother would try to stop him, and then he could very well beat her too.

We lived in constant fear of his hair-trigger temper. We matured in an atmosphere of terror which also, sadly, corroded our love for our father (or maybe it was only my affection for him that was conflicted). I respected him for his art and his intellect; I dreaded him for his ready violence, which the most minuscule *faux pas* could detonate.

There were no guarantees. If Bill Clarke encountered a neighbour or a buddy en route to our door, we'd overhear his comic ripostes, his joviality. But, as soon as he'd take leave of the friend or passerby, frowns would crop up; and then it could be time to pummel his children or smash down our mother; or attack us all (if she dared to interfere). A good mood was more likely to persist, once he returned from work, if he had a nice buzz going with his suds. Then, he'd relax, smile, and joke with us, and be *unnervingly* friendly, husbandly, fatherly.

But too many were the crises, still, when, once the "high" was gone, he could tear into us boys with his belt or into our mother with his hands. Growing up with him was like being on tenterhooks, walking on eggshells, tiptoeing through a minefield. There was no assurance that his love or affection would be displayed daily, especially once we'd graduated from nightly prayers and a bedtime kiss goodnight.

Bill Clarke's love always seemed tentative, always on a knife-edge, where it could teeter into wrath or a sabre-slashing verbal put-down, and often without warning. We all had to be circumspect, seen-and-not-heard, or, better still, not-seen-or-heard-at-all. His moods were as treacherous as April weather: sunshine, then thunder; warmth, then a blizzard.

Maddeningly, the same hand that could draft a portrait of me, aged five and a half, with something like tenderness in the charcoal pencil lines, was also the same hand that could shellac me, or any of us. He'd say, while whacking away, "This hurts me more than it does you!" Well, the obvious perversity of that statement suits dictators far better than it ever should parents.

Nowadays, psychologists might analyze or diagnose my father as being bipolar or manic-depressive. Such a case could be made; his mood swings too often ended in punching swings or belting swings—slaps, smacks, smack-downs.

Although I don't excuse my father's terrorism towards us, I tender an explanation. Many black men, "back in the day," held jobs where they had to exhibit civility, gentility, and even docility and servility: to grin when "nigger" got spat in your face. To be real nice to white people and real careful around white women. It was not possible to "get uppity"; whites would take umbrage, and you'd find yourself living hand-to-mouth and down-at-the-heel. Or else the cops would give you a lick with a baton and/or hustle ya into the hoosegow. And then, how could you feed your family and keep clothes on their backs and a roof over their heads?

Because the results of contesting or speaking back to authority could be dire, men like Bill Clarke had to act nicey-nice, beam light-house smiles, and exude affable personae. They all had to play Uncle Tom and Stepin Fetchit or Sambo: to suggest that they weren't rapists or robbers, and so deserved white trust to incentivize white tips. Yet, treated like boys and called out of their names, they tamped down their rage over humiliations until they trudged home.

My father pretended to be harmless, helpful, and "white"-mannered, but seethed with black turmoil within. He, like many black men, was gentle and genteel with whites, but brusque and brutal with his family, ruling with iron fists and casting off any notion of velvet gloves. He accommodated white trespasses and transgressions by inflicting cruelty on his own black flesh and blood. It was the "brown behind" that needed "tanning"; it was the black child who was "the pickaninny"; it was the Coloured wife who was a bitch who had to be walloped or "tapped" and put in her place.

I recall now a petite, beige neighbour woman being pummelled right through the front door of her home by her irate railway-worker hubby: the door splintered and she spilled, lacerated, into the street. Her assailant was a gentle giant as a railway porter. But at home, as a husband and father, he was a thug. Or he could be. I was twelve. Neighbours—women—wives—came running to help the struck-down woman, to clean her wounds and console her over the fracas, and then take her back home to her now silent (and maybe sorry) husband. No one thought to summon police.

Having witnessed my own mother being mauled, all of us children knew that husbands could exercise such power—even if the circumstances were so unfair, especially to a child's mind. After all, our neighbour was over six feet tall and must have weighed closer to two hundred pounds of muscle than to three hundred pounds of fat. His fists looked as big as his size-twelve shoes. But he had punched a five-foot, slender woman right through the wooden front door of their house—and so hard that she tumbled down the stoop steps and onto the sidewalk. I remember feeling paralyzing pity for the lady, for I was so horribly powerless as a child. Yet, because black men could control little else, the idea that their home could be their fiefdom (not merely a "castle") was held dear—often with vile—and ugly—consequence.

Then again, most of the black men—fathers and husbands (our neighbours)—worked for the railway and owned their homes and had their wives and children fed, clothed, and sleeping under their roofs. On our street, Maynard, there were at least half a dozen households (including our own) that portrayed this demographic. These men, who may have grown up poor and fatherless (like so many black people, freed from slavery but not from slave-like treatment), had toiled and scrimped, accepted slurs and pretended gentleness, to be able to achieve a more-or-less middle-class lifestyle and *paterfamilias* position. They were resolutely impatient, then, with any sign of disrespect or hint of misbehaviour in their zealously secured domiciles.

So, we ricocheted among Bill Clarke's enthusiasms—model-kits, World War II memorabilia (he'd been a paperboy by the end of that conflict, and had saved the most historic headlines), the Jackie K/ JFK/ RFK Kennedys, auto races, his paintings and drawings, classical music, CBC Radio—and his rages, though they were less predictable than his passions. Unfortunately, however, Gerry loved to shop, and Bill Clarke was a skinflint, a tightwad, as miserable as any miser (not related to Midas). Many of his assaults on our mom were sparked by her sneaking to buy us (and/or herself) new clothes (often on "layaway"), while he'd insist that hand-me-downs—or darned this and patched that—were fine.

A dreadful occasion occurred when Bill Clarke, pleased by having obtained extra cash money for some duty of the night before, smilingly, gleefully, waved a handful of cash bills in our faces as he pranced about our kitchen. I was eight or nine years old, and it was about 8 a.m. Breakfast—oatmeal and brown sugar (sometimes with milk) and toast and margarine and cinnamon sugar—was over, and my brothers and I had soon to trek about fifteen minutes to Alexandra School to our respective classroom grades—likely four, three, and two. We'd all been happy for his apparent windfall, but I remember keeping my own pleasure in his pleasure just a tad reserved, for one never knew when vitriolic rage could follow delirious happiness. Surely, it was a stressful moment because he was exhibiting an unusual amount of gaiety—practically cha-cha-cha-ing with his ka-ching, ka-ching, ka-ching.

Sadly, my mother, whose own girlhood was prosperous as opposed to her husband's boyhood, believed she could take advantage of Bill's good humour, and snatched up a couple of the bills—maybe fives, maybe tens—herself. She explained quickly that she required the cash to buy us new clothes, but my dad's attitude shifted just as quickly as she had grabbed her "share," as she imagined, of the moolah. No longer beaming, but now looking dire, monstrous, our father demanded that our mom return the bills. She refused.

What happened next is vague—except for impressions. Shouts, cries, screams; the kitchen table gone airborne along with bowls and unfinished porridge; a mess splattered or clattered on the linoleum; our mother soon went down too, hitting the floor, but still refusing to return any of the money that she had bunched, clamped, in her fist. We boys were all crying: we had no other viable recourse or response. I'm pretty sure our mom must have been able to get to her feet and hobble—limping quickly—up the stairs to the bathroom. Maybe she'd planned to lock our father out and talk him out of his rage. It didn't work. I remember him walloping her—half in, half out, of the dry bathtub, as he insisted on uncurling her fingers and reclaiming *his* money. My brothers and I were weeping madly and tugging at him to try to get him to stop, but he shrugged us off as he knocked her about.

These harrowing scenes played out six or so times a year. It taught us to be careful. To be reticent. It taught me to smile; to compromise; to try to be a peacemaker; to be studious; to agree with the patriarch's tastes so as not to run afoul of his temper. I also learned to "respect authority"—even if disreputable authorities deserve revolt, rebellion, or just plain, honest-to-goodness, deliberated disrespect. Yet, there was always some confusion about my father's behaviour: he was always so courteous and polite outside our home, and measured, for instance, in taking the taxi driver to court who'd slapped Billy's fingers. Also, in regards to the US Civil Rights Movement, he preferred King's non-violence stance to Malcolm X's defiant and aggressive postures. Yet, there was a marked difference between his domestic comportment and his cordial demeanour outside our doors.

Only thrice did I see Bill lose his cool regarding others. Once, we had walked—all of us—including my mom, despite her length-compromised, right leg—some blocks from our Maynard Street home down to a bus stop on Gottingen Street, en route to see an older man—a friend of my dad's (who looked like Uncle Ben—and served us Uncle Ben's rice once we arrived). But we just missed the bus. My father—likely about thirty-one or thirty-two at the time—ran to try to stop the bus from leaving without us, but as the operator pulled away, my father leapt and struck the side of his bus with his fist. It didn't stop, and we had to walk several more blocks to the dinner engagement.

On another occasion, a Saturday or Sunday, Bill took his three sons to a movie matinee, at a Gottingen Street cinema, where there was a black usher in a burgundy uniform. After we'd seated ourselves and had our treats—pop and popcorn—the usher came by and shone his flashlight in our faces. My father quickly exchanged words with the chap, to express his annoyance with our being checked out as if we were suspect vandals or movie cheats, and the accusatory beam of the flashlight quickly sought a more receptive target. I don't recall exactly what Bill said, but it was something like "This is what happens when a Coloured chap lets a little trumped-up authority go to his head." (Looking back on that moment, I'm guessing that the Coloured usher felt as humiliated by his job and my father's reaction as my father felt—at least sometimes—dealing with disrespectful white folks at the train station.)

A third instance of my father's outrage was again merely verbal. Thanks to an article in our home's *Encyclopaedia Britannica*, I had diagnosed myself, at age ten, with myopia and was shepherded—reluctantly—by my father to an optometrist who confirmed, to Bill's chagrin, that I'd been nearsighted since birth. Next stop was an optician, who furnished me with precisely what I wanted, a set of black-plastic-frame, Buddy-Holly-nerd-style glasses. Graduating three years later to a new pair, pink-tinted, I soon lost them while conduct-ing my paper route (I was thirteen), and Bill called a local radio station to ask that they broadcast a notice of the missing spectacles. Well, the station operator refused my father's request, and he slammed down the telephone receiver, complaining that the refusal was due to class.

Also threatening to me was Bill's insistence that we sons needed to be toughend up by enrolling us in military "cadets"—a space where we'd get called nigger incessantly and have to brawl and brawl and drink too much beer and rum and where the only literacy would be cussing. Thankfully, it never came to pass. (Once, he did try to force us into swimming—a skill he himself lacked—but when we showed up at the public pool, it was—to my vast relief—closed.)

Strangely, Bill told my brothers and I, from the time we were old enough to understand, "I'll only respect you when you're old enough to beat me!" Even as a child, I knew that this utterance arose from some curious sense of machismo that he never manifested, except for terrorizing his children and his wife. He also said, frequently, from our youngest ages as boys, "When you're eighteen, you must leave!"

So, when my brother Bryant was seventeen, and stayed out two or three nights in succession from our home, Bill Clarke was waiting for him on the morning that he returned, and punched him in the face, in the doorway. He shouted something like, "You think you're old enough to stay with women? Collect your things and get out!" Although Bryant wasn't eighteen, and hadn't fought back, our father still deemed his behaviour insubordinate, insolent.

That same year, 1978, I was eighteen and still at my father's home, though Bryant had been punched out and then tossed out. I'd graduated from high school, but was working as a grocery clerk, and had a room in my father's basement. By this point, my parents had divorced; he was remarried and had a daughter; and though I respected his wife—I'll continue calling her Pammy—she was never—in my eyes or mind—my stepmother. No way. The simple idea was perfectly repugnant. There was no way that Pammy could ever replace my mother. Gerry was elegant; Pammy, slovenly. Gerry had elocution; Pammy—despite her wealthy parents (who wintered in Florida)—spoke a garble likely evacuated out the Miramichi. Pammy could glam up at times; she was a curvy, voluptuous blonde; I could see why my dad liked—or loved—her. But she was vulgar—french fries, hamburgers, cigarettes, bingo cards. To me, she could not equal Gerry's poise and erudition.

Anyway, one Friday night that summer, 1978, I came home from the late shift at the grocery store, and found both Bill and Pammy intoxicated. Usually, my father would be jovial thanks to having had a few beers. This night, Pammy had said or done something that annoyed him awfully, though from experience I knew that whatever it was, it may have been, in and of itself, a trifle. Nevertheless, he thrashed her on the sofa and he beat her up the stairs to their bedroom, and he continued to wallop her on the bed. I'm ashamed to say that I tried to ignore the fracas because it was his house and she was his wife and she was not my mother. Besides, in the course of this latest domestic assault, Pammy had blurted out—blubbered—"Why doncha go see your whore in Cherry Brook, you nigger!"

I had to intervene because the beating intensified once the "n-word" nagged so nastily at Bill's ears. I entered the bedroom and was able to pull my father off his howling wife. The moment was ironic: I now was big enough to stop Bill Clarke's whaling on Pammy, whom I unfairly resented for displacing my mother, though I'd never been able to stop him from hurting Gerry. The other irony: Pammy had slurred my mother as much as she'd slurred my father. And those days, given my unreflective adoption of Eldridge Cleaver's misogynist teachings and Malcolm X's masculinist preachings, part of me felt that Pammy's drunken cussing merited her physical upbraiding. Their analysis decried the fact, in the white man's racial-sexual hierarchy, the white woman rated higher than the black man, while the black woman was on the bottom. To hear a white woman calling my father a nigger and my mother a whore was—theoretically—righteous cause for a whupping. (After all, hadn't I been beaten for piddling snafus never based on insulting my parents?) Yet, I understood also that Bill Clarke was definitely in the wrong, no matter what Pammy had said or done—just as he'd been wrong, in my boyhood years, to unleash his rages on my mother and his sons.

Bluntly, Bill Clarke was an acerbic, assault-prone hubby and daddy. He seemed to take "spare the rod and spoil the child"—that biblical proverb—deeply to heart; and his attitude toward his wives (and perhaps his mistresses) was just as miserable. And yet I can say openly that I loved and admired that man—and emulated him—in art and politics. I loved his dash, his derring-do as an amateur artist with some belief in his own talent; and his credo that eloquence and literacy—and historical consciousness—are vital to any freedom-loving citizen. (In one of our last conversations, in 2005—only two years before the global liquidity crisis struck—he condemned the international banking system for its definite bias against the commons.)

Decades after I'd left home, an uncle told me that that my father and a sibling had been placed, temporarily, in the Nova Scotia Home for Coloured Children, a segregated orphanage for parentless children and/or merely needy kids, which became notorious for practices of beatings, starvation, and rape. (Ironically, Bill Clarke's grandfather, WAW, had been instrumental in founding the institution.) Was my father a boy-victim of such abuse? Did he then transfer this abuse to his own toddler and then schoolboy sons?

Another rationale for his short-fused temper and explosive rages was to try to prevent us—his sons—from becoming wayward dropouts, spiteful hooligans, drug addicts, drunk delinquents, or petty thugs resentful of white folks, for any of the above would have made us prey to white cops, the white (I mean, anti-black) justice system. Perhaps he deemed it better to try to batter us into docility, into submission before authority (parents, teachers, coaches, cops), than have us act uppity or condone criminality that would see us placed in reform school or, worse, sent to prison—all the distinct fates that white society historically holds in store for black boys and lads and men who go afoul of the razor-sharp (for us) straight-and-narrow.

(I remember how amazed the Homeland Security agent at Buffalo, New York, was when upon my applying for admission to the US, in August 2013, to teach at Harvard in 2013-2014, he photographed—mug-shot—and fingerprinted me, ran my visage and my digits through a super-duper, criminal-identifying computer, and received the results that—presto!—I ain't got no record and no warrants seeking my apprehension. How bout that?)

One lesson of black-male survival that Bill took to heart was to be non-threatening in behaviour and non-gaudy in appearance and unflashy with his accoutrements—briefcase, wristwatch, solid-coloured suits, Windsor-knotted, conservative ties; or, a shirt-and-tie-and-pullover combo. His shoes were polished to mirror quality; his vocabulary was all dictionary decorum—euphemism where essential, plus puns productive of mollifying levity. His interactions with cops and bosses (robbers?) were always respectful and stolid-citizen-casual. In public, his behaviour was composed; he dressed as natty as an executive; and his all-business stride (no showbiz strut) and clean-shaven physiognomy (save for a trim moustache), all suggested that he was almost boringly *bourgeois* (no cannabis under his front seat—ever!).

Thus, a prime reason for Bill's thumping his sons was that we were being "defiant." Defiance—"insolence"—had to be squeezed out of our marrow. It was the existential sin: that gumption to stand up to "massa" could absurdly easily lead to our being jumped, smacked about, or shot dead. He would've known that a careless glance could cause a cop to deem a black man insubordinate; that stubborn or manly resistance could be interpreted as presenting a bad or surly attitude, as having violent intent, as needing to be "corrected" or—like an animal, "put down"—for one could be a menace, a danger, a peril . . . only God knows how many black men in the Americas have been executed by police or lynchers just because they didn't say "please" or "thank you" or "yes sir" or "yes ma'am." (Recall the case of Emmett Till.)

But the contrast to Bill's usual projection of best-foot-forward *Négritude* was a single night in 1978 when he wielded his fists in a barroom brawl, alongside other waiters, versus white drunks. On that singular instance, when the constables materialized, they sided with the staff. Chairs got busted; noses got bloodied; white men got cuffed and handcuffed; white property got destroyed but black (and white) labour got validated. When he got home that Friday night, Bill sat in an armchair, just staring at his fists with a mix of awe and respect. I remember that he had the granite-jawed aspect of having finally gotten to star in his very own James Bond or John Shaft flick; that he had asserted himself pugnaciously—in the brouhaha—and had won: no acceptance of pacifism; not this time. Instead, he was standing up and meting out a beating to his tormentors. I'm not sure how many (white) drunkard, insult-mouthing faces he punched, but I'd like to imagine that each blow was delivered with a lifetime's worth of pent-up aggression. He sat musing, thoughtful, in his living room, but seemed proud that he'd had an opportunity—at last—to flex a little muscle, to engage in fisticuffs—*and* have the flatfoots in his corner. As someone who had mainly preached non-violence (outside the home at least), that moment of physical triumph over some of the shape-shifty spectres spewing disrespect and belittlement seemed meaning-ful—and even uplifting—for him. But I was eighteen and about to exit his home for good. If that one instant of "coming to blows" had helped my father hold his head higher and meet white men one-on-one with an assured look in his eyes, I can only wish that it had happened sooner—but with the same, helpful alliance with white constabulary, so that he could have confronted his real demons, not beat up on his wife and children.

ii.

Having described my father's harshness and explained its causes (as best I can), I need to emphasize now his other side—for the sake of bal-ance and truth—and to negate any inadvertent backing of stereotypes about black males (since I am one myself). Lookit: Bill Clarke was also capable of producing much merriment. There were good times a-plenty: being borne up on his shoulders, so we were suddenly tall, could almost touch the sun or the clouds! Another terrific joy was being swung about, his big hands clutching our thin wrists and wheeling us about, becoming horizontal propellers, watching the world giddy speedily around us. When he'd finally tired and let us regain our feet again, we wouldn't quite get back our footing, for our heads would still be spinning, and we'd lurch and lunge and stagger about, blissfully wobbly as gravity and balance too quickly returned.

To scare us, he'd play the bogeyman, extra-terrifyingly at night, and would shine a flashlight up under his chin, and, simultaneously, use one thumb and hand to pull up his nose; the effect was grotesque, Gothic: a gargoyle face appeared, and we'd have to cower, gleefully horrified. Then he'd let us reproduce the same effect, and then he'd have to pretend to be scared.

He was an implacable tickler of the soles of the feet; and he'd clutch our legs and hold our feet together and up, and tickle away, while we squirmed and cried and pleaded and cried giggling tears to try to get him to stop. Eventually, we'd gather enough strength to wrench our feet away, or he'd just get tired of the fun.

When we were older boys—nine, ten, eleven—Bill would help us build backyard tents with some of the other neighbourhood guys. He'd take an old wood pole, a broomstick or mop handle, stake it into the earth, then nail together a couple of blankets at the top of the pole, and then spike the four corners of the tent into the soil. We were then allowed sleeping bags, coins to buy pastries and pop, and the flashlight, to sleep out in our backyard with a couple of friends. Using the flashlight for illumination, drinking ginger ale and eating pound cake, and telling each other all kinds of jokes and stories, and guffawing loudly. At least once, we were a tad too rambunctious and/or the stories told were a tad too raunchy and/or the laughter was too uproarious, and Bill had to come out and tell us to calm down. At least once, too, we caused the tent to collapse, and Bill came out and told us we'd just have to make the best of things, even if we woke up with dew falling on our faces. But it was all okay. Most sincerely.

Bill was a long-distance walker, and he led us, including my mom, despite her bad leg, all over Halifax. Private property was off-limits, but public property was ours to explore—parks, gardens, the waterfront, crumbling fortresses, museums, the Commons. None of it cost anything, but all these ambles and rambles were still adventures. He'd tell us stories from history or from his own life in relation to the places we'd tour, so that they became parts of our imagination. We learned that the police chief used to live inside the old Town Clock; and that Prince's Lodge was built for a real-life prince; and that the Halifax Explosion blast-force split the bottom of the harbour. He'd also take us on tours of construction site fencing—so we could admire the amateur paintings (some of them quite good) that sprang up as temporary public art displays on the wooden-plank barriers—hoardings—separating passersby from the workplace. He took us on a tour of a submarine—and also of Canada's only aircraft carrier, the HMCS *Bonaventure*, and I remember riding the giant deck elevator from a bottom floor up to the flight deck.

Similarly, Bill (and Gerry) ensured that we three brothers attend a summer camp at Chezzetcook, NS, operated by Brunswick Street United Church. We spent three or four summer weeks there between 1968 and 71, and I remember being thrilled by the unusual July visits of Santa Claus, bereft of reindeer, but with a satchel brimming with toys. There were about fifteen boys and equal number of girls attending Camp Brunswick. The guys would bunk down in the main house, while the gals had a separate residence. I was too shy to participate in most of the activities—arts-n-crafts and sporty games. So, I'd spend my time reading through a parlour library of Thornton W. Burgess tales, such as the exploits of Reddy Fox or the story of Blacky the Crow. Or I'd bother the parlour piano, inventing a melody that, as far as I know, is only mine (though I can't think how it could be written). I enjoyed conversations with one of the main, adult attendants, Graham, who let us rap our knuckles upon his wooden left leg. (He would also hoist his pant leg so we could study the gleaming, pine-coloured wood.) I also loved taking tall glasses of whole milk before going to bed. It was the very same milk that I had at home. But, somehow, in the country, it just seemed richer—frothier, colder, creamier. (Also there were instances of disturbing violation: One white teen female counsellor stripped one of us brown boys utterly naked. I can still see him trying to hide his penis and testicles from her eyes, but she batted aside his hands while he bawled.)

Perhaps because Bill had exulted in the pleasures of the open road as a Bohemian, bon-vivant, bachelor motorcyclist (he'd reject "biker"), he figured that we'd benefit from travel. Free passage as a railway worker allowed my father to take us to Montreal, for Expo 67, but also on to Winnipeg in 1969. In 1970, he loaded up our station wagon with camping gear and a gaggle of kids—somehow squeezing ten of us into its confines—and motored us, including Gerry, up to the steep heights and cliffs of Cape Breton's Cabot Trail. (My mother told me later that, when we stopped in pouring rain for the night, we parked alongside the edge of a precipice. Bill didn't realize our peril until dawn when he roused Gerry and asked her to awaken us all and get us out of the car—on his driver's side and from the back—so he could then manoeuvre it out of the awaiting clutches of reckless, hooligan gravity.) After exploring those vistas, we drove through a chunk of southern New Brunswick, stopping to goggle at concrete dinosaurs or to saddle up ponies and trot about. The trip lasted but a week, and it demonstrated Bill's unfettered cosmopolitanism—his interest in spurring us to roam the world.

(This is not a minor aim. Next to being able to have and hold onto our children and spouses, what freedom is it that black people most value? Mobility. That's precisely the liberty that yesterday's slave masters and today's police seek most strenuously to curtail.)

I would be remiss were I not to record here some of the ways in which my father showed me his regard. Noting my scientific pretensions, he not only gifted me chemistry sets, but also two microscopes, a crystal radio, and a film projector (accompanied by *Mr. Magoo* reels). Having developed a model-kit mania, ages ten to thirteen, for film monsters and spacecraft and fighter planes and tanks, he put up shelving so I could display the items. When I wanted a pet guinea pig, he built a cage for the animal as well as a tray to catch its droppings. He took me to see *2001: A Space Odyssey* (1968), but also *Barbarella* (1968)—just he and I—and I found both memorable (for astronomy in the first, but anatomy in the second). When my first bike was stolen, he replaced it readily. When my brothers and I got flats, he patched the air-leaking, inner-tube punctures but also showed us how to fix them ourselves. He was fierce—and his emotions fickle—but he was also devoted to us—in our early years.

When I was ten, in 1970, Bill and I toured what was formerly Africville, the community having been totally reduced to rubble by that year. (The demolition was effected 1964-70.) On the spring day of our visit, there was fencing up all about and signs warning of hustling, bustling rats—even in daylight. I'd always known about Africville, heard about it (for one thing, Great-Aunt Portia had taught school there), but, curiously, had never been taken to the seaside enclave—a Lil-Harlem-on-the-North-Atlantic, so to speak. Its population had numbered four hundred, and Africville supported its own church, school, corner store, and post office. Most adults were employed as domestics or day labourers, but the residents owned their homes, kept farm animals, tended vegetable and floral gardens, and—just like the plutocratic Caucasians on the Northwest Arm—could boat, fish, and swim in waters practically lapping at their front or back doors. Also, because most were Baptists, they could hold outdoor baptisms pretty close to home, thus testifying to their *Salvation* just steps from their own stoops or thresholds.

Though no Africvillers received welfare; and though they kept their homes spic-and-span; the City of Halifax never accepted the existence of this maritime Black community. The city collected taxes from Africvillers, but extended no water or sewer services. Instead, as if to demonstrate supreme contempt for Africvillers, the City of Halifax located its open-air dump—the largest in Atlantic Canada—within spitting distance of Africville homes. Also constraining and contaminating the village were train tracks, a slaughterhouse, an infectious disease hospital, toxic factories, and the city prison. Africville sprang up around 1815; but by 1962, Haligonians were labelling it a segregated slum, and the city decided it should bulldoze the homes and "relocate" the residents to public housing projects and/or to downtown, racist-ass, slumlord properties. Although the "Africville Relocation" was billed as Liberal Welfare-Social Work-Urban Renewal, Africvillers perceived it as veritably the demolition of an Africadian community by white folks who declared a waterfront, black-peopled village an "eyesore" and who were intent on accessing land pertinent to the approaches to a new bridge spanning Halifax Harbour. (By 2004, the United Nations agreed that Africville's destruction was an expression of Euro-Caucasian racism and judged former residents as deserving of reparations.*)

It is telling that my father brought me to see the ruins of Africville, for he considered its removal to be, in fact, a progressive measure. He didn't say much about it during our visit; indeed, he was more keen on the construction of the "New Bridge," the A. Murray MacKay. His 1959 *Diary* attests to his dislike for Africville; he considered it a redoubt of "ignoramuses." Later, in the 1990s, he wondered aloud to me why so much fuss was still being made about its razing, given that "Sailortown," a district serving white sailors and their ladies and layabouts, had also been knocked down by the City of Halifax. But Africville was a 150-year-old village, a community, not a clutch of flophouses, tattoo parlours, bars, and brothels serving a transient population who might bunk in the port

---

* On March 1, 2004, Doudou Diène, Special Rapporteur on racism, racial discrimination, and xenophobia to the United Nations Commission on Human Rights, delivered a report declaring that Canada practices racism in particular against people of African-Negro heritage and Indigenous peoples. Dr. Diène also recommended reparations be paid specifically to ex-Africville residents. See UN Commission on Human Rights, *Report on contemporary forms of racism, racial discrimination, xenophobia and related intolerance: Addendum Mission to Canada* (2004).

for a few days and then be off. I think my father's prejudice reflected his sense that he belonged to a better class of black people*; yet, ironically, he was the one who grew up in a barn, while Africvillers resided in houses.

Although my father—Bill—was a flawed human being (as all of us are), I can't be sorry that he was my first and steadiest role-model—as an artist. No one's conversation was ever as expansive as his. After he became a taxi driver, and I'd fly home to Halifax, I was always hopeful to see, upon arrival, his lit-up roof sign (though he'd never let me pay for a lift): YELLOW 321. His Yellow Cab number gave him his final nickname, "Blast-Off." After he died in 2005, I was still surprised—and troubled—for some years after—to not see his taxi idling right across from the Arrivals area.

iii.

Though my mother was the certificated teacher in our home, Bill decided that he would experiment with his own child-rearing (or son-raising) techniques. Since I was the first-born, I was subjected to the deny-son-maternal-affection experiment, a notion that was either self-generated or picked up from reading one of the he-man adventure mags, so popular in the 1930s-60s (until the nudie mags drove em from the stands and racks).† In any event, while I was just a few months old,

---

* Documents such as *Condition of the Negroes of Halifax City* (1962) verify that Negro residents of Maynard Street earned more than Africvillers. However, Africvillers owed no mortgage or rent, and controlled an independent, semi-bucolic community (despite the dump). So, who was better off?

† Indeed, if my dad picked up this idea from a men's mag, it must have been some screed denouncing the "maternal deprivation" theory proposed by Brit psychiatrist John Bowlby in his influential *Maternal Care and Mental Health* (1951). Bowlby held that infants best develop in a warm and loving bond with a maternal figure. Without that relationship, Bowlby thought, a child so deprived would perhaps fail to develop any true affect. Ironically, given her expertise in Early Childhood Education, it was my mother who'd have read Bowlby directly, but who was thwarted in establishing her bond with me by a man whose opposing theory likely arose from a back-page squib attacking "coddling" as leading to producing "mama's boys," or "pansies," or some such rot.

Bill forbade my mother to hold me, nurse me, caress me; and ordered that I be locked away in a room to cry myself to sleep—so as to make a tough guy out of me. Well, his approach failed. I might have harboured fantasies of becoming a pugilist, but I became, as a youth, a runner. I starred in spiking grass, not throwing punches. My fists were feathers, but my legs were lightning.

I used to train in a small gym in the basement of Brunswick Street United Church, for its minister, Rev. Rod MacAulay, once a Navy signalman, had decided to champion potentially wayward youth by giving us a track to trek, a team to join—the BUCS (he wouldn't write it as BSUC because it could be construed, by the gutter-minded, as "Be-Suck"), and meets to race—and, in my case—giddily, vehemently—*win*. (In 1975, Rev. MacAulay officiated at my father's wedding to his second wife, Pammy. A couple of years later, disturbed by the high rates of black teen pregnancies, he advocated to me—with repressed humour—that all black teen cocks-o-the-walk—myself honorably excepted—be castrated.)

My trophies have long gone missing, but I still have a box full of ribbons and medals for having dashed the 1500 metres, the mile, the 800 metres, the half-mile, and cross-country (up to two miles long) faster than most of my competitors. My diet was mustard and bologna sandwiches, orange juice, milk, and two chewable, orange-flavoured vitamin-C pills.

I trained by running around the mile-long perimeter of the North Commons, often on the asphalt street (thus melting down the cartilage in my knees, to cause me much current grief in my seniority), often at night, even in winter, with ice forming from the sweat bands around my wrists. (I would also run—*not* jog—across the mile-long span of the Angus L. Macdonald Bridge, Dartmouth-side to Halifax-side, on winter mornings, with a spit of the Atlantic churning, frothing, smoking, darkly far below.) The BUCS track meets could entail overnight travel to Horton or to New Glasgow: terrific, out-of-town adventures. My pre-race warm-up was pious: pray, pray, and pray some more. Then, I ran. Fast. My last meet was in 1977, a mile race, at age seventeen, and I won—without training for it, but praying vehemently for my victory.

So, I didn't become—as my father wanted—a macho man; but "maternal deprivation" still inflicted harm. Indeed, up to my late thirties, until my daughter was born, I had trouble forming genuine and profound emotional attachments. I was too worried that my friend's or lover's love would disappear. Thus, I was reserved, aloof—even within committed relationships. I had to strive to build meaningful bonds. Maybe my affliction stems from those toddler years, and the isolation and loneliness imposed upon me.

Years later, Gerry told me that her parents, who loved me as their first-born grandson, would travel to Halifax, hoping to look in on me and hold me, but Bill would deny them this wish. He'd only allow them to look at me through a window, no matter how much I cried and no matter how much they pleaded. They'd have to return to Newport Station, Three Mile Plains, their grandparents' hands empty of the weight and feel of my little body.

Yet another Bill Clarke experiment was his decision to parade his *Playboy* mags before my brothers and me.* Maybe it was a naïve Age of Aquarius approach to boy-raising: by giving us nude models to ogle, he essayed, I guess, to assure our heterosexual inclinations. Yet, I did find it confusing—if not disturbing—because the Black Baptist Church insisted that nakedness was sinful, and both my parents were members, and my father had been president of the entire Halifax-area Baptist Youth Fellowship in the late 1950s. Still, right along with *Kool-Aid* and *Crayola* crayons and Saturday morning cartoons, we got to leaf through snaps of white-breasted, pink-nippled pixies; to juxtapose

---

* After my father's decease in 2005, I found that he had saved four precious, playmate centrefolds: Miss November 1967 (Ms. Kaya Christian), Miss February 1968 (Ms. Nancy Harwood), Miss March 1969 (Ms. Kathy MacDonald), and Miss June 1969 (Ms. Helena Antonaccio). These bodacious beauts numbered three redheads and one strawberry blonde.

the Playmate of the Month with Walt Disney's movie-of-the-week. Given this exposure (pun intended), it was possible for me to imagine Mary Poppins kissing Malcolm X; Cinderella entertaining Bill Cosby.

That experiment came to a crashing halt when, having been given license to talk about tits and bums, I was the one who applied this liberal lingo to an adult woman friend visiting my parents. I think I was seven or eight at the time. I still remember her shocked face when I jokingly made use of the permission to speak of these body parts in a slangy way; and I remember my father's abrupt decision to revoke the license at once, inviting my brothers and I to an immediate conference where we were lectured sternly on the inappropriate, indiscriminate use of such vulgar, anatomical terms. It was a wise decision, but it also seemed like a yo-yo move—maybe a local, scaled-down amelioration of the kind of chaos then underway in the Great Proletarian Cultural Revolution in China, where fervent attempts to make red traffic lights mean "go" did not advance the working-class, just caused fatal accidents.

In any event, Mr. Clarke's decision to sequester me from maternal affection as well as to expose my child's mind to topless, white, young women likely served to spark a dream that I loved to try to recall throughout my childhood. It involved my entry—*via* a rabbit-hole of sorts, into a fur-covered cave, pink in tint, where a naked, white lady awaited my ministrations, which were all, absolutely, witlessly inno-cent, no more than stroking and smooching, because I had no other idea what to do with this sylph, other than kiss her, snuggle with her, and be caressed and kissed in turn. She was simply *there*, in my mental cave, delectable in its fur and warmth and pink and silk and satin, a preface to the serious boyhood crushes that I had for all my grade-school female teachers. I did crave adult female attention and affection as a boy, and the best way to attract it was—strangely—in the same way that I courted my father's: to excel at scholastics. (Gymnastics was out of the question.)

Because I was usually a gold-star pupil, achieving A's and 100's in my schoolwork and projects (Bristol-board extravaganzas, heavy on trans-parent-paper-tracing and pastel and/or coloured-pencil highlights—and insights *via Encyclopaedia Britannica* or Herbert S. Zim), I was teased by being called "Perfessor"—which indeed became my nick-name—and also a "teacher's pet." The latter epithet rang true, for, in the mid-1960s into the mid-1970s, to have a brown-black pupil, in Halifax, regularly scoring 90's and 100's on most tests, including mathematics, must have been a boon for many of my white teachers who were likely overly familiar with black-brown pupils who were struggling in school—and who acted out as class clowns or trouble-makers. I got laurels—and they got the strap (the smack of a length of leather across an open palm—hurtful enough to summon "girlish"—thus shaming—tears).

I had learned well—from home—how to avoid incurring displea-sure, and those lessons guaranteed scholastic success: to be affable; to never dissent from prevailing (adult) opinion; to work hard to score the smile and the pat on the back; to memorize answers and spew out truisms—enthusiastically. That's not to say that I didn't merit the plau-dits. I was that kid who built dioramas of Vikings, of Aztecs, of the Halifax Explosion, of British coal miners; I was that kid who built mini-volcanoes around test-tubes and then poured in the vinegar, bak-ing soda, and food colouring to make the object issue "lava." I was that kid who drew see-through models of the heart, the brain. I was that kid who asked the son of the corner store guy to give me sulfuric acid so I could use it to make white sugar burn black. (That the corner store owner's son gave me the acid brought about a hurried conference of my parents and the school principal and the storeowner: No more H_2SO_4 for me!) Maybe that experiment appealed to me because I knew—in my own family—that racialized colours were unstable: blacks could be whites; whites could actually be blacks.

Yet, in my teen years, I was sensitive to being called "high yellow" (in my high-water pants to boot), which was a derogatory term for a gold/ brass-tinted black. Gerry advised me to tell my detractors, "I'm tanta-lizingly tan"! But I did not find that easy to do. I kept regretting that

I wasn't just black—licorice-black, tea-black, coffee-black, tar-black: Definite. Defined.

While Gerry tried to help me accept my tint, Bill addressed no such concerns: only that I not fall prey to peer pressure—to smoke, to cuss, to drop out, to bum around. To him—and this measure did back his "race-less" bias—a person was what he/she did or achieved or acted, and was never a function of "race," or class, or ethnicity (though gender/sex was—in his mind—yes, determinative). So, one was a "crook" (like Nixon) or "classy" (like JFK); one was "uncouth" like Ali or "unconventional" like Christo and Jeanne-Claude—the artists who loved "wrapping" large structures, and whom my dad idolized. Laudable—partly—was this concept: Why convince black youth that they could not be accepted for themselves? Better to let them learn who they were as they made their way in the world, asserting their equality. Yet, this approach also denied reality: That no matter how "raceless" we imagined ourselves to be, the world was not going to see us that way. Even more problematic was the idea that we couldn't—shouldn't—foreground our "blackness," but appear to be "just like everyone else." The problem with that view is that it seems to project shame about who we are. As if to say, "I'm black, but I wish I could be invisible"—or non-existent—or dead! I have to say that I preferred—ultimately—my mother's view that we should be black and proud, and damn all opposition!

Bill did allow one exception in terms of celebrating our blackness: Bill Cosby's comedy albums of the 1960s, as well as his Fat Albert cartoon special, which aired on TV in 1969. It was us; it was our hood; it was our friends and our ways of talkin and havin fun and our games and our adventures with sabre-tooth junkyard dogs, and garbage-rich lots, and sloppy slouches and baggy pants and saggy caps and sneakers. It was a revelation to us that—right there on television (so customarily broadcasting whiteness)—there was our neighbourhood, ourselves, in glorious Technicolor. An unforgettable moment of self-recognition in an (African) American mirror!

iv.

Growing up in the Black—blue-&-pink-collar—North End, I encountered many folks whose "true" names were nicknames. Some were pseudo-African, such as "Googie," who was also the head of the Bum Gang (so called because its *modus operandi* was to "bum"—ask for—coins or candy or cigs or the like; and if the target didn't cough up the moolah or the goods, well, then he/she—mainly he—would get "beat up"). Try also "Huckabuck," "Tuppy," "Kishie," "Airk," "Skookee," "Gooey Linda," "Puppy," and "Brother." Others were elementary—but still African-grammatically-based repetitions: "Bun-Bun," "Lee-Lee." Some were given names that may as well have been nicknames: "Junior"; "Bruno." Some names related to personal characteristics such as "Skip" (for a way of walking) or "Herky" (short for Hercules, given for the boy's way of making muscles with his flexed arms) or "Plums" (a mix-up for "plump"—because he was plump as a boy). Other names came from complexions: "Smokey" or "Inky." Two black girl twins who attended Alexandra School with my brothers and I were—to our minds—"The Tootsie Girls"—a name that represented our scrambling up of "Watusi," borrowed from the title of a 1962 hit song, "The Wah-Watusi," by the Orlons.

True to form, though, Bill Clarke was very suspicious of adults who still carried nicknames, believing them to be infantile—no, infantilizing. (His own later-life nickname, "Blast-Off," was the creation of his fellow cabbies, not one that he bruited about.) Then again, my father—and I myself—would be slagged by that most demeaning epithet, Oreo, which is meant to denote any black or brown person who spoke or acted "white." But Bill would have shrugged—or laughed off—the allegation. He would never have viewed his behaviour, tastes, or speech as being "white," but rather as adept, responsible, reasonable, and—conscionably—adult.

Yet, I also got tagged with the cognomen "Bucky," given my protruding upper front teeth—a *Bugs Bunny* look—that made me shy. Yet, when my parents planned to have my overbite "corrected," I resisted: I was sensitive about the cost of braces, and I was conservative about my body. Translation: doctors/dentists shouldn't monkey with what God hath wrought.

v.

In keeping with saluting Bill's adoration of smarts, when I was nine or ten, I decided that Albert Einstein would be my hero. The reason? I was usually considered the star pupil, and so I needed to identify with a white, German Jew with a white afro, who represented the acme of intellectual acumen. As a black kid, coming from a community where boxing gloves were more prized than scribblers, it was meaningful to worship Einstein. I admired his eccentricities also; it gave me the sense that an intellectual could be unconventional; that the "life of the mind" was valid; that I didn't have to be an army cadet or be a boxer or do any of the things customary for a black male out the labouring-class. I also liked photos of Einstein's beach-walking—being a Nova Scotian, with beach and surf quite handy, it was easy to imagine myself into such heroic vignettes, racing the combers along a beach—even though I couldn't swim.

Around the same time, aged ten, I also gravitated toward another German role-model, weirdly enough: Baron Manfred von Richthofen— famed as "the Red Baron." I cottoned on to the lone-wolf aerial assassin, the director of the Flying Circus, because of Charles Schultz's *Peanuts* cartoon character, Snoopy, who is always jockeying his doghouse (as a secretly souped-up Sopwith Camel biplane) into a dogfight with the Red Baron (haunting the heavens in his Fokker Dr-I, crimson-painted triplane.) But I also seconded his penchant for solitude—and his scarf, a garment which has always symbolized for me the rakish, the devil-may-care, the dashing get-up of someone with places to tour, dolts to escape, and adventures to experience.

I grew up as a buck-toothed, brown-skin "Brainiac," with a white enemy-alien and a white ethnic-minority-group member as my default, go-to heroes, justifying my own loner self, my bookworm aptitude, and my wish to soar above the bullying and squabbling that constituted the sweat-and-fisticuffs world of Haligonian, North End black boys. Besides, I had a tuft of white hair in the back of my head: maybe I had a teensy-weensy bit of Einstein back there?

True: I lacked serious black heroes. I appreciated George Washington Carver because he was a scientist who had discovered a plenitude of commercial uses for peanuts. As a boy having to eat a lot of jam-and-peanut-butter belly-fillers, Carver came to mind whenever I had to have one of those "samwiches."

Although black heroes did not loom large in my mind, I did love a *Classics Illustrated*-like comic book titled *Great Negroes*, which I read incessantly. That's where I learned of Phillis Wheatley—the first book-length-published black poet in English (1773), plus Carver, plus Alexander Pushkin—Russia's greatest writer and poet, and Frederick Douglass (the anti-slavery crusader) and Harriet Tubman (liberator of hundreds of slaves). They were enthralling.

My father's library included John Howard Griffin's best-selling memoir, *Black Like Me* (1961), which I read both as a child and as a mid-teen, marvelling at Griffin's transformation from white to black (a metamorphosis achieved by chemicals, radiation, and a to-the-roots haircut). In this skin-deep disguise, Griffin went deep cover (as it were) throughout the segregated South to emerge months later with a book-length report, including convincing photographs, on his first-person-verified, Negro experience of Dixie's discriminatory treatment. Griffin's first-person journalism helped to convince white northerners, otherwise sceptical of the Civil Rights Movement, that the South really was oppressive and that Negroes were not content with their lot, but were seething with resentment.

As a boy, I twigged to the story's sci-fi quality, which, again, reinforced for me the notion that racial categories were more myth than truth. I had white friends and white-looking relatives; I had white friends who acted black, and I had black role-models in my family whose tastes were European. At sixteen, I returned to Griffin's book, but it was in the light of reading Cleaver's *Soul On Ice* (1968), also in my dad's home library, which hit me with the force of truth: that to be a black male, even in officially "tolerant" Canada, was to exist in a state of existential "cool" under relentless socio-economic and political and justice-system pressure. From that perspective, Griffin's report amazed me only because of the very idea that he imagined his reportage was necessary. Certainly, his book is a modern equivalent of Harriet Beecher Stowe's *Uncle Tom's Cabin* (1852), a white northerner's fictitious treatment of slavery that persuaded other white northerners that the system was diabolical and had to be overthrown.

My movement into adolescence had to summon black heroes into my consciousness. That's not to say that I was ever utterly unconscious of "race." Nope. In fact, when I was five, and spending afternoons with a caramel-complexioned lady I knew as Aunt Donna (who babysat me after downtown pre-school sessions until Gerry or Bill could pick me up), some Coloured kids came running up to me on the sunny afternoon of Monday, February 22, 1965, shouting, "Malcolm X got shot!" I recall that moment with crystal clarity—it was the first time I'd heard his name, and I wondered whether Malcolm X was really Malcolm the Tenth.

Fast forward to Monday, February 21, 1977: I had just turned seventeen and was sitting in the back of my grade eleven Advanced English class at Queen Elizabeth High School, and I was *not* following the excellent teacher, Fred Holtz, and his lesson for that day. Instead, I was reading Donald Reeves's memoir, *Notes of a Processed Brother* (1972), which tells of his teenage radicalization into Black Power consciousness and activism. At one point, he narrates the impact that Malcolm X's assassination had on him, and he reports the date: February 21, 1965. I realized that I was reading about it on February 21, 1977. I couldn't believe my own ignorance of X's death date. I began to cry. No one knew it. I was—if I recall right—the only black kid in the class. I looked outside and white snow was coming down, topping every black, leafless tree and the black asphalt of the street, and whitewashing everything with its Caucasian-associated chill. I suddenly felt suffocated by the overwhelming whiteness all about me—and by my own self-asphyxiating ignorance of black history—meaning African-American history. My search for deeper knowledge began with that moment of a tearful snowfall.

I should witness here that there is a persistent theme in African-North American life-writing of any sort, that moment, which usually arrives in childhood, where one becomes aware of oneself as Coloured or black, and that one's "race" is subject to discriminatory abuse. It's indelibly described in autobios by W. E. B. Du Bois, in Malcolm X, in Barack Obama, and in many others. But, as of the 1960s, there's a sub-theme solidifying that transition to racial self-recognition, and it is the impact of Malcolm X's life and teachings and violent martyrdom upon his followers, disciples, and long-distance and much-later readers like me. I think the power of the awakening lies in X's disclosure of his own former ignorance about—and disbelief in—the innate majesty and congenital equality of black people(s) and his slow but steady acquisition of a higher consciousness, leading him from the occult dogma of the Nation of Islam to adopt a quasi-socialist Islam. The impact of that life-story—of intellectual salvation *via* a project of profound (re-)education—is vital to almost everyone who comes under X's literary or auditory influence. Check out the memoirs of Obama, yes, but also Amiri Baraka, and even the Chinese-American saxophonist and musicologist Fred Ho. The racialized political awakening of all is catalyzed by reading X's *Autobiography* (1965).

Due to his representation of the power of self-recognition, X was vital to me as a teenage nerd: he made Dilton Doiley eyeglasses "cool"; he made usage of correct speech and employment of punctuation (and punctuality) progressive ideals; his suits and wristwatch and telegenic appearance and fire-breathing rhetoric made him not only an icon of "respectable" black masculinity, but also foregrounded the power and sanctity of literacy, of smarts, of intellectual endeavour as a form of peaceful combat. He was really the Guerilla of Education—of Knowledge as the Key to Self-Knowledge and Power; as if Daniel Webster was really

Toussaint L'Ouverture or Nat Turner in disguise. I could not have articulated this idea as a teen, but Malcolm was, really, as "correct" as my father in his insistence on education and self-discipline; yet, he was also unlike Bill Clarke in being able to confront—visibly and audibly and directly—white aggression. He could be—was—another role-model father-figure for me—a source of motivation and encouragement for not only classroom ascension, but for attaining an epiphanic consciousness of self as a being amid History, responsible *oneself* for attempting to upset and/or repel forces of political subjugation. Because of X's example, I adopted as a teen this motto: *Ingenium ad imperio* (Talent equal to power*). Amen!

I didn't get around to reading X's *Autobiography* until 1978, after turning eighteen. But that moment with Reeves's book in English class served to propel me in X's direction, and I remain to this day a satellite orbiting X's radiance, while repulsing his self-besmirching faults (misogyny, homophobia, anti-Semitism). To gravitate from Albert Einstein to Malcolm X[†] only took seven years, that crucial period of transitioning from Coloured kid to black teen, i.e., moving from being seen as cute to being seen as threatening . . .

vi.

Like Bill, my mother, Gerry, was also experimental with my rearing, albeit differently. She loved to take me to see movies, just the two of us, and they were sometimes beyond the not-yet-existing 14A (age fourteen with adult accompaniment) MPAA rating. I loved those moments in those vast, darkened rooms because they were instances of mainly silent but almost holy communion with my mother, from whom I had been separated so often, in infancy, by my father. I also felt sanctified—a bit

---

* Google translate says, "Ability to command." I prefer my original, untutored translation.

† E=MX²: Einstein= Malcolm X as a "Square"?

more grown-up—to be trusted by her to be able to process these projections of adult life, the glamour and insolence, the terrors and jests, the
styles of comportment (dazzling and demure, retiring and startling).
I bonded—or tried to—with Bill by liking the entertainment that he
liked. But my mother's pedagogy emphasized sharing experiences, and
I think that was one reason for our cinema outings. (Gerry didn't mind
letting me try even adult things: My first taste of wine—Mateus—was
downed hurriedly—in the backyard—in a shot glass that she filled for
me, just as Bill was arriving home—oblivious to the escapade. The fla-
vour was grapes set on fire. I was thirteen; Mateus still holds for me
that nostalgia-tinged tang and spank and pang.)

So, when I was seven, Gerry took me to see the fifth Bond film
release, *You Only Live Twice* (1967), and I remember feeling sheepish
about the scene in which Bond (Sean Connery) uses a scalpel to cut
the shoulder straps of a black, sparkly gown worn by assassin Helga
Brandt—played by Karin Dor—and then the later scene in which Brandt
is slid into a pool of ravenous piranha fish. I wasn't sure if I should—as
a Sunday-schooled African Baptist boy—relish the suggestion of nudity
in the film, while the murder scene seemed baroquely Gothic even to
my comic-book-violence-satiated eyes.

Also branded in my brain is the visit to a theatre, back in my birth-
place of Windsor town, where, in 1969, my mom took me to see
Hitchcock's *Topaz*, a film in which Karin Dor starred again, in the role
of Juanita de Cordoba, a character who is also murdered, shot in the gut
by her revolutionary lover. Classic is Hitchcock's depiction of her sinking to a parquet floor while her dress blossoms about her like a burst of
royal-purple blood. But what mattered more for me were the unfurled
Soviet missiles being rolled through the supposedly Cuban countryside: the unveiled threat of a thousand Hiroshimas, a thousand Halifax
Explosions, ready to be launched from hundreds of silos to put us in our
millions of graves, those negative wombs.

The last movie that I took in with my mother—just she and I, during
a visit to Windsor—was *The Sterile Cuckoo*, also a 1969 film. I remember

finding it very strange—it being a romantic flick, and I being just nine—about a nerdy girl who attracts a nerdy boy, but a lad who wants to be a somebody and not (too soon—and not with her) a dad. The movie was digestible for me because of the Sandpipers' soundtrack hit "Come Saturday Morning," which did tug at my precociously sentimental heart-strings, even if I was out-of-tune with the schmaltzy plot.

I wondered, sometimes, why these flicks appealed to Gerry and why she thought it was a good idea to bring a child along to watch em. But there was romance for me—for us (maybe)—in ordering up the hot but-tered popcorn (the thicker the drool of that molten gold, the better) and the thick, red Twizzlers licorice, and, for her Coca-Cola, and for me, in fealty to my father's taste, ginger ale. Maybe attending those films together was one late-childhood way to try to repair the lonesome isolation to which Bill condemned the infant me when I was literally crying for my mother.

Later on, in my teens, Gerry and I would watch TV movies jointly. Two were instantly poignant for me because they seemed to trace her sorrows and her regrets, though she never discussed the evident—to me—biographical symmetry. *The Glass Menagerie* (1950), with its limp-ing heroine, Laura (played by Jane Wyman), and her lovelorn, withdrawn self, reminded me of my mother's own "crippled" condition, and the pain that she felt in walking, but also the heartbreak that she experienced with my father—and then, later, with the lovers with whom she tried, as a divorcée, to forge pseudo-marital relationships. I thought that Gerry could see herself in Laura, but maybe she didn't. For one thing, despite her hobbled gait, Gerry liked to dance, to dress fashionably, and was engagingly sociable. She was no wallflower. Nevertheless, the depiction of Laura still affected—saddened—me because I saw, in that dramatiza-tion, my mom's vulnerability to emotional hurt, to being just as lovelorn, as was the silver-screen character.

The other film that Gerry and I often watched was *Valley of the Dolls* (1967), which traces—in florid colour—the depressing saga of several starlets ending up as shooting stars, dropping into addictions to barbiturates, booze, or too-fickle adulation, and then suffering ripped-apart hearts, suicidal illness, self-sabotaged careers, and smashed-up marriages. I wanted to identify Gerry with the stellar survivor of all the wrecks, Anne Welles (played by Barbara Parkins). The last woman standing—literally—she retreats to New England after surviving suicide-by-overdose and sinking into the sands of a Pacific shoreline featuring insurgent and luckily revivifying surf. The feminist ending and the West Coast scenery enabled me to imagine my mom surviving all tempests and tantrums, standing tall—intact—indomitable—on an Atlantic beach while oceanic commotion unfurls, roaring and roiling, all about.

Yet another film that helped me feel close to Gerry was *Daddy Long Legs* (1955), a Fred Astaire dance extravaganza in which he plays an aloof guardian who is suddenly all twinkle-toes and starry-eyed for his fey waif charge (Leslie Caron), who seems thirty years younger. I loved watching the elegant, dandy, coat-tailed Astaire moving like a pinwheel—cartwheeling—in his ecstatic, hearty leaping. That it was just my mom and I, absorbing the spectacle, lodged the film in my heart at age four, and I did not see it again until I ordered it from Amazon, some 55 years later.)

Those theatrical hours—just she and I—were also a kind of extension of those hushed and hurried conferences during childhood, when she would call me to her side to ask to borrow money from my little five-and-dime bank account so that she could make up for a shortfall in her pocket money (because she'd bought a new dress or blouse). She wanted to avoid a stressful scene with my miserly father, a bickering back-and-forth that could end with him striking her—a sight and sound that I dreaded. Surely, Gerry and I had an unstated alliance against Bill, but one that, for me, was meant to forestall his meanness against her and/or his hands hitting my mother, whom I viewed as fragile, beautiful, and too elegantly dainty, and much too loving.

vii.

As a boy in my mom's Head Start-program kindergarten (the first that she founded), housed in the basement of the Cornwallis Street United Baptist Church, I wasn't coddled by her. She let Alexa Shaw (later McDonough*), my teacher, be a—the—pedagogue, and I was never aware that my mom was the boss. I was just glad that she was about, but I was also a bit confused, as a four- and five-year-old, because I had a secret crush on Miss Shaw, and I was wondering how I was supposed to square those feelings with my love for my mother. (The pattern repeated itself with all of my grade-school women teachers. I had crushes on all of them—surreptitiously, poignantly, and irredeemably, and treacherously, given my supposedly primary, maternal devotion.) Enjoyable, though, was Miss Shaw's praise of my boy-wonder precocity, which I believed also made me more likeable to my father.

Upon exiting kindergarten I was given, by Miss Shaw, a blue Dinky car, and then went to see Bill at the train station, with my mom. I endured the hard plastic seats in the waiting area by roaming and speeding my little toy car all about the edges and the top and bottom of my chair. My best remembrance of Miss Shaw and Gerry and me? One day, Miss Shaw took us out on the Northwest Arm in a canoe, hers, I guess, and we paddled about (I think I had on a life jacket) in late afternoon, warm, golden (maybe September) light. It was likely a half-hour adventure, and then, we retired to Miss Shaw's home for lemonade and cookies. It was a magical day—with my favourite adult women (alongside my Aunt Joan) in the world.

Though I attribute my schoolboy precociousness to an eagerness to please my father, Gerry deserves the most credit (or blame!), for she was the expert in Early Childhood Education, and she spent many hours with my brothers and me, at home with us, for several years,

---

* My ex-kindergarten teacher, as Alexa McDonough, headed the Nova Scotia New Democratic Party (1990-94) and the Federal New Democratic Party (1995-2003). I was a red-diaper juvenile!

while Bill went out to work. She was always planning little jaunts like going down to Point Pleasant Park in the deep South End of Halifax to scrounge up pine cones, spruce needles, and fallen leaves—to make things out of em or paste em into scrapbooks. We'd also pick up dead, stiff starfish, dried-up and hollowed-out urchins, and gull-smashed-open mussel shells. Out on the Northwest Arm, she'd take us out to try to dig up mussels to steam and eat, though I've no recollection of whether these *sorties* were successful. She'd also take us out back of our house on the Bay Road to pick blueberries or strawberries along the shale cliffs overlooking the railroad tracks, or she'd let us help her plant lettuce and carrots and peas in our front-yard garden. The crisp, leafy lettuce, spiced up with salt and pepper, seemed richly fresh because it originated near our own stoop.

Despite my mother's success in founding three daycares (really pre-school education sites)—Cornwallis-Brunswick pre-school (early 1960s), the Children's Development Centre (1970), and the Centre for Exceptional Children (1971), I was sixty before I learned that she'd been applying Maria Montessori's methods—pioneered in Rome's slums—to us North End Haligonian underprivileged, poor, underclass children and waifs—black, brown, and white. Not only that, but my mother's pedagogy was informed by the research of (and likely correspondence with) Prof. Barbara Clark, an expert in brain-based, child-education stimulation.* (If I recall correctly, Dr. Clark studied my mother's methods and travelled to Nova Scotia in 1980 to interview myself and Ms. Wendy Bond, the two "graduates" of my mother's Head Start program who had gone on to university, fifteen years later.)

Notably, Mrs. Geraldine Clarke, equipped only with her teachers' college certificate and a few summer courses taken at the University of Ottawa in her early thirties, pioneered the importation—for marginalized, proletarian, and racialized Haligonian children—of both the

---

* See Barbara Clark, *Growing Up Gifted: Developing the Potential of Children at Home and at School* (1979).

Montessori emphasis on freedom of movement and independent study and the Clark focus on nurturing "giftedness" so as to augment intellect. My mother understood that the best way to boost lifetime earning potential was to "mother" a child's IQ. In fact, her second and third daycares, both government-funded, relied on a communal model of instruction and interaction, with parents and interested citizens volunteering to assist the paid staff consisting of Gerry—"the founder," an assistant director, three trained teachers, one assistant teacher, and a cook. I now know that, having experienced the formal school system, my mother believed that "slow learners" had few chances to succeed therein, and so could lose—perhaps forever—any interest in engaging curiosity and finding its breathtaking satisfaction (which is what constitutes effective learning). She felt that it was best to "mother"—cajole, inspire, cuddle, and encourage—her charges into wonder, exploration, and undaunted reading and writing and speaking.

My Aunt Joan, who organized and ran for thirty years (1986-2016) the North End Parent Resource Centre, in Uniacke Square, Halifax, focusing on aiding single-parent families, also applied her sister's ideas. (In fact, before illness kept her housebound, Gerry used to spend time at her sister's centre, aiding with the children, whom she loved spontaneously, always.)

My own schooling owes much to my mom's prodding and pushing and urging. When she attended my Ph.D. convocation at Queen's University in October 1993, she stood with tears in her eyes. It was an emotional moment for us both. She also inspired a girl who came under her tutelage, and she is now Barbara Hamilton-Hinch, a Dalhousie University professor; ditto for a youth, Christopher Bundy, who is now a senior attorney with the Public Prosecution Service of Canada. To be clear, Gerry didn't "teach" either Barb or Chris, but Barb has told me that she took them on a memorable car-and-ferry trip to Maine that did expand—literally—their horizons. One of my mom's pupils at her later daycares, Troy Adams, is now an Africadian actor; another, Craig Smith, is an Africadian historian and a Mountie at the rank of Sergeant. Many,

many, are the lives of those Gerry touched, improved, and nurtured—to want to achieve high marks in school and make their marks in their careers. She advocated that children need to know that they are loved *somewhere*—in school, assuredly, if not at home.

She taught a few years in the early '60s at what was still a segregated school in North Preston, ten miles or so from Halifax, across the harbour. She took me with her there at least once, and I remember spinning records—45s—on our portable record player. Soon, the sound of pop music received interference from the call of nature, but I was too shy to ask the location of "the little boy's room." Well, nature called stridently, and I answered—in my pants—and then began to bawl because I was so ashamed. No problem: a couple of older girls took me by the hand back to my mom, who got me into dryer clothes and soothed my upset with one of her patented peanut-butter cookies, which did sweeten the bitterness of my embarrassment. Later that day, I crossed Halifax Harbour with her on the ferry home, noting the cool, gloomy fog which had chased away the warm, original sunshine of my big-school expedition.

A few years later, at the end of grade three, when I was eight, I happened to be at home alone and picked up the ringing phone's receiver on a late June afternoon. The caller, a woman, asked to speak with my parents, but they were out, and I asked politely—as I had been taught—whether I could take a message. The lady responded that she had wanted to talk to my parents because my test scores had been startlingly high, and she had wanted to share that fact with them. I don't believe she left either name or number, though I did report the call and the message to my parents, who then began to talk about enrolling me in the Halifax Grammar School—a private school—founded in 1958. They asked me for my opinion, and I shook my head no. First, I was concerned about the potential cost; secondly, I didn't want to be separated from my chums; thirdly, I fretted that my sacred identity as "the smartest kid in the class (who also happens to be Coloured)" would be lost were I immersed with a lot of junior bluestockings and "brains." My parents decided not to pursue the possibility, and I remained among my peers.

It was likely about then that our local "ghetto" grocer—Sobeys— offered hardcover, science-oriented encyclopedias, a dozen, for about $2 each. Well, my parents bought em, and gifted em to me. But how weird it was that a grocery store whose floors were black with dirt and whose greens were often brown was bothering to offer its welfare- payee clientele science encyclopedias—and Great Masters art repro- ductions (which my parents also bought).

Another incident that pinpointed me as a public school whiz-kid occurred when I was ten, in grade-five. Out of all the Haligonian pupils available, I was chosen to answer a letter from a ten-year-old American, from California, who had written randomly to "any Halifax school" to sound Canadian perceptions of the U.S.A. Unfortunately for my pen- pal, I was a nascent nationalist, thanks to being sick-and-tired of American books dominating library shelves. Not only that, but the Guess Who's anthemic—and anti-American hit—"American Woman" (1970) had impressed itself on my inner ear. My answer to the Californian was also highly critical of his country, and I likely cited the Vietnam War, riots, and assassinations, not to mention Yankee domination of English-Canada's arts and intelligentsia, as good reasons for Canuck rebuke of our southern neighbours. It still bothers me that my inter- locutor did not respond to my letter; then again, he was likely shocked by its contents: More George Grant than George Washington . . .

viii.

Naturally, it was my mom who took me to the Halifax North Memorial Library in the winter of 1968, when I was eight, to pick up my first library card. We lived on Maynard Street, approximately four blocks from the library, and she trusted me to get there and back, with an armload of books, often twice a day. Then again, my parents knew I could lead my brothers, and later Aunt Joan's daughters—Geri (named for my mom) and Donna—to school and back. So, after that initial library trip, I was free—in concert with my mom's investment in Maria Montessori's teachings—to make my way solo to and from that palace of vertical, word-imprinted spines—the pillars of imagination and information, but also that gallery of pyrotechnic book covers, each of them a stained-glass window onto fantasy, sci-fi, or factual science.

North Branch librarian Miss Dee (Adelia) Amyoony took note of my prodigious capacity for borrowing and reading and returning heaps of books, and, once aware of my frustration of not having anything new or interesting to read on the elementary side of the library, gave me early permission to cross over onto the adult section. Yes, I'd exhausted all the kiddy holdings of Greek, Roman, and Norse myth; plus Alice and Oz and Narnia; plus world-war narratives; plus all Isaac Asimov and Herbert S. Zim books on touchy-feely robots, alien worlds and the psychopathic, sabre-toothed T. Rex; plus spooky books—mysteries and horrors (Nancy Drew, Hardy Boys, Sherlock Holmes, Poe); plus Canadiana up the yin-yang (Pierre Berton, Sheila Burnford, Catherine Anthony Clark, and the like). Normally, one had to be fifteen to borrow books from the adult wing, but Miss Amyoony permitted me that leeway when I was ten, for she knew that she could eye whatever titles that I was scouting, and hold back whatever could be too amoral or immoral for my tender eyes and budding mind. I'm sure she did a responsible job of double-checking my desires, but I did take out one book—a crime-thriller-mystery—in which the fascinating, scientific-looking word *pudenda* appeared. It became as much of a thrill to possess as did another scientific term, *tachyon*, which I also acquired that summer of 1970.

Like Miss Amyoony, Terry Symonds was a vital overseer of my reading interests. More importantly, he was "black like me," a dude from our blocks, and in the mid-1970s he was added to the library staff—at first—to stymie delinquents who might want to act out their disaffection with home-and-school by disrupting the library's patented QUIET. Terry could parley frankly with everyone, and he'd been to Africa—to Ghana, and had returned as an avid spokesman for black uplift and pride. So, he wasn't just a bouncer—if that had been his first role—but an in-house griot, who saw it as his mission to give us "young bloods" some guidance.

By 1977, he was screening films expressly for us black youth—after the library had closed for the day—in the auditorium. Thanks to Terry, I saw *Lady Sings the Blues*—Billie Holiday's bio elevated to Hollywood-scale, Technicolor treatment—in 1978. It was an electrifying experience: there we were, a gathering of black kids or young adults, finally becoming attuned to our heritage. Terry also screened for us the Bill Cosby-narrated, 1968 documentary *Black History: Lost, Stolen, or Strayed*. In addition, Terry would rap about "real life"; explain why it was important to be an in-the-home father; why we should complete school; why we should go to Africa. He was of us—the hood, the people, and the "boys": he even played basketball. (After his premature death in 1990, a provincial sports championship got dubbed, in his honour, "The Terry Symonds Memorial Invitational Basketball Tournament.") But Terry and I had a personal bond. Whenever he thought my afro was becoming "a fright," he'd summon me to the library basement, grab his clippers, and give me a free haircut on the spot! So, the library was not only a second home for me, but also a barbershop, a cinema, and a schoolhouse for lessons in Diasporic African history and culture—from Nigeria to New Orleans to Nova Scotia.

Poignantly too, in 1977, the library's Africadian janitor—a matrilineal relative—was cleaning up, after hours, on one winter night, when he bent and picked up a piece of trash, straightened, studied me, and said, "Georgie, I hope you make it, so you can give me a job and I don't have to do a job like this!" He then discarded the waste in a garbage can, sheer disgust animating his expression and his deed. I felt perfectly conflicted: How was I to "make it"—and what could I possibly achieve that would allow me to hire this older man—to do exactly what? I was only in Grade 11, only 17, but now was summoned to assume responsibility for this adult stranger's life. How was I supposed to navigate a society and a system—successfully—that had relegated him to what he saw as a loathsome post? Yet, the next year, being a grocery clerk, I'd be tasked by my father to achieve yet another seeming impossibility . . .

(In 1980, my summer job, under the direction of Ms. Janet Doyle, was to administer the library's programs, and I did so with gusto, preaching kiddy-level Maoism *via* the puppet shows [I penned the scripts], and even nurturing sunflowers and green beans in boxes on the library's roof. When my employ ended, I was allowed to keep a retired sign that once emblazoned the teen-oriented library shelves, "Young Moderns": it now sits atop my University of Toronto, Department of English, office desk.)

My quick-eyed reading speed and expansive (and expanding) vocabulary also made it possible for me to scan, surreptitiously, my mother's "bedside" novels. When I was nine or so, I leafed through one—secretly—about a cigarette girl who'd make her way among nightclub patrons, vending cigarettes from a tray, but who'd also end up—frequently—being bent over her boss's desk or being pressed and pretzeled behind the coat-check by a patron. I didn't understand most of the verbs—even the four-letter ones; but it seemed enticingly smutty, though I could not imagine anything more muscular than kissing in those hurriedly, sneakily perused passages about tempestuous, romantic gymnastics. Gerry also devoured *True Confessions* and *True Romance* magazines, which were notable for their black-and-white snaps of bleached-out gals in bras and repulsive, hairy-chested guys, all of whose eyes were blacked out by narrow rectangles. (Later, I'd spy similar black-barred faces in the detective and crime mags abounding in my buddy Wayne's home.) These depictions accompanied tales of marital or love-affair woe. I couldn't think why my mom liked these "stories" (her word), for they did seem grotty, disreputable, with their suggestions of wham-bam shenanigans and tween-the-sheets skullduggery.

One of those trashy stories appealed to me because there was a facing photo of a rocket—an Apollo mission Saturn V—and so I expected the tale to be Space Age-scientific. Instead, whatever connection it had to the NASA, moon-shot program, it centred on a young woman suffering hallucinations because an unchivalrous gent had spiked her drink with LSD, presumably to launch her into his bed. The effect of that story was that I became convinced that every swig of Kool-Aid or Coca-Cola could be similarly spiked. I don't think I bothered with my mom's mags after encountering that story. Still, I did approve the risqué element, the spicy odysseys disclosing hidden knowledge—either about moon rocks or hard drugs ...

So, once I began to read, there was no stopping me. I read everything—without much discrimination—just because it was delightful to enter the worlds of history, fantasy, mystery, theology, science, just pure story as narrative, fiction, non-fiction, comic books, a galaxy of paperbacks, a cosmos of hardcovers. Imagination was reading; reading was excavation. It was also genealogical. It brought me closer to my father (or so I felt). He liked the Bond films, sure, but he had a full set of the original Fleming novels. So I read em all—at age ten—though I didn't get the sex references (including the peculiar chapter title "How to Eat a Girl" in *Thunderball*). The point is, I was a vacuum cleaner-type reader: I hoovered up everything.

So, in grade eight at Bloomfield Junior High School, Mr. McFee, a white Cape Bretoner with a bushy afro, turned his English class into an adolescent Encounter session.* Desks were banned; we had sofas and beanbag chairs, plus comfy rugs spread over the regulation vinyl-square flooring, and even a sawed-off tree trunk that served as a stool. Rather than lecture, McFee asked his rocker buddies to class, and lead discussions for us twelve-to-fourteen-year-olds on such subjects as feminism. (Once he asked: "Are women just seminal inlets?" Not because he thought so, but to try to get us young'uns thinkin and talkin.)

---

* *Theoretically*, we early teens were supposed to evolve our authentic identities (psyches) and sense of personal responsibility through *encountering* each other *via* frank conversation about our reading or subjects raised. So, books were encountered (if not read), conversation rambled and gamboled, and grammar—that Unholy Terror—got exquisitely exorcised ...

McFee was a devotee of "Progressive Rock," and so his long-hair, Hippy jammin friends did a couple of electric organ/synthesizer sessions with us. Emerson, Lake & Palmer and Rick Wakeman's *The Six Wives of Henry VIII* (1973) were heard, if not studied *per se*. But the most important feature of Mr. McFee's ultra-freewheeling class was that all we had to do was read—either the hundred-plus books and comic books (of all sorts) in his hangout realm and/or library books. He kept score of pages read, and I did want to arrive at year's end as having read the most, which was true. But this notion of quantitative reading (sort of like quantitative easing) also saw me ignore qualitative differences: Shakespeare was equivalent to *Sgt. Rock* (comic book); Arthur Conan Doyle to Edgar Allan Poe; *Archie* (comics) to *Archy and Mehitabel* (another book—by Don Marquis—in my father's possession). I still prefer to read that way (apart from what I need to read for research and/or teaching): smidgens of anything pulled from everything—the *smörgåsbord*—available.

Assuredly, McFee's class was an advance—I thought so—on the former English teacher at Bloomfield, who was so strict a grammarian that he kept an alarm clock on his desk, sported Coke-bottle-glass-thick-lensed horn-rimmed glasses (to try to see his eyes was like peering down the wrong end of a telescope), and resembled a forty-year-old, tweedy version of Clark Kent. Although the teacher was professionally punctilious about comma splices and dangling modifiers, he could not discipline the class—in spite of his pointer, alarm clock, and elbow pads. We were too rambunctious: it was 1972, and the black pupils, led by fifteen-year-old and sixteen-year-old teen moms (with mewling babes in arms), initiated an anti-racism protest march and one-day student strike that mandated the wholesale, immediate sacking of the upper echelon of school administrators. (It was our own version of a Children's Crusade or, maybe, Mao's Red Guards rampaging through North End Halifax.) Given such a context, of classrooms of stone-cold "hot-heads" whose grammar was slogans and slang, our old-school English teach went bonkers—said the schoolyard scuttlebutt—and found asylum in the Nova Scotia Hospital (the provincial bedlam). The new administrators and the new English teacher were younger, "hipper" people, while our rebel leaders got suspended or separated out to lily-white schools. Thus, we had McFee and anything-goes talk-fests instead of exams on semi-colons and predicates.

(It was in Mr. McFee's class, in spring 1973, that I wrote my first poetic work, a Hilroy-scribbler of songs and poems and a hand-drawn portrait of a Greek-Canadian classmate, a girl, with braces "in," to whom the work was dedicated. I stole her surname for my questing hero, the chivalric "Benny." I don't remember anything else about it, except that it filled a whole scribbler, and I likely did show it to Mr. McFee, but not to my classmate so "honoured," for I was—yes—too shy do so. The point? All that miscellaneous reading or various congeries erased any prohibitions for me of what could be deemed literature, and so I stole from Shakespeare, from Elton John / Bernie Taupin, from detective novels, Vampirella [her costume no V-neck, but a breast-cladding, deep-plunge, tear-drop-shaped, belly-baring opening from neck to almost navel] comic books, generous excitements, to weave that adolescent fantasy, whatever it was.)

Unlike Gerry, her sister, my Aunt Joan was a devotee of Harlequin romance novels. When I was fourteen, I read through three or four, and soon found the plots identical: nurse leaves home for distant employ; finds her doctor boss distasteful, unlikeable, cold; a crisis ensues and the doctor proves considerate and gentlemanly and "in like with" the nurse; she ascertains that he's available, though she's still iffy about love; a secondary crisis unfolds and the pair embraces, blurting confessions of how they've "always" loved each other; marriage follows; the End. I read the Harlequins because I was curious about their romance scenarios. Maybe, also, by age fourteen, I wanted to understand adult relationships, including that of my parents, who had separated by then and would divorce in 1974, that same year. Given my parents' split, I could not suspend disbelief enough to trust in either love or happy endings—though I craved both.

ix.

Because he had been a paperboy, my father took me, Bryant, and Billy, aged twelve, eleven, and ten, down to the *Herald* newspaper offices on a Saturday afternoon, and scored us all paper routes, threaded throughout the North End. So, every weekday after school, between 3:30 and 4 p.m., we'd each collect a bundle of *Mail-Star* newspapers, or pick up a bundle of *Chronicle-Herald* broadsheets on Saturday morning (around 9 a.m.), and deliver them to the three-dozen-plus households on each of our routes. Mine included decaying, 1867-era, three- or four-storey flophouses, smelling overwhelmingly of boiled cabbage, wet dog, musty draperies and carpets; plus a beer-odoriferous private club and a tavern; many tidy, private homes and a few mysterious apartments. I also delivered papers to rooms in dark, rancid, Victoria Regina-era houses that had somehow survived the 1917 Halifax Explosion and were still doddering on, with their tottering staircases. One such pile was situated right next to the Schwartz spice warehouse and smokestack. So, the aromas therein, of aged newspapers and cat-food-dining pensioners, mixed, now and then, with pepper or curry or cinnamon or vinegar or mustard. A zoo of smells.

(But Halifax was such: the Moirs chocolate factory right downtown addled the streets with that sweet-and-tart stench, which competed stomach-churningly with oceanic odours of mackerel or lobster; while, elsewhere, there was the Hebraic-manna aroma of fresh bread from Ben's, just off Oxford Street, and the Social-Gospel-smell of ale from the Oland's brewery off Agricola Street. If you were starving, Halifax would either be a place to go to imagine a feast or a place to avoid because the scents of potential satisfactions would drive one batty.)

My paper route zigzagged a swath of the district. My southern border was Cogswell Street; my eastern border Brunswick; my northern border should have been Charles, but I pushed it, unilaterally, to Almon Street—to follow our local Black Panther-radical, anti-racism activists Rocky Jones and wife Joan when they moved to Windsor Street from Cunard. The day I'd first dropped a newspaper at their Cunard Street address, I was taken aback by a life-size black panther poster—a circle—which depicted the animal leaping towards me, above a slogan that read, "Move On Over! Or We'll Move On Over You!" Having only ever *read* about the Black Panther Party for Self-Defense or seen news items about their "violent" proclivities, I was nervous about bringing papers to the Joneses, save that I never glimpsed Rocky or Joan, but only their beautiful daughter, Tracey, who was, a few years later, my brother Bryant's girlfriend. I think it was Tracey who paid me the weekly rate for the delivery. Ironically, Rocky and Joan later became major influences upon my young adult life, even though my first encounter with the "Black Power" power-couple was as a scaredy-cat-fearful-of-Black-Panthers paperboy. Yet, I must have been intrigued by their aggressive politics—threatening bullets rather than tendering boring bulletins—because I went out of my way—literally—to continue to sling the daily newspaper their way, even when their address had shifted to a distant—by-foot—abode.

To continue: my route's western border was, I think, Robie Street (which again I elongated, to Windsor Street, pursuing the Jones family move). Despite the outside borders of my quadrant, most of my route fell within a central hodgepodge or maze: Cunard, June, Moran, West, Agricola, Maynard, Armory Place, Creighton, Maitland, Cogswell, but then that final, long-distance jaunt to Windsor @ Almon, past the Forum on Almon and past Pilcher's Flowers (with a neon-lit rose above the window), adjacent to the Jones's demi-mansion.

I kept the route from the spring of 1972 to the fall of 1974, and I earned approximately $13 per week in my take-home pay for the forty-five minutes to one hour that it took me, each weekday and Saturday, to slam the paper down on doorsteps or thresholds. Out of that baker's-dozen of bucks, I could treat myself to "health food" (emphasizing honey and whole-wheat bread), paperbacks (sci-fi), and a record album—anything by Elton John (I'm ashamed to admit) because my father liked "Honky Cat," and I had to honour his fanhood. I'd had a Royal Bank account from the time I was ten years old, so I probably banked my savings. However, my mom was terrible with money, and so, more than once, I handed over my earnings to her to help pay off some small bill or another, and/or to avoid Bill Clarke's miser-vs.-spendthrift wrath.

Lugging the dark-blue Halifax Herald Limited canvas bag, through rain and snow, sun and hail, and the stack of newspapers talking of Watergate, the Yom Kippur War, the Turkish invasion of Cyprus, and the medley of domestic politics—Stanfield almost becomes PM (fall 1972), Gerry Regan wins a second term as Nova Scotia's Premier (spring 1974), and Pierre Trudeau wins a new majority government (summer 1974)—I got extra-schooled in world and domestic affairs. I say "extra" because I'd already been suckled on CBC Radio and reared on the *TIME/LIFE* magazines my parents swore by. I didn't read the daily paper daily; I was too busy delivering it; but headlines burrowed into my mind. I recall the first attempt by the Turks and Caicos isles to join Confederation (1974). Amazingly, some subscribers told me, blithely, "I only get the paper for the obituaries." As a youth, I couldn't appreciate their placid morbidity. (Now that I'm sixty, as my generation begins to pass on—at first slowly, and then in earnest—I now fathom my patrons' interest in knowing who was still a taxpayer and who was now a corpse.)

Even so, and thanks to Bill Clarke's interest in the Senator Sam Ervin-chaired Watergate hearings (which had established that Prez Tricky Dicky Nixon was, ya betcha, a crook*), plus the endless Cold War tensions (despite US-USSR *détente*), I found my own geopolitical consciousness expanded exponentially—by radio, not by press.

---

* Bill Clarke was intrigued by false fronts—such as Nixon's (but not JFK's), which is one reason why he was so fascinated by Clifford Irving's attempted forgery of an autobiography by Howard Hughes, a news story that played out between December 1971 and January 1972.

x.

Between ages ten and fourteen, I listened religiously (pun intended) to the 9:30-10 p.m. broadcasts, on CJCH (the Halifax CHUM-network radio station), of the Herbert W. Armstrong and/or Garner Ted Armstrong thirty-minute sermons dubbed *The World Tomorrow*. Their apocalyptic Christianity prophesied Jesus Christ's imminent return, "not to bring *Peace*, but to wield a sword," as could be divined by Russian-Cuban intervention against South African *Apartheid*, Mao's People's Republic rabid to lob hydrogen bombs at Pasadena, California (headquarters of the Armstrongs' Worldwide Church of God), and the constant turmoil of the Middle East. (This was the era of Carlos the Jackal, the Entebbe raid, the September 11—1973—US-backed *coup d'état* in Chile, the hostage-taking of Israelis at the 1972 Munich Olympics, the Nixon landslide of autumn 1972, and the dissolution of South Vietnam as the Yanks vamoosed, by April 30, 1975, so that Saigon could be rebranded as Ho Chi Minh City.)

I did write to a Vancouver, BC, PO Box address to acquire many of the pamphlets and booklets published by the Worldwide Church of God (WWCOG), including *The United States and British Commonwealth in Prophecy*, *The Modern Romans*, and *Does God Exist?* I was keen to receive such printed matter—all free—because all seemed keys— portals—to wisdom about world events (presented as fulfilling biblical revelation). Then again, the emphasis on imminent apocalypse made sense because, first, I lived in a city that was a NATO naval base (and so likely targeted by some Soviet warhead); secondly, my parents' marriage was unravelling. "Impending doom" was no cliché—in either circumstance.

I still own those WWCOG publications, which I house with Government of Canada Emergency Measures Organization pamphlets such as *Survival in Nuclear War* and *11 Steps to Survival*—all *Diefenbunker*-era publications with nifty illustrations. (The latter depicts a chap—in black—tucked into a highway culvert while a red mushroom cloud—looking more like a tulip than a doomsday omen—blooms nearby.) I shelve them together, I guess, just in case one of the Armstrong prophecies of nuclear Armageddon comes to pass. (You scoff? Well, as you read these words, a few thousand dudes are patiently circumnavigating the seas, their submarine missiles set, awaiting a presidential command to fry you wherever you are . . .)

The Armstrong *père et fils* religion appealed to me because the preachers were scholarly and secularist theologians who detected biblical prophecy unfurling—as scheduled—in the slow approach of European Union (which the Antichrist would head), and also in affirming that their brand of Christianity was the real McCoy. But I had sympathy for end-o-world scenarios, anyway, for Halifax's North End district had vanished instantly under a mushroom cloud, thanks to the explosion of a French munitions vessel in the harbour on December 6, 1917.

I was seven when the fiftieth anniversary of the Explosion was commemorated, and the Halifax *Chronicle-Herald* issued a special insert that year, wanton with haunting images: houses punched down as if by a gigantic fist; a fire truck evaporated except for its steering wheel; babies with Band-Aids for eyes; schools and factories with their windows gone and snowy winds blowing through; streets become unrecognizable rubbish. Moreover, there'd been minor disasters within the larger Disaster: a tsunami off the harbour; then firestorms (triggered by houses collapsed onto stoves still flaming for heat or for warming food), and then a blizzard (to freeze to death anyone who hadn't burned.)

My awe at this tragedy only intensified when my father told my brothers and me about his experience of the *almost-second* Halifax Explosion, in 1945, when a naval magazine jetty on Bedford Basin caught fire: ten-year-old Bill'd been relieving himself in a lavatory (a word that he taught us to use as boys) when one of the "small" explosions from the detonation caused the plaster in the ceiling overhead of his refuge (the Armoury—to which North End residents were about to be evacuated) to crack and crumble and rain upon his head.

But there was that other strident reason for my keeping disaster in mind: my parents were dividing, 1972-74 (during the same period of my paper carrier career). So, I hewed to the extolled, Armstrong sentiment, namely, "The Family That Prays Together Stays Together."* I hoped, as an early teen, that *Faith* and *Love* could be an antidote to the domestic tragedy (at least for me) at 2357 Maynard Street. And that parental turmoil, playing out against the usual world turmoil, was yet only allegory for the turmoil of my transition from boy to youth.

xi.

If a grab-bag education in politics and world affairs was one consequence of hefting the *Herald* newspaper sack, so was incidental schooling in rambunctious heterosexuality. One afternoon, stopping at the paper-box to pick up my bundle (I may have been thirteen), I opened the wooden lid of the chest (located behind a service station at Robie and Cunard Streets)—only to let it blam shut an instant later: I was shocked to see a black boy and a white girl, his pants down, her skirt up—maybe five, six, or seven years old, exploring the male appendage and the female orifice. When I lifted the lid again, the blonde girl looked up at me, a big, sheepish grin on her face, as both children tugged up their drawers, scrambled out of the box, and scooted off, giggling. Thanks to Armstrong-*père* and Armstrong-*fils* sermons, I yelled at them to skedaddle, and I may have scolded, "Don't be so dirty!" But my puritanism was as phony as my prudery.

Once, on my paper route, I'd rescued a scuzzy, scrofulous document, a photocopied leaflet, *How to Pick Up Girls*, blowing along a street. It was a typical North End Haligonian porn distribution: let the

---

* Ironically, Armstrong *père* had to defrock Armstrong *fils*, at least once, for the son was susceptible to Adultery. Then again, Garner Ted's voice was kind of Nashville-satiny promiscuous, and so defiantly more seductive in tone than were daddy Herbert W.'s church-organ-wheezing pipes . . .

merde blow through the streets and/or cross the Commons—end up on school grounds—and up-end kids' innocence. (All presumably sailor detritus.) Yet, my introverted thirteen-year-old self did study that leaflet because I did want to know *the Secret: How* do *you pick up girls—I mean, get them to want to go out with you, like you, kiss you?* I was a klutz, a "spaz," unable to sing, play basketball, or dance—a one-youth, singular, Oreo refutation of all the black-male stereotypes. The leaflet—which was explicitly pornographic in writing, not imagery—was no help. I was too terminally shy to try anything, and though I was the kind of smart-ass who could score 100 percent on a gym-class Sex Ed test, my lived experience of the subject was nil and my insights were nonsense.

The older paperboy who had introduced me to my route testified—from day one—that I would encounter elder women who, mindless, would fail to fasten their house-gowns, thereby exposing their breasts, when they answered the door. (They also failed to clean up the cat poo dotting their linoleum floors.) As an unbaptized African Baptist-raised youth, I was scandalized by this information, but also hypnotized by it, for it was true. Being "a good boy," I did indeed avert my gaze—as much as I could—and pretended not to notice those older breasts as they swung in my direction. So, I did adopt a tacit, mental chastity in those encounters, focusing on the bucks in my hands rather than the paps before my eyes. I exercised scruples, repented my immature lust, and felt sorrow for the addled biddies who were my customers. Yet, I was also a teen boy. So I admit to feeling some excitement when, in that long-lost era of blissfully braless, second-wave feminism, I'd spot—inadvertently—a taut nipple or two as a perky housewife sashayed to the front door, not bothering to properly sash her robe or clasp a housecoat.

I must exalt one spectacularly busty black lady, whose white hubby seemed miniscule next to her swishy girth. He was a short, bearded Jack-Sprat-type, white-collar bloke. But his wife seemed to spend her day—on money-collection Fridays—in voluptuous and ravishing lassitude, lolling on a sofa, a *zaftig,* chocolate doll in a satin wrap that barely

draped her "brick house" self. She'd always be viewing a soap opera or
The Price Is Right, and was so perfectly self-possessed she seemed a
female pasha, who deserved to be carted about on a sedan, dispensing
lottery wins or death sentences with equal aplomb. Certainly, her head
was as haughty as Cleopatra's. Nor could she ever be critiqued as nar-
cissistic, for it was not her fault that she was so operatically composed,
and it was only justice that she be coddled and cosseted like the notes
of a climactic aria fluting from a soprano's silvery throat.

I also recall a classmate, whose parents also took the paper, who,
on one fantastic billing day, stretched herself out, pushing against the
doorframe, yawning her creamy, sable-haired self lengthwise like a cat,
while eyeing me, smilingly, while I just gulped stupidly and flushed
hotly, unable to veer my eyes away from her fourteen-year-old swelling
bust-line, displayed in crimson-clad profile. Strange, but even though
we'd shared the same classes at one point, I'd never noticed, prior to this
moment, that she was a beauteous teen version of Raquel Welch, if given
to chewing a lot more gum and blowing a lot more bubbles. At once, the
dull, frankly silly phrase *va-va-va-voom* acquired electric, urgent, deno-
tative applicability. And even though I was, out of my fealty to Brit rocker
Elton John, wearing pink-tinted, aviator-style spectacles, glitzed up
with the stuck-on, good-behaviour stars that teachers gave kids back
then, I was still able to make out all the roundness and curves and trajec-
tories of that *young lady.* I yearned to see her on every succeeding Friday,
for she and I were attending different schools by that point. However,
I don't think I ever gazed on her again beyond that indelible moment.

Carrying the paper let me scope out the larger world, *via* headlines
and (front-page) photos; but it also gave me entrée into my neighbours'
lives, at least when I paused to banter with them or to collect their
payments, a process that let me glimpse—through doors either cracked
or flung wide—their private, personal, and intriguingly separate lives.
I knew the habits and dreams and problems of my neighbours and
classmates and chums and relatives; but my newspaper customers
were strangers to me; and though I was no voyeur, their partly—or

fully—open doors revealed shards of their otherwise utterly mysterious and foreign existences.

Along with the musty odours and creaking stairways of hovels and slummy fire-traps and pubs, there was also stubborn *Beauty*, startlingly omnipresent—in the fashions and chat of women (or girls edging into womanhood); or in gents prosperous enough to wile away time in taverns and private clubs (beer smells courting tobacco smoke, or pinball blings and bleeps serenading televised sports); in the sea breezes off the harbour; in the taste of the almond-chocolate bar to which I'd treat myself at the end of every run. I wasn't Atlas toting the world; but, with the newspaper, I did carry *a* world, one that brought me within the orbits of strangers.

(I also rambled a zone of eccentrics. One stubby, chubby, pasty-faced, and bespectacled and fedora'd fogey, a stogie always boogying in his choppers, held his alfresco court on a street corner, but his cigar flummoxed his raspy aphorisms. Minus his glasses and hat, he'd've been Elmer Fudd. Another white chap, also senior, sported slicked-back grey hair, silver-wire-rim peepers, and favoured grey pin-stripe suits. A consummate executive type, what was unorthodox about him was his out-of-kilter gait, which was explained once one glanced at his feet— both beige-nylon'd and encased in screamingly scarlet pumps boasting an inch-high heel. A third character was black, up from the States—he was affable, though shambolic in dress, if not shabby. Reputedly a piano wiz, who made a living by tuning and testing the instruments that posh shops retailed, he was tall and commanding in stature, gravel-voiced and easy-going, with smiles always uplifting a face, framed by silvery and black-peppered dreadlocks. His oddity was that he wore his great, black coat, fingerless gloves, and long-and-thick rainbow-coloured scarf year-round, even on the most torrid dog days of the summer when actual canines would lie panting in any slip of shade.)

But hostility also flared. One day, on my route, I came across an abandoned shopping cart, strayed from the store to which it belonged. I flung my newspaper sack inside: it fit perfectly! Feeling slick and resourceful, I began to wheel the papers about in the cart, and my customers complimented me on my sharp delivery vehicle. But the cart was not long mine. A cruising cop spied me blissfully pushing the cart, screeched to a halt, rolled down his window, and barked, "Hey you, Coloured kid, leave that cart where it is! It's stolen property!" Unaccustomed to being chastised by a peace officer, and though peeved that my harmless helpmate had been criminalized, I obeyed. So, I left it right where it was—in the empty lot on the northwest corner of Gottingen ("Got-a-gun") and Falkland ("*Islas Malvinas*") Streets, back in spring 1974. It must still be there, rusted down to tetanus-toxic waste. Even so, I implore you to return it to the nearest Sobeys grocery store. I'm sure they're missing it!

xii.

When I was ten, I found myself in puppy love with a grade-school classmate, Sibyl, who was a pint-size and bonier image of my mother: ivory skin and black hair. As streamlined as a drinking straw. I can't recall now how she first came to my attention, save that, somehow, I learned that we were both the "smartest" kids in our class. Magically, she lived on my street—just half a block away. Her parents got along well with my parents (our friendship brought our households together), and she and her brother and cousin (who lived with her folks) and her young sister all became playmates with my brothers and me. My parents were better off, for we had our own house, while her parents had to share their maternal in-laws' house.

We were, for two solid years, 1970-72, "best friends" and "school chums"—except that I was so-in-love-with-her, but strove to keep the secret. We hung out in each other's homes; we biked all over Halifax and Creation together; we were inseparable in most games and summer fun; and she knew my upstairs bedroom in my home as well as I knew her parents' basement-apartment in their in-laws' house. I don't know how either of us managed to dispel the kids' games of teasing, of making fun of (would-be) prepubescent boyfriend-girlfriend, but we did; partly because I—or we—maintained the grand illusion that we were—honest—just friends.

But her parents (like mine) knew better. One afternoon, in spring or summer, either 1970 or 1971, I called on Sibyl, and had to wait for her in her grandparents' living room where her parents were cuddled, lying full-length (and fully clothed) on a sofa. As Mr. & Mrs. Z. palmed one part of an anatomy and probed another, I sat in an adjacent armchair, trying not to look, but also not feeling that they were doing anything all that different from my parents' loving touches. Then, as Mr. Z. swung a leg over Mrs. Z.'s legs, he asked me, and he may have winked too, "What do you think of Coloured guys marrying white girls?"

Well, due to my Junior Einstein persona, I tried to answer with as much sophisticated nonchalance as I could muster, while trying not to blush (and I can feel flushed, despite my brown skin). Essentially, I said it was "okay." But I knew—could sense—that the interrogative was intended to ferret out whether I had any designs on Sibyl—though we were only ten or eleven, and I felt protective of what I thought were *my* cryptic longings, and embarrassed, anyway, at having been so clearly found out. Luckily for me, Sibyl arrived, and I was able to retreat from the living room with the feigned air of happy-go-lucky friendship.

And so our innocent alliance continued, through all four seasons, at least twice experienced. But never did I not look at her with anything less than heart-pounding, pulse-throbbing, brain-painful ardour. She was lean and lanky, sweet and good, and scored equally high marks, and also outscored me at times. I liked her so much that I was sometimes jealous when she'd prefer to spend time with her brother or sister or cousins. When I had to be apart from her, I wanted only to be within the arc of her smile, the precincts of her gaze.

When we were twelve, Sibyl came along for a car drive with my father and our other playmates. She sat in back, me in front. But "I only had eyes"—in the back of my head—for her. A sunny, spring Saturday. We motored down roads with the radio playing, Bobby

Vinton, "Sealed with a Kiss," Looking Glass's "Brandy," and Paul Anka, "Diana," and the Jackson 5, "ABC." I knew—suddenly—that those songs were for me—and *her*. After that car ride, nothing was the same. For some reason, I was alone in my house afterward, and I took the radio (battery-charged) and lay down on my bed—sunlight streaming in the west-facing window—tuned to the Hit Parade—and fantasized about me and S. Z.—first kiss, first dance—none of which was ever to be. But I could never again be parted from music.

That same year, that summer, Sibyl came over to my house, came up to my room, closed the door, and lay on my bed, and unzipped her pants. Just that. She didn't remove them, but she lay on the bed before me and closed her eyes. I was astounded, way too flabbergasted and silly to figure out that she was expecting a romantic moment. I didn't do anything but just gaze at her—so stupefyingly lovely. But I was as weak and tepid as winter sunlight. No, the sunlight coming through the window at that instant had more spunk, more spine, more unfettered and committed power than did I. I stroked her sex—gingerly—through her panty, and then she zipped up her pants again.

Suddenly, my amorphous yearnings had taken shape. Yet, I couldn't decipher the meaning of her inclination, her posture, her act: lying on my bed, her black hair on my pillow, her face shimmering, her eyes closed, lips parted, her zipper down and the flaps of her pants spread, and I was utterly mystified about what should—or could—happen next. I was as spineless and boneless as snow—despite feeling, for the first time, the fiery wholeness of the blood in my veins. And yet, I felt love in that instant, too, for she knew that I loved her, or she could not have trusted me as she did. My restraint—or paralysis—was out of fear of having to take responsibility for feelings that I wasn't quite ready for; or, rather, there was a part of me that did not want childhood to end; that there was talismanic safety in that cocoon of being told what to do, as opposed to assuming the shattering liberty of seizing permission for myself.

Sibyl and I never discussed that moment. Then, suddenly, she was thirteen, and she was twirling plaid skirts and looking leggy and lithe in sheer black pantyhose and was wreathed in perfume and stepping in high heels and appearing extra vivid in makeup. Geez, I was dismally awkward in figuring out a response, even though I remained furtively enamoured. Still, every time Lulu crooned out the radio "To Sir With Love" (1967), and that line about a girl's going "from crayons to perfume," it was instantly tear-jerkingly sentimental for me. For I could see Sibyl maturing beautifully, right before my eyes, but I just wasn't courageous enough to tell her that I'd been in love with her for three long years, that all our play together was really me play-acting. That I didn't want to be a black-boy-Einstein-teacher's-pet anymore, that I preferred to be her "man," her fella, her boyfriend, her guy—the type of *mec* that Mary Wells sang about.

Bill harrumphed his way through "the Talk" that summer of 1973. No, it wasn't the "talk" about police that many black parents must give their children. It was, rather, the traditional talk about maturation that fathers grant their sons. In our case, it boiled down to, "It's time for you to start wearing deodorant" and "I'm sure you've looked at books on biology." It was childhood's end, yep, but the gent who'd thought it nifty to introduce me to *Playboy* at age five did *not* have much to say about my changing body or my insurgent interest in sexuality. He sat beside me and appeared sheepish and discombobulated himself about going through the motions of speaking about a boy edging toward manhood. All his eloquence that day degenerated into mumbles. Really, he spoke to his own feet as opposed to addressing me, his first-born.

I teared up as he talked because I knew this was supposed to be a defining moment—the Speech—from father to son about glacially approaching manhood. But I think we both flubbed the moment—maybe because we were both cognizant of its attendant Bar-Mitzvah-like transition-marker, but also because I wasn't quite ready yet to stop calling him "Daddy," or for him to stop thinking of me as his readily obedient "boy."

True: girls move toward womanhood faster than boys do manhood. Yet, whatever our rates of maturation, Sibyl and I grew into our teens on separate tracks. Indeed, after starting grade seven, at twelve, in September 1972, at different schools, we saw each other less and less, and then never. Maybe her parents told her, at some point, that we shouldn't be as close anymore because there could be no real romance between us. Maybe. I'm only speculating. The truth is that we were suddenly growing apart as we sprouted into our later adolescence. And maybe it was due to "race"—or maybe class. Or maybe both . . .

A few years on, when I was eighteen, I saw Sibyl for the last time. It was a sunny spring day and she was helming a convertible—either hers or her guy's—and her cigarettes and blue jeans (and the muscle car) signified to me that she wasn't much interested in acing school tests anymore. She gave me a lift to the supermarket where I was working as a carry-out-boy and shelf-stock-boy, now quite her junior—economically and, likely, sexually. Still, on that day, on that short drive, from near Citadel Hill down to the near-South End, with the top down and her hair streaming, I still couldn't tell her how much I'd hankered to hold her and kiss her, all those grade-school years before.

xiii.

But Sibyl wasn't the only subject of an abortive, pre-adolescent and early-teen *amour*. In grade seven or eight, ages twelve to thirteen, I fell in like—due to wonder tinged with excitement—with another classmate, the daughter of a soldier or sailor. Like Sibyl, Alma was chalk-skinned with dark hair, but had a spicy, sassy, exuberant freshness in her demeanour. Her face was as white (though freckled) as a skull. She was an ocean breeze—so bracing in her windbreakers, salty in her speech (all fuckin this and friggin that), and an urgent whirlwind of jumpy energy. She was bony—or splendidly slender, but also flighty, nervous, her hands flying off every which way. Her step was a giraffe's gait—a loping glide—as she cruised along sidewalk or asphalt, in flat shoes or sneakers, pacing, marking off her territory. Sitting still in the classroom, her mouth would work chewing gum as loudly as a machine-gunner rat-a-tat-tatting down enemy troops. She let me know that she liked me by alternatingly hugging me and then playfully punching a shoulder. I classed her as surely, purely desirable, all devil-may-care pizzazz, and wiry where she wasn't just spaghetti-skinny.

She lived right round the corner from where I gathered newspapers for delivery, so I got to walk her home from school a couple of times, and I got to stroll by her house (or her and her father's rooms in the building), roughly six days a week. Even if the sun was glaring on its front stoop and staring at the front windows, that house—really, a rooming house—was always dark, always dank-smelling (a stale-beer and mouldering-newspaper scent, a rude and repellent odour), a place where sombre shadows were prowling. So, I was constantly amazed when she'd emerge, all big blue eyes and gleaming brunette hair, and looking so scrubbed she seemed laundered—soaped and bleached— herself. Even so, her scent was more cigarettes and bubble-gum than it was "99$^{44}/_{100}$ percent" Ivory Snow "pure." Her mouth exuded spearmint chewing-gum and nicotine.

Intriguingly, Alma didn't seem to have, nor did she ever speak about, a mother. However, that her father loomed large was never in doubt. The ill-humoured figure lurked in overbearing, juggernaut-gargantuan shadows.

I did screw up the nerve to knock on her door once, to ask for her. Her father answered. I have no recollection of his looks, just the sound of the door blamming, yes, in my face, and a voice yelling, muffled by thick wood and frosted glass, that he did not want "niggers" about.

His sentiment did not prevent Alma from smiling my way or clasping me for a playful split second, or tapping me on my shoulders, and I was pleased by the attention, though she was no gold-star or A-plus classmate—I mean, someone who I might have thought that Bill would like. Yes, Alma's pops wouldn't tolerate me, but I never considered whether my parents would like Alma. I liked her—and that was good enough. Still, I was awkward—being lanky, skinny, "Bucky," four-eyed, a "brain," a nerd, and a "goody two-shoes." Nevertheless, I invited her to my street, Maynard, just a few blocks east (toward the waterfront) from her digs on West Street.

It was early fall, 1973, and, stars just studded the night sky. Alma sauntered over to my neighbourhood on a plain-as-day date—though I'd not have dared term it that. She was a glow-in-the-dark skeleton, and also *Insouciance* and *Insolence* calling upon—in me—the model of (purported) *Propriety* and *Prudence*.

We hung out for an hour or two, just talking or playing children's games—hide-and-go-seek (I think), which did permit frisky grabbing amid the thrilling chases, while I kept trying to get up the nerve to angle for an official kiss, a real-close hug. But the rendezvous ended abruptly when my father called me indoors, since it was on or after 9 p.m. Alma defied his summons to me, and said so, loudly. I'd never heard anyone but my mother ever backtalk my father. Instantly, Bill, rejecting Alma's rudeness, ordered her to get on home. She refused to budge, standing her ground as a thirteen-year-old—every inch her martial father's daughter—daring to lecture Bill that the sidewalk and street were not his to police, and that she could go when and where she wanted (and I think she suggested that I could do so too). Sassily, these legal perspectives were laced with four-letter interjections. Yep, she swore "like a trooper"—or "like a sailor," and she'd likely inherited some of her dad's blue-streak diction. I was astonished that Bill ceased to argue with my bratty, would-be sweetheart, but just closed our door in her face—for I was indoors, which was his interest, and she was outside. Thus, his mission was accomplished. To keep me from her. Bill Clarke committed the error that parents are wont to commit, forbidding me from associating with "that foul-mouthed girl."

I recall Bill's words well, for I'd not considered Alma mouthy, or lippy, just eminently kissable. However, the flirtation collapsed when I reconnoitred her, one Friday night, lounging in the arms and lap of one of the other military-born classmates who was brawny enough to make the football team, whereas I was scrawny enough only to take to track-and-field. The twain were all hugged up in a school doorway, and Alma—her voice as smoky as her cigarettes—yelled out to me as I was running past, in training for a race. I was stopped in my tracks by the sight of the pair, two pale shadows in the foggy night, snuggled, tightly twined, really naked—except for still wearing clothes. Was I ever grateful for the mournful, nocturnal shroud, for it helped me hide my perturbation behind a stoic mask. But, maddeningly, I was heartbroken.*

Yet my infatuation—frustrated—with Alma was also the beginning of a process—that was to last for decades—through which I could finally accept myself as being both a black (Afro-Métis) intellectual writer/ scholar and a "raceless" individual who could pursue (elusive) happiness. Although I inherited my mom's predilection for a fully "black" identity and my dad's expression of independent, unaffiliated selfhood, I remained confused—almost all my adult life—about whom I might best make happy or who would grant me a measure of happiness.

xiv.

My infatuation with my maternal second-cousin, Mona, who was from Five Mile Plains (incorporating Three Mile Plains), just down the road, westbound, from Newport Station, and seventy-five kilometres, westbound, from Halifax, had as much to do with place as with person. Mona was a beaut: high cheekbones, blonde hair, green eyes, and a slim, trim figure. Because she was so pretty—and yet—like many Africadians— part-black, part-white, part-Indigenous—my Caucasian-looking mom, Gerry, took a real liking to Mona—her Aunt Laura's second-oldest daughter—as representing the girl she couldn't have and would never bear herself, given her distorted pelvis. My mom loved us three boys, her trio of sons, but she also hankered for a girl. Moreover, I think she wanted to afford Mona and her siblings a big-city-release from the

---

* I must've been right some jealous. Thus, I'd've been sweating on my nose! Yep: twenty years later, an African-American woman told me, "You sweat on your nose: that mean's you's a jealous man!"

cramped quarters of living—four children and their mom—in a two-room cabin. True: while my mom had grown up fairly well-off, her aunt had had two families with two men—one black, who *could not* provide for her and their two children, and one white, who *would not* support his four children. So, Mona's mom was hard-pressed to provide more than food, clothes, and heat in winter. Despite electricity, the dwelling seemed smoky; assuredly, it smelled of hickory smoke. Bluegrass music and Baptist hymns sprang out the radio like endless rhubarb, or nettles.

My mom brought Mona and sometimes her siblings to Halifax to stay with us—for a weekend or even a week. Due to Gerry's indulgence of Mona—buying her clothes, helping her spruce up with makeup, and encouraging her dating—I found myself smitten by my cousin. Yes, I viewed Mona as a rival for my mother's affections, but I also saw her incandescent blonde beauty. Flagrant was her incendiary-lemon-solar-inflammable self! Not just Latinate pulchritude, but brazen, Scotian *Beauty*! Surely, my obsession with Mona started when I was nine while, in the midst of mourning Grampa Johnson's passing from Black Lung Disease in 1969, I was sent to gambol with other Three Mile Plains/Five Mile Plains chillun, the denizens of Green Street and Panuke Road, in that field of hay adjacent to the Johnson homestead. We played hide-n-seek; we wrestled; we played tag; we tussled; while the adults mourned. Did we scuffle amid the wheatfield? Somehow, I got cousin Mona's gold hair mixed up with late-afternoon gold light and the gold colour of the tall grass, all that gilded shade just smiting and smiting. But I must add that her voice was indescribably husky wisps of speech, half-whisper and half-growl; it was tar and honey; or scabby with syllabics, the melted—now airy—chunks of consonants. Or it was shafts of laughter, all cascading, tumbling, down, one upon the other. She had a dimple in her chin; her very walk was gold light, thrusting into, furrowing, the air; or she would tilt into a dance—like 18-karat-gold flames leaping at a log. Only lovingly could anyone glance upon her cheekbones. Pastoral was her gentility; blowtorch-flame yellow was her hair. I couldn't believe that Eric Clapton had written the plangent, ethereal "Layla" for his mistress, Patty Boyd (Mrs. George Harrison). Not when the melody and squealing guitar riffs were crying out, "Mona, Mona!" Tears sounding from eyes; sounds tearing at ears . . .

Mona represented—pictured—for me my birthright connection to the country, to Three Mile Plains, to that ¾ acre of wild spruce and pine and anthills and blackberry bushes that's now mine, on Highway 1, the Evangeline Trail. I romanticized her—shamelessly—from the get-go because she was the Pomona of my honest-to-goodness homeland, where I was born, and her name could be a moan—a train's moan—my own heart's moaning for a place of plenty, and peace, and rest, and cheer, and honour, and *Love*. She could be all that to me, and yet she was also a girl who I rambled roads beside, who served me Tia Maria and milk, who teased me mercilessly, and who lisped words like "land-sakes" as if she were Elly May Clampett from *The Beverly Hillbillies*. Whenever she came to Halifax, there was a sense of fiesta, of escapade, flourishes of fashion and flauntings of that achingly aspirated accent. My mother would have a grand time dressing Mona as if she were a model, anything and everything stripped off the mannequins and slipped onto her bod. And she was always grateful and gracious in her assent to be made a rightful fuss over. To stand out: primped and pampered. To preen, righteously.

Yet, eventually Mona'd have to go back home; to that too-small-house where her soon-teen self had no privacy; where she'd be just another country chick to be preyed upon and/or seduced by no-count hicks, mean users of substances and abusers of herself. Her world may have seemed beautiful to me—a wanna-be Beat/Romantic poet; but, for her, it yielded few options.

I know she carny'd—in the late 70s or early 80s—with a travelling fair, but seldom were jobs anything other than seasonal or part-time. Despite the perpetual instability in her life, however, she symbolized for me the stability of a pastoral ideal, which is to say that I ignored the reality—the challenges besetting—her life. (My romanticism? The yearning to get back "home"—to Newport Station, to Windsor. And yet,

I won't likely get back there until I'm buried in the plot I've purchased beside my mom.)

In our later thirties, Mona and I kissed once—on the lips; but both of us were married to others, and that was that. I could see her as a fixed point, a homing beacon, but we were on irrevocably separate planes: due partly to our being cousins; but also due partly to class. Yet, her limited prospects entailed accepting a boyfriend who was incarcerated; then, she experienced angst—anguish—that laid waste her dreams: despite later marriage and maternity. She came to know in her own life (as did Gerry) that *Beauty* is not enough, on its own, to ward off the terrorism of bill collectors, Unemployment Insurance clerks, careless doctors, suspect attorneys, and suspicious cops; that *Beauty* can hardly ever soothe pain, let alone neutralize it, or displace sorrow with satisfaction.

So, I was devastated when she—Mona (Pomona symbolizing the Annapolis Valley)—while sitting on a chair before her trailer, committed suicide, by gun, in September 1999. Or maybe it was accidental. Or maybe always, as gilt-edged as a sundial, she was prone to lean toward dusk? But it's impossible that such lemony, dawn-piqued sunlight is obscured by grave dirt! (Yes, her grave is hard to find.) She thrives still in blossoms . . .

When I heard that news of her self-death, her dead self, I was haunted by my failure to keep in touch, to write or call, to maintain communion with a woman I saw as the Muse of my own patch of terra firma, my own prairie and tundra and jungle, and my fundamental, bottom-line, no-nonsense self. Could I have allowed us (if she'd agreed) to carry further that single, illicit kiss, to have somehow fulfilled that child's childish dream, fixation? Surely, it would have ended disastrously? Still, yessum, my tears rushed down. Immediately, words gushed into a journal; I let unfurl some flawless, mournful humming; rampant heart flutters, some antiphonal conniptions; to eulogize all the good blues guitar-pickers and even the weeping mean drunks—all those scalawags who chow down on fried mackerel and who salt down their ale.

I knew her death—Mona's death—was prophecy of all of ours—the Coloured wretched, *les misérables*, of Windsor Plains, half-Injun, copper-or-ivory-or-mahogany niggers, the last-hired-first-fired, not-wanted-anywhere-near-Windsor-town peoples. That's us: the despised by the despicable—those who love to see the lichen overarch our tombstoned names, those of us laid low by Black Lung, by belly cancer, by the sugar diabetes, by stroke, by emphysema, by tuberculosis, by alcoholic driving, by fucking in bad cars with the motor left running so the carbon monoxide poisons us in the midst of the act, by the heart attack, by the gun, by the knife, by the fists, not to mention homicides by cop or jail-guard. Mona was—for me—our Black/Back Country Madonna of *Struggle* and *Beauty*.

disintegration and d-i-v-o-r-c-e

i.

Whatever inchoate concept I had—as a teen—of heterosexual romance and coupling was soon troubled by an emotional and psychological domestic Götterdämmerung: my parents splitting. No salve, no balm. It was like a mountain imploding; like an earthquake spawning a tsunami.

Dissolution began due to the collision between my father's patriarchal tyranny, which included his doling out money, stingily, to Gerry, on a proven-need basis, and her activation of feminist ideals by putting her teacher's certificate to use and earning an independent income. The tension between these two polar notions within the marriage increased significantly when, after studying anew child development theory, *via* summer study, solo, at the University of Ottawa, in 1969, at age thirty, Gerry became, in 1970, the director of one and soon *two* day-care centres located on Cunard Street, just round the corner from our house on Maynard Street.

Suddenly, our mom had an office, a desk, and a staff. She was the boss! She could no longer be a domestic serf to Bill, now that she was responsible for employees that she charged to implement her pedagogy (which had been approved by government funders). Perhaps she saw herself as living out locally a role similar to that of Mary McLeod Bethune, the pioneering African-American womanist, philanthropist, educator, *and* university founder. Like Bethune, Gerry was a proud, unrepentant "race woman," active in the Congress of Black Women of Canada from its Halifax founding in 1976. Like Bethune, also, she knew that *Education* is the crucial means to engineer class and race uplift.

Gerry's success discombobulated one person: Bill.

I can't say what my mother's income was from her daycare directorships, but, even if it was less than my father's, it was hers, and he couldn't control her access to money anymore. No longer could he, in no-uncertain-terms (to use one of his pet phrases), dominate unquestionably our household. Gerry modelled the "New Woman": sexy (halter tops and hot pants), independent (her own paycheque), empowered (directing underlings), and, yet, also maternal—caring for her boys, but also several foster children that she and Bill brought into our home.

(A fine aspect of both my parents was their willingness to take in three foster children from the Nova Scotia Home for Coloured Children: Deno, Darlene, and Leelee—a boy and two girls. Then, relatives of my mom were suffering marital strife, and we took in their two daughters—Donna and Debra. So, between 1969 and 1971, our household consisted of two adults and eight children. I was blessed to have my own room, but we all bickered, while still trying to get along, and Gerry provided nutrition and nurture, while Bill doled out "discipline.")

In contrast to Gerry's professional progression, Bill was still a drone—a prole—at the Halifax train station, a thrall to CN passenger rail (not yet VIA Rail). He neither commanded his own office nor bossed others. Yes, he'd attended Labour College in 1967, in Montréal, taking courses in Economics, History, Sociology, Political Science, and "Theory and Practice of Trade Unionism," but none of that—nor one term at the Nova Scotia College of Art and Design in early 1970—proved sufficient to let him escape his—in Marxist lingo—wage-slave status.

Change—which had arrived at our doorstep originally *via Playboy's* live-and-let-live libertinism (hedonistic liberalism)—was now arriving *via* Simone de Beauvoir's *The Second Sex* and its offshoots. But Bill sought to maintain the *ancien régime*.

Once my mom returned to the workforce, she could not prepare our lunch or tidy up. The solution? To hire a maid. But we had to hire two to end up with one.

Our first maid was a mousy-looking white woman with cat-eye glasses and a busy-bee, stove-scouring-and-cooking ethic. Our kitchen was small, but she hustled and bustled in rustling up lunch and muscling through the cleaning. I can still see her hunched over the oil-stove, scrubbing and rubbing, removing char and grease, although nothing could eliminate the stubborn fragrance of bacon fat percolating in a frying pan. She lasted but two weeks. In a hushed conference in our living room, she tearfully told my parents that her husband had learned that she was working for "Coloured people," and so had put the kibosh on her employ. Although they were on welfare, our maid's husband could not stomach his wife working for us.

We were a "Coloured family" engaging a white maid. Even as a 10-year-old, I realized it was an unorthodox arrangement.

Keep in mind, too, that the usual set-up in low-income, Africadian households was that the unlettered father and husband would do catch-as-catch-can, unskilled labour jobs, while the wife and mother would hold down a low-wage, but steady post as a maid (cook and cleaner and nanny) for a well-to-do (or just middle-class) white family. Often, the black "help" would be employed "in service," which could mean that she'd spend up to six days per week with her white employers, requiting every need and whim, while only being able to see her own husband and children on her day off: Sunday. Did white fathers or husbands or sons or other males "take advantage of"—seduce, entice, coerce, rape—the black women who were, well, "at their service"? Assuredly. So, it was a point of patriarchal pride for Africadian men— like Bill—to see his wife and the mother of his children "safely installed" in his own home as opposed to being exposed—potentially—to the empowered lechery of white-male employers.

Too easy it is now—though, yes, appropriate—to sneer at the ambition of black men like my father to idealize the *paterfamilias* model. The separate-spheres notion (woman controls kitchen and cradle, man controls dollars and decision-making) also made it possible for much sexual and physical abuse to occur: from brutality to all to obedience extracted from all. Not to mention practices of intermittent— even whimsical—paternal denial of cash, food, clothing, shelter, and affection—as a means to punish recalcitrant wives and/or children. This socio-economic order oppressed women (and children); yet, mainstream white society upheld it as the "norm," as a God-given mode of family structure. Many black people thought these social relations "progressive" because slavery had made it impossible for them to have *any* stable family life, and poverty had hindered their aspiration to attain and or sustain such households.

Additionally, ideals of Christian propriety and bourgeois decorum— along with fealty to capitalist propaganda extolling hard work, thrift, investments, self-reliance—were adhered to, consumed like manna, by betterment-oriented Black North Americans. These ideas became a series of mantras to enable one's ascension from economic servitude and segregated marginalization into an *Ebony*-magazine aristocracy of suave and moneyed men and churchy and accomplished wives and mothers. I believe that this was Bill's cherished dream: to preside over an orderly, obedient household (wife included), and pursue middle-class aspirations, while never letting *his* wife fall prey to the lusts of middle-class white men (who viewed their black maids as automatic playmates) nor letting his children ever need to bow to—kowtow to— any domestic authority but his—or that of close relatives.

True: many Negro musicians and dancers, entertainers and scofflaws, plus crooks and scoundrels, outright rejected white bourgeois morality (which they scoffed at as a lot of church-organ huffing and puffing, much hooey and hypocrisy). They preferred lifestyles of jive talk and hooch, jazz and silk, blues and cigs, hard knocks and easy money, a rough-edged equality between men and women, and tolerance for same-sex couples, and not giving a damn for Bible or bosses or blue-uniformed thugs. But that wasn't Bill's way; he'd striven to achieve *Respectability*. Nevertheless, now our family was altering that white-patriarchal schema of male domination and female submission. We would hire a white maid—and now *she* could be subject to the (black) male gaze and the symbiotic positions of objectification and subjection. (Patriarchy thus continued in our household, but with a reversal in race-and-class power.) Gerry must have been aware of that possibility—or threat, but most likely discounted it . . .

Enter our second maid, Brigitte, who was blonde, busty, and exuding tons of bonhomie with a dollop of gusto on top. She was Québécoise, bilingual; had been a bar-maid—and had a bellowing laugh. Her girth was generous and her mirth was voluptuous. Indeed, she was chubby, and I used to tease her relentlessly about her physique, to show off just how snarky—or bratty—I was. She responded good-naturedly to my ribbing, seemingly. But, one day, a few weeks after she took over our kitchen, my father took me aside and asked me to tone down my poking fun. I relented, for he was right. And I feared being on his bad side. What I didn't know (nor did Gerry) was that Bill Clarke had quickly begun an affair with Brigitte.

It all made perfect sense. One way for my father to firm up (pun intended) his masculinity in relation to his wife's rise in status and independence in income was, as it turned out, to exercise authority—financial and sexual—over a maid. That she was white—and forbidden—made the situation all the more alluring and steamy.

What do I mean? Well, to begin, Bill would have loved that first-ever, big-screen, interracial, bedroom scene between Jim Brown—ex-football star—and Raquel Welch—the "It Girl" of the 1960s—in *100 Rifles* (1969), given his own Eldridge Cleaver-style, *Soul On Ice* sensibility that a black man is not "free" until he can "have" a white woman without any fear of white reprisal. (In the film scene, the much taller Brown, pulling Welch towards him, seems almost to absorb her into his chest. His masculinity is further signalled by a machete that, elsewhere in the film, he rests nonchalantly on his shoulder in a kind of imitation of one of Tom of Finland's outlandish, cartoon phalloi.) Decades on, when O. J. Simpson stood accused of murder of his white ex-wife in 1994-95, my father sported his own personal portfolio of newspaper clippings about the case, for he was convinced—like 95 percent of African-Americans—that Simpson was innocent of any crime save that he'd had the audacity to wed and sire children with a blonde "babe." Yep, my father's gut—instinctual—feeling that Simpson had to be innocent, had to have been set up, had to have been railroaded, that the L.A. cops (who'd infamously pummelled Rodney King only a couple of years before) were more than capable of planting evidence against a black male superstar, was supported by the facts that he sussed out of the news reports. But his perspective was really driven by his own experiences as a teen, who'd heard about the near-lynching of an Africadian man, round about 1950, for having bedded a white fisherman's wife and slain her husband in Italy Cross, Nova Scotia. (I've never been able to document this story, but he mentioned it to me one day, when I was in my forties; and I could sense then how his attraction to white women was mixed with both dread of white reprisal and a desire to "take" from white society the glamourized trophies of Caucasian pulchritude.)

Notably, in Bill's 1959 *Diary*, he describes an incident in which a newspaper photo of himself and a white bro, depicting them standing behind three young white women leaning—bent down—stooped* over a table in the foreground (a positioning most likely staged by the photographer) occasioned a tacit reprimand from his white railway bosses: They summoned him to their offices, to admonish him against thinking that he could rise above his station. Although the photo depicts a local Baptist youth club and identifies Bill Clarke's position as president emeritus, it is also a snap that could tempt "the unspiritual mind" (to quote C. I. Scofield) to espy therein coital implications. My

---

* I have to use three verbs because their questionable positioning is so adamantly awkward.

father knew that the reason for his "dressing down" from his bosses was that he was standing too close behind the trio'd white women, that the image conveyed possible intimacies that should not be his to contemplate, let alone enjoy.*

(Though I'm now sixty, I recall—photographically—that, once, while accompanying my white, teen girlfriend along a Halifax street, we passed an older black man, at whom I nodded, signifying respectful acknowledgement; he smiled in return and, unbeknownst to my ladyfriend, *winked* at me. I knew instantly that he was urging for me the—or a—"conquest" that may have eluded him. Yet, such lovemaking would not have been about love, in his eyes, but about a settling of accounts: to kick a white man in the groin by kissing a white girl's lips.†)

The Victorian aspect of Bill's affair was reflected in its class dynamics. Bill was working-class—definitely, as was Brigitte (who was, in comparison to him, *lumpen*). But he was also an autodidact intellectual, one who carried and conducted himself with *haut-bourgeois* dignity. Although he was black, and thus possessed less social capital than did white women, his erudition and his earnings rendered him patrician—in his mind, yes, but perhaps also in Brigitte's, whose position as a Francophone in a WASP-ish city, would also have empowered my father—in their affair—due to his linguistic alliance with the local English-speaking elite.

Bill and Gerry were, together, marginally middle-class. That fact was established by their ability to employ a maid. I have no idea whether

---

* Thus one of the books in Bill's home library was Clem Kovak's smutty *Casebook: The Interracial Sexualists* (1971), which, purporting to document "affairs between men and women of different races," is a non-stop, orgiastic sex-fest.

† When I was a grocery clerk, my boss—Swan—called all us stock boys to the back room at closing time, one summer Saturday of '78, and handed us each a beer, an unprecedented generosity. As we sipped, he sobbed: He'd just "disowned" his daughter. Why? "She's shackin up with a black guy." Being the singular black guy present, I had to observe, "But she's your flesh and blood." "What if she gives me nigger grandkids?" "They'd still be *your* grandkids, *sir*," I answered.

Brigitte obtained income in any way beyond being our domestic, but, presumably, she felt some prestige in being loved by a classy, suave, black gentleman of modest financial means. They were, sort of, in class terms, James Earl Jones coupled with Anna Nicole Smith. Black gravitas and blonde voluptuity.

Bill and Brigitte likely pursued their secret love in 1970, and it went on, maybe undetected—if even suspected—by Gerry until 1972. However, she did not confront Bill about his lover, though she did fire Brigitte once her suspicions were aroused. Gerry's further revenge was to take a lover herself, R. J., a Jamaican-born Dalhousie University student, a decade junior to herself. Gerry had found a lover younger than her husband, more highly educated than her husband, and darker-complected than her husband. But Gerry kept her affair secret too.

She also kept two other secrets which represented her studious betrayal—or rejection—of Bill's patriarchal order. She took driving lessons—on the sly—and purchased—on the QT—a brand-new, forest-green, two-door 1972 Ford-Mercury Comet.

Not only was Gerry, then, by the summer of 1972, her own boss, with an office, her own income, and a staff, she also owned chattel separate from her husband—i.e. the car—and she had a lover who was, by incipient lettered degrees, Bill's better—a fact that would have rankled my dad. (R. J. boasted that his family's neighbour back-home was none other than Sidney Poitier.)

This state of mutual, secret affairs plus a secret car and a secret "superpower" (i.e., Gerry's ability to operate a motor vehicle) was akin to the mutual stockpiling of dynamite to be set off as marital dooms-day-blasts—whoever first decided to make an issue of the other's lover. When the explosion happened finally, that summer of 1972, it disintegrated our nuclear family,* but the damage occurred in slo-mo,

---

* By this point, our foster siblings had returned to the Nova Scotia Home for Coloured Children, and Donna and Debra had gone home to their parents. We were once again a household of five (if not for much longer), not eight.

metastasizing over twenty-one months, almost two years. My brothers and I went from a state of suspended terror—in regards to Bill's haphazard rages—to a steady state of alarm—as bickering, crying, cursing, slaps, threats, and damnations scored the classical music and the Motown that had once washed over our ears.

It began with the revelation of the "stealth" car. (A minor accident, with R. J. at the wheel, exposed the stab-wound facts—for Bill—that Gerry owned a car and had a lover.) All this came spilling out during a tense supper in which one or both parents spoke the absolutely *verboten* F-word, and Bill ended up waving—dramatically—a steak knife in Gerry's face. This memory is so terrible that I wish it were open to doubt. I can still see him hauling the knife out of a kitchen drawer and pointing it at her cringing head and face, while my brothers and I sat at the table—stunned, transfixed, horrified, paralyzed. What were we to do? What could we do?

Shortly afterward, Bill went—*bam!*—out the front door—to cool down, or, more likely, to seek out R. J., to treat him to a kicked-in skull. Wasting no time, Gerry gathered up us three sons—now twelve, eleven, and ten—and took us to A&W for a fast-food supper and then to a rooming house, where we all shared one room for the night, interrupted only by the appearance of R. J. under the dismal, disgusting room's single light bulb. It recalled those cracked-plaster, peeling wallpaper decors so prevalent in *Looney Tunes* cartoons. It was so depressingly appropriate a setting—of decay, of dirt, of disease—that it was for me the perfect illumination of our family's precipitous disarray.

No matter how nasty Bill Clarke could sometimes be, he'd never have allowed us to witness the fly-by-night squalor in which we were now sunk. He'd striven to protect us from cockroaches, the rats, the vermin, that always await a Negro who has fallen from socio-economic grace. Yet, his mean behaviour had made inevitable our flight. Whatever Gerry's culpability for the unfolding drama in which we were caught up, my brothers and I were her natural-born (pun intended) allies. We'd all suffered together; we were all escaping together.

R.J.'s materialization that night in our man-child lives marked perfectly our passage from the prosperous tyranny of Bill Clarke to the relative pauperdom—if with funkier LPs—of life with R. J. and Gerry. Certainly, that first night "on the run" from Bill was the beginning of an endless succession of moves for Gerry and us sons. We would never know again any domestic tranquillity until we had established our own households as either a family man (Bryant) or as a student (me). (Through his high-school years, my brother Bill lived with our father and his second wife, Pammy.)

That same traumatic evening, Bill gathered—Gerry related later— a few of his brothers to waylay R. J. and treat him to a drubbing. But I think the student stayed indoors, in his own flat (well-supplied with beer and nudie mags), and so didn't have to answer to my dad for his adulterous liaison with our mom. Perhaps R. J. considered the "affair" to not really be his "affair," for it was not up to him—as a mere twenty-something undergrad from Jamaica—to ask a woman in her thirties to reserve her favours for her husband. If a wife wished to stray, who was he to commend her to prudish *Morality*? After all, it was the 1970s: The "Me" Generation was coming into its own, and that anything-goes-era meant a Canuck PM's estranged wife could be snapped kicking up her heels, pantyless, at a Manhattan disco on the same night that his government was defeated.* Anyway, R. J. kept his pretty, ebony face aloof from Bill Clarke's fists, though not from the smooching adoration of Bill Clarke's wife . . .

Following that first weekend of our being a broken-up family, a mutually, parentally smashed family, my father—I believe somewhat chastened by his wife's obvious disaffection with his regime and his regi-men—attempted; or, rather, they both attempted—a salvage operation: they'd been wed for a dozen years to that point, and had felt enough affection to have three children and also strive to improve our lives

---

* Cf. Anna Biller's *Viva* (2007), a satire on the sexploitation films and the love-the-one-you're-with ethos of the 1970s.

economically as well as in terms of social status. So, the efforts to repair things were genuine, except that neither was really ready to give up his and her lovers. They found—in others—what they no longer found (if ever) in each other: *Acceptance, Adoration, Ardour.* Whatever, it all added up to *Adultery*, that mirage of marriage, that blighting massage.[*]

After we'd gone up home (to Newport Station) for a couple of days, Bill came calling to collect us and return us to his roof and his governance. I know that my mother and he wept (and it was heartbreaking to see that proud man cry), and talked, and promised to make things better. The sun was standing over him as he called out to my mother, that summer day, to come back to him. His shadow seemed longer than usual: It was a *High Noon* shadow. A shadow that could shatter a sundial. Or a shadow that could be shattered by sun-lit *Enlightenment*— my mother's assumption of *Equality* and *Independence*; or our boys' own shrugging off of a domineering father's too-strict state?

So, we all traipsed back to 2357 Maynard Street. Our mother's still-new, if slightly-damaged car now sat perched in front of our house, looking sleek and gleaming as much as avocado paint can gleam. Even if it was a sombre green rather than a fluorescent emerald, it still outshone my father's decade-old and rusty station wagon, that he'd patched up with putty and had spray-painted patches of different-hued blues. (A medley of sapphire and turquoise rectangles, squares, and smears: the vehicle resembled an abstract painting set upon rubber tires. All as Day-Glo as a Warhol and as brash as a Mondrian.) I don't know if my father had ever owned a new motorcycle, when he was a motorcyclist; but I know he'd never owned a new car. If he was jealous about Gerry's car, one remedy was for him to drive it—as one way of trying to mend the double (fatal) wound that his wife and he had inflicted upon the marriage.

---

[*] Why don't tears, heavier than heavy water, splotch this page? While I critique my father, do I not also confront his first-born son, that Adulterer, that *Scarlet-Letter*-branding-his-chest hypocrite?

So, Bill gathered up my brothers and I to take us on a one-week jaunt through New England to New York City. I got to sit beside my father—in the passenger-side beige, bucket front-seat as his "pilot." It was my job to check maps and verify directions.

ii.

Our family self-therapy entailed motoring through pulp-and-paper-stinky Maine, not to mention all the saint-dubbed backwaters (Saint Thingabob and Saint What's-Her-Face and Saint Thingamajig-de-Ha!-Ha!) of righteously goddamned New Brunswick (so cursed due to its lumber-baron-ruined roads), and then through New England spruce (for which Humbert Humbert pined) down to New York City skyscrapers. The last time that Bill had made this trip was by motor-cycle, in the summer of 1959, when I was a curled-up fetus inside Gerry's womb and he was oblivious to my looming entry into the world.

An emotional journey, truly. I wanted my parents to stay together, but I also questioned how a week apart could work that miracle. At that heady time, the era of my joint infatuations with Mona and with Sibyl, I'd begun to fuse—in my mind—radio pop songs and the possibilities and issues of romance. So, in between checking routes on maps, I soaked up the Top 40 songs like the synthesizer-composed "Popcorn" by Hot Butter and "Ben," Michael Jackson's prophetically (for him) per-verse, weird, crooning, squealing love song—for a rat, i.e., a rodent.

But another big hit that summer was "(If Loving You Is Wrong) I Don't Want to Be Right." Every time it cried out of the radio, I thought of my father, at the wheel beside me, maybe thinking about Brigitte, for the lyrics talked about the fatherly adulterer having a wife and children "depending on me too." The wah-wah sound effects and thwacking guitar licks in that song underlined the central dilemma. There really didn't seem to be any way out for the male singer—Luther Ingram's persona—to disavow the lover's touch that he's a-hungerin for, although he's disappointing his own blood-and-flesh. I mused on how my father was hearing that song, how it was ricocheting between his eardrums and his heartbeat.

Being only twelve—though it is that Jesus age of intemperate, impertinent query—I had no understanding of the inimitable intimacy of coitus (to grasp and clutch, to clasp and touch, to pounce and bounce, and then to kiss deeply, fondly, and sleep, spooned together), of how bodies blend and join, form outta each other a tight cocoon. Still, I sensed that a solemn trust—the private, avowed, physical, primal bond between two people—had been broken; that sacrilegious acts—much dirty fussin—had occurred; that sneaky lovin—"runnin roun causin misery"—was not a sin that a song could explicate or ameliorate.

(But I was also struck by Neil Young's tune "Old Man": I couldn't have imagined then—or maybe I did—that one day that song would define for me my own mixed emotions toward Bill as well as my horror—and thrill—that I was more like him than I could ever care to admit.)

Did we enter NYC through Harlem? Must've! I do know that it was scary and exciting to tour a city of black people. It was scary because the Blaxploitation film fad had crowded our heads with images of guns, mangy dogs, trash heaps, fire-escape ladders dangling off tenements, and, of course, the requisite pimps and "hoes" (pronounced *hose*). Compared to Harlem, Halifax was sedate—if the North End was the closest thing to Harlem that Canada could boast—with our record of race riots, cop skull-busting, drug-kingpin assassinations, Chitlin Circuit soul singers, Black Baptist preachers, and Black Panther Party imports, plus a prostitute "stroll" that rolled right—tight—round the provincial legislature. While my brothers and I had delighted in seeing the Fat Albert cartoons on TV, we were also taken by *Shaft* (1971), with Richard Roundtree playing a black Bond-type amid Harlem's garbage and gunfire. So, to be there, in Harlem, meant that we had to separate the images of filmmakers reducing African-American life to a cavalcade of crime—the movie-set scenes—from the observable lives of the people about us.

(When *Shaft* played Halifax cinemas in 1971, my brothers and a buddy and I went to see it. Though late for the first show, we were in time for the nude scene—a white woman in a shower. Excellent! We watched the film twice more. When we got home late that Sunday night, Gerry and Bill asked why we had stayed to watch the film thrice. What excuse did we concoct and mumble? They only figured out our interest once they went to see it themselves.)

Once the brand-new car broke down—due to a flat or our running out of oil—Bill had to enlist the aid of black male strangers—Harlemites. And they did help. And they were clearly not silver-screen stereotypes, but real people. It was comforting and it was consequential. It would be a long time before I would see again so many black people in so concentrated a space. (Driving from Ottawa, ON, to Washington, DC, in December 1991, I almost ran off the road when I saw, coming towards me, in the opposite direction, driver after driver who was black! Think about it: it is—or was—a rare event in Canada, thirty years ago—to see "drivers of colour" dominating a highway or street.)

We rolled down to the Taft Hotel, a lofty pile (a bright contrast to the rooming house in which Gerry had had to install us temporarily). The next day, during a ferry ride round the harbour, I saw the World Trade Center craning toward the status of being the tallest building on the planet—a fact that I rued because I'd always esteemed the Empire State Building for claiming that cachet. Bill took us also to Radio City Music Hall where I got to ogle the Rockettes, whose sequined gams, high-kicking, were the perfect segue for the film *Last of the Red Hot Lovers* (1972), a Neil Simon sex-comedy, yet also a sad reminder of our road trip's impetus. How weird: to hear Luther Ingram beltin "If Loving You Is Wrong" and then to watch a film about a middle-aged bloke tempted to spice up his humdrum life by capering among bedrooms.

We left New York on a Saturday morning, but stopped at New Hampshire's Mount Washington come afternoon, after six hours on the road. I suspect that my father was revisiting memories of his last

summer of freedom (before marriage) when, in June 1959, he participated in the annual motorcycle rally at Laconia, NH. He said he
wanted to stop at Mount Washington so we could ride the famous
Cog Railway ("an engineering marvel of the 19th century") to the peak,
the highest in the northeast US. Sunshine matched the swank of the
spectacular ascent. Yet, a half an hour into the incline, the train shud-
dered, screeched, and began to roll backward. It came to a raucous
halt, at a seventy-degree slope, with the twenty or thirty passengers
aboard at the sudden mercy of gravity and an emergency brake. Bill
said he turned around when he heard the first signs of trouble and
saw the train engineer blanching with fear. He later told us boys that
he was prepared to throw each of us out the window if the downhill
acceleration had continued. (He was right to be worried: a 1967 accident had slain eight. However, the most grievously injured then were
those who had jumped from the backward, downslope, careening
train!) We were stranded until help arrived, about an hour later.

In the meantime, passengers divvied up available food. One white
woman gave us an orange, and I can say that the fruit and juice never
tasted better. Once we were winched downhill, Bill received a full
refund for our tickets, but he said that, given the safe ending, he'd have
been okay with forgoing the dough.

After that, we loped doggedly straight to Halifax, arriving the
next day in the afternoon. I recall that we slept at night in forever-
sulphurous, forever-hellish, forever-backward Maine, in the car for a
few hours (save for a midnight, knock-on-driver's-window-with-
flashlight inquiry from a state trooper), and then we booted through
bootless New Brunswick.

At odyssey's end, we found that not much had changed. What did
change—at least for me—was that Bill was no longer a paragon of
moral authority. He went from being the boss, the know-it-all tyrant, to
being merely life-size fatherly, yet never buddy-buddy.

iii.

Instead of our parents reconciling, our home became a revolving door through which each spouse left, to live apart from us, at different times. Neither cut off their side loves.

First, Bill exited. I can still see him going out the door with a leather coat on his shoulders, tears in his eyes, and a midget suitcase in hand. I regretted his comeuppance, for he seemed so diminished, no longer the awesome despot whose word was almost God's. He was gone for a couple of weeks or a month: long enough for the Temptations' "Papa Was a Rolling Stone" to register as a radio gospel-sermon for my brothers and me. Just as it had been spooky to hear Ingram whine "If Loving You Is Wrong" that previous summer, so was it now upsetting to audit the Temptations talking about an archetypal Af-Am male, some dude's daddy, noting "bad talk" claiming that Papa had several kids by different ladies, including a common-law wife. My pops didn't have an "outside" child (not yet) and "another wife" (not yet), but central conceits of the song seemed right on: the man had ceased to have any claim to rectitude, even if he still had a claim on love. So, the grunt of bass, the wah-wah of electric guitar, the stratospheric fluting of violin, the steady pulse of drum and cymbal, plus the song lyrics divulged the "truth" about a man who womanized, who drank, who got into fights, and who was shunning his legit spouse and kids. When Bill'd left us—with his dwarf suitcase and fedora—he did seem a "rolling stone," but definitely more like the Temptations' version than Bob Dylan's Beat heroine. (I wondered if, on some inaudible frequency beyond the tinkly, churchy glockenspiel of this classic of pop bathos, Bill himself recognized the song's partial, autobiographical significance.)

By October, Bill was back (ta-da!); then Gerry moved out, taking an apartment on the Dartmouth waterfront, just across the mile-wide harbour from Halifax. It was surreal to go there, with my brothers and my dad, to chow down on the fantastic treat of Kentucky Fried Chicken, which we knew all about from Man-from-Glad-spic-n-span-white-suited Colonel Sanders' TV ads, but had never before had so much as a whiff. (Even so, the ads had sold the sizzle so well, it was a let-down to get to the meat—despite its boasting "11 herbs and spices.")

If "Papa Was a Rolling Stone" sketches—for me—a once-Ten-Commandments-intoning father gone rogue, the song that most befit Gerry that autumn was Helen Reddy's feminist anthem, "I Am Woman." Truly, Gerry was living that paean to independence by being literally her own boss, being able to tool about in her own car (tooting "toodle-loo" to Bill in the process), living in her own home-apartment, exploring a lifestyle likely closer to the sparkle of her girlhood than anything she'd known under Bill's penny-pinching regimen.

Yet, she was "separated"—technically "single" (as was Bill)—and did not have to answer to anyone except—eventually—the bank that financed the car buy and the landlord pocketing her rent. Other than those debits, she was *liberated*—at last, and was still canoodling with R. J. Were there moments during that fall of '72 when she could amble to the Dartmouth side of Halifax Harbour, right at her building's front door, and survey Halifax and wonder about her sons (now living with a wifeless father, now radically lenient in his treatment of his boys)—or simply contemplate the strange—brave—new world to which she could now claim entrée?

Regardless, now Gerry could bring her young cousin Mona to her place, to grant her a week's reprieve from rural sorrows—in her peda-gogue's effort to intervene in Mona's life, to suggest to her that she could be educated—improved, that she could blossom. For my part, it was ecstasy to go to a cinema, sit beside Mona, and watch *The Secret Garden* (1949), and imagine that we were its child heroes discovering *Beauty*, *Vivacity*, and *Joy* and familial reconstitution in an enclosed garden (*hortus conclusus*—as is trumpeted in the Song of Solomon).

After the film faded to black, and we returned to my mom's water-front abode, we went running and jumping and skipping all about the many grassy knolls that were the topography of the grounds. Moonlight shimmered silver upon Mona's golden hair, and there was exhilaration in my—maybe our—laughter, a moment for me of breathless and breathtaking glee in the midst of the trauma that was taking scissors to my family photo album and also slashing at my heart . . .

iv.

Yes, these trying times—for my brothers and me—were also a Special Period of suddenly suspended restrictions. To try to palliate the discord roiling us, both Bill and Gerry were avid about treating us boys to outings to A&W, to the local drive-in pleasures of Sunnyside (Bedford, home of The Chickenburger), to the still-brand-new McDonald's. Onion rings, milkshakes, burgers, soda were now weekly fare, not the once-in-a-blue-moon treats of the patriarchal *ancien régime*. Maybe Bill and Gerry were vying for our loyalties for the division-of-household approaching. Still, these precious moments were lulls in the maelstrom besetting us.

Now, Bill's nightly curfew was 10 p.m. Perhaps he realized he'd been too hard on us. Maybe he suspected that when the Family Court attorneys would ask us which parent we'd choose to stay with, we'd all vouch unhesitatingly for Gerry, and for an elementary reason: she was nice to us; kind, not stern, not full of rebuke, or too-easily catalyzed rage. Still, Bill's relaxation of once-rigid rules and duties was disorienting: how far could we now go? Like our mother, we were now "liberated," but we could still worry, surely, about when the congenial ex-dictator might resume despotic command again, or cancel liberties and generosities and charity that still felt tentative and ephemeral. Weren't we merely living in the eye of the hurricane?

Come Christmas '72, my prayers got answered: our mother came home from Dartmouth—for the holidays. She still had her apartment, but it seemed as if she and Bill would try to recover their love. On one of the pre-holiday mornings, I came down from my upstairs bedroom and found them cuddled together under the covers of the hide-a-bed sofa, and I felt some slight relief, some hope, that we would all be reunited, and that Bill's former domestic terrorism would transform now into a Utopia of tenderness.

Come December 23, 1972, I was helping my mom decorate our tree when, on that grey, drizzly, chilly afternoon, arrived stereotypical dread. The gloved fist of a taxi driver thudded on our front door to announce a delivery. My mother asked about the sender, but the taxi driver just shoved this ribboned-and-bowed item past my mother and onto the hallway floor, and then skedaddled. Gerry picked up the gift-wrapped box and she began to cry—no, to bawl—horribly, as she ripped it open in the living room. I tried to play matter-of-fact detective about the sender. But my mother guessed that it was from my father's lover, and that Brigitte had taxi'd it over, on an afternoon when she knew (thanks to pillow-talk) that Gerry would be there, and would divine the intended message: Bill was no longer hers, regardless of the Xmas normality that Gerry—and maybe Bill too—had thought they could conjure. I confirmed my mom's suspicion by locating and withdrawing—from the open box and the wine-red man's cardigan that it proffered—a single, long strand of yellow hair.

The fallout from the cardigan—or bomblet? Toxic! Gerry got in Bill's face about this evidence of his ongoing affair with Brigitte, but he denied, denied, denied, asking, rhetorically, "Why am I always the bad guy?" When he threw out that question, I felt a pang of regret for his predicament. I'd resented and feared his domestic dictatorship, but I didn't believe he was a "bad guy"—a Western movie villain with a black hat.

Somehow, we made our way through that Christmas, but the hope—maybe mine alone—for parental reunification did not end up as a gift under-the-tree, but merely as high-tension-under-wraps. So, in January 1973, my mother left again, this time scooping up her three sons, and moving us into a grand (by our standards) house on Chebucto Road, in the tony, upper-middle-class West End. It was our first time to live outside the North End since our very early boyhood days on the Bay Road, a decade before.

v.

We'd only just settled into the three-storey house when R. J., Gerry's swain, also moved in—while still keeping his apartment near Dalhousie University. (Even when my parents accepted weeks of trial reconciling, neither cut off his or her lover.) Suddenly, I had to make room in my Elton-John-clouded ears for the jazz-rock of Miles Davis, the reggae of Bob Marley, the African warblings of Miriam Makeba, and the pure-funk of James Brown. I couldn't really interpret the bleeps, toots, wah-wah thwackings, and electric this and electrified that of Davis's *On the Corner*. But it was soon blasting from the stereo in that huge, drafty house, with a fireplace crackling out flames in the living room.

I suspect it gave me a different grade seven experience than that of my peers, whether black or white. In Halifax, jazz—of any sort—was an underground, subversive music—unheard in school precincts, nor heard on radio or in clubs (save for coteries of hipsters). Most black kids bopped to soul, funk, r-n-b, disco, gospel; white kids clodhopped to rock, country, Top 40 pop. To have jazz fusion percolating and bebop-ping and ping-ponging out the stereo or portable tape recorder was the aural equivalent of "snap, crackle, pop" becoming notes rat-a-tat-tatted from a machine-gun. (Contradictorily, however, R. J. was also a fan boy of the fey, fair-maiden singer, Judy Collins and the sultry warbler Maria Muldaur; and he lauded the reggae riffs of Eric Clapton's "I Shot the Sheriff" and Elton John's "Island Girl.")

Well, R. J. was in synch with the Me-Gen *Zeitgeist*: to be preco-ciously decadent and pretentiously avant-garde. So, ten years our senior, R. J. changed up our teen wardrobes by lending us his threads. Instantly, we were sporting bouffant afros, polyester shirts with hyp-notic patterns and tear-drop collars, po-boy caps, and clunkin bout in platform shoes. We quit Bill's police state and entered the People's Republic of Cool: afro picks, trumpet squawks, Afro Sheen, Funkadelic beats, mood-rings, bell-bottom pants, *Soul Train* on TV, and 8-track "TSOP (The Sound of Philadelphia)" in the car. We escalated—or

downgraded—from Portia White to Barry White. Flexing his complexion of dark chocolate and his diamond-scintillant black eyes, R. J.
could deck himself out in skinny blue-jeans, a polyester indigo shirt,
a grey po-boy cap and an earring, and show up rhinestone-stud-flashy
in any circumstance. Sagely, R. J. never tried to play dad, for that was
still Bill's singular—unceded and unsuperseded—role, but now exercised only when we stopped by his place—2357 Maynard—after school,
from where Gerry would pick us up to motor us to our new, near-
suburban residence.

I liked R. J.; for one thing, he represented, not so much exotic
Jamaica, but exotic university study—the possibility of that pursuit.
Yes, my mom had gone to teacher's college, and other relatives—Uncle
Sock and Uncle Gerald—had done the same. But R. J. was closer to me
in age and part of the household, so it was intriguing to hear him parley
bout exams and profs and cramming; too, his bachelor apartment—an
upstairs corner unit, close to Dalhousie U—was laid-back sincerely: lots
of wicker *bric-à-brac*, books (including a spoof version of *The Joy of Sex*
which asserted that pregnancy could result from swallowed semen),
smells of curry and coconut, beer in the fridge, Guccione's *Penthouse*
mag on the coffee table, Lady Marmalade turning raunchy on the stereo. R. J.'s set-up? Idyllic, though better for lovemaking than for study.

R. J. was the first adult I got to see up close living that tuition'd life-
of-the-mind. And he respected my teen-ponderings. Often, he'd push
back a chair, balancing on the back legs, while detailing musicological
critiques, and exclaiming "Lawd, oh Lawd," between sips of brew, and
flicking his wrists or snapping his fingers as if either or both were casta-
nets. He was also exorbitantly funny, and never funnier than when he
tried—in vain—to back my mom's authority by up-voluming his voice
and slashing his eyes at us as if they were machetes. Too, he was self-
conscious bout his short stature, and so sported skyscraper platform
shoes for apt uplift.

Assuredly, Gerry's passion for R. J., which included spinning lots
of Al Green and Barry White—particularly the slow jams, those

blue-light-in-the-basement waltzes that simulate having-coitus-while-fully-dressed-and-standing-up—was only partial revenge against Bill, who was more and more an ex-husband without fully being x'd. Even so, Gerry was "separated," but R. J. was a single: no quotation marks needed. He was a solo "international student" for tax purposes, and he saw himself as a bachelor in his love life.

So, not long after R. J. joined us, he and Gerry began to have many moody moments. She suspected that he was seeing "girls"—women nearer his age, classmates. (He had "a room of his own," yes, and a heart roomy enough to host other congenial ladies.)

The pop songs that orchestrated their relationship best were ones they both loved, namely, Roberta Flack's renditions of "Killing Me Softly with His Song" and "The First Time Ever I Saw Your Face": there was romance, yearning, strife, and sorrow, and that was the yin-yang of their affair.

Because R. J. had "side-ladies," Gerry began to see other men, a fact that R. J. loathed. In spring 1975, he was so incensed by Gerry's independence, he entered our home, bounded upstairs, then kicked down the door of her bedroom—to disrupt her would-be communion with another fellow, who was augustly dapper, with a Sherlock-Holmes (not Hugh-Hefner) pipe, but who was assuredly no fighter. He was a railway porter who served in uniform, but liked to dress lavishly when free of the train tracks' tedium.

R. J. was charged for breaking-and-entering into our home—or, specifically, my mother's bedroom. I attended the trial—but Bryant had to testify. Yet it was 1975—and a man's jealousy of another man trumped—for the trial judge—my mother's rights to security and privacy. However, I don't think she minded overmuch that R. J. was acquitted: they still kept company.

vi.

Maybe due to R. J.'s discreet-but-detectable philandering, Gerry soon returned to Maynard Street and Bill in the winter of 1973 for what was to be the final attempt at reconciliation. We boys thus witnessed the worst disturbances of their torturously slow—maddeningly drawn-out—breakup.

I think we'd only been back with Bill a week before a vicious, no-holds-barred argument—a house-shaking brouhaha—erupted, with objects hurled, eyes directing stabs, jaws tossing out curses like grenades. The screeching, hollering, screaming, and yelling sounded a worrisome din—like a war movie exploding—at cranked-up sound—from a living-room TV.

Amid the chaos, Gerry told me to call the cops. According to how I'd been raised by my parents, it was proper: we'd been taught to trust the police; ask them for help if ever in danger; and obey adults and authority figures (except for strangers, who could be child molesters, though that threat was never spelled out).

Maybe I also wanted to demonstrate my supposed maturity. Maybe I relished exercising relative authority in the instant. Whatever the ultimate reasoning (perhaps simply because I'd seen Gerry beaten too many times before), I dialed the police. I can't remember what I told them; it could only have been that Bill was pummeling walls, not my mother, and my brothers and I were scared and worried.

Well, Halifax's Finest did swagger onto our premises, a few minutes later, and magic happened: Bill and Gerry were all sweetness and light—smiling, laughing, assuring the two officers that everything was fine. There'd been a misunderstanding; only. If the constables tried to ferret information from my mother that could've allowed them to arrest my father, she did not yield it. She was as adamant as Bill, with whom she'd just been most violently quarrelling, that all was well. Satisfied that neither assault nor murder were in the offing, the symbols of martial authority over the marital commons retired to their squad car.

That afternoon soon knew a degree of peace. Denunciations were now mutters; damnations were now murmurs. I think that both of my parents withdrew to their respective corners and tried to repair or sweep up whatever physical objects had broken and pick up whatever intact objects could be retrieved from the floor.

Neither Bill nor Gerry said a word to me about my summoning of the police. But, I now know, I had committed a colossal stupidity. True: I had obeyed my mother—partly out of concern for her safety. But her request—and my acquiescence to it—had put us all in mortal danger: had my parents not stifled their dispute and donned faces of equanimity and attitudes of reason, my father—in particular—could have been assaulted, humiliated, beaten, arrested, or even shot. I can only imagine how he, the once-tyrant of his castle, must have felt seeing the uniformed deputies of *White Supremacy* standing in the master bedroom of the house that he'd striven to wrest—through sheer sweat and assigned humility before the white patrons of the railway—from the clutches of bankers and other unforgiving overlords.

Although my action would be applauded in many white households, conceivably by wives and moms facing assault (or worse) from husbands and/or lovers, the police—white-controlled and white-dominated—are *not* neutral entities in the eyes of Black (and Indigenous) communities. To us, the police are sufficient monsters, efficient terrors. This statement is no contention; is not—given history—contentious. For me to have invited such, well, probable poltergeists into our residence was almost as bad as opening our doors to the Ku Klux Klan or to arsonists, and then handing em dynamite, matches, and gasoline.

Yet, my error was that of an obedient boy who, up to that point, had not been asked (or taught) to understand the world as a miscellany of dangers for black people. Ironically, it was Bill Clarke himself who advocated pacifism toward white authority, so that his sons could survive the ever-present threat of fists and batons and guns and handcuffs and jail (if not bullets).

vii.

But that moment of potential peril was not as bad—for me—as what happened a week or so later—on another March Sunday. It was winter still, but with an upside of sunny, hypothetical warmth. Ice was thawing, if not melting. In our home, there was no thaw; instead, there was a smash up. Literally. At the top of the stairs of our two-storey house, my father hefted the cedar chest that he'd just given my mother as a Xmas gift, and threw it down the steps. He wasn't aiming it at me, but I happened to be at the bottom of the stairs looking up. I can still see that flimsy wooden furniture tumbling and crashing and disintegrating, all simultaneously, in my direction, and my mother's baubles and lingerie come flying out like dogfighting aircraft. As I witnessed this destruction—frozen in place, not by fear but by stupefaction—my father pointed a finger at me and said to my mother, "I only married you because of him."

In truth, the sentence was not a surprise, though still disturbing, and I ran away from home—pedalling my bike quickly away—for the afternoon. I shed traumatic tears, gouts and gluts of tears, broken-dream-bloodied tears. When I returned home with nightfall, I don't remember that anyone asked where I'd gone (down to Point Pleasant Park to hole up in an old World War II-era pillbox), and the house was cemetery-peaceful: it was the dread peace after the guns have fallen silent because everybody's dead. Still, everything had changed for me. I was born George Elliott Johnson. "Clarke" was an add-on. I was Bill Clarke's son, but I wasn't really a "Clarke." And even less was I a "White"—the premarital surname of Nettie.

The clues had always been there, but I'd never bothered to think them through. My birth certificate, with surname "Clarke," was issued in 1965, not 1960, not even 1961. My brothers had baby pictures from the instant of their births, but I did not. My parents' wedding and honeymoon pictures were dated June 1960, but I was too young—or deliberately repressive of the truth—to bother recognizing that these events occurred four months after I was born. But now I knew for sure that I was, really, a tacit "Clarke," a tangential "Clarke." When I was christened at Windsor Plains United African Baptist Church by licentiate-Baptist-would-be-minister Greg Cook (later a poet and head of the Writers' Federation of Nova Scotia), it was as a Johnson, an heir to the local Avon River, not Shakespeare's, but a sapphire tributary that became studded with ochre mudflats whenever the Bay of Fundy tide was out.

So, there I was, just turned thirteen, and aware now that I had been born a bastard—because my parents hadn't yet married. Did their eventual marriage frustrate the application of that hateful term to myself? Or was a born bastard always a bastard? It was a profound problem for me, for the most-common term of derision among Africadians was not "cocksucker," but "bastard"—and "black bastard." My ears were so innocent of curses and the real meaning of slang that, though I'd been called a "bastood" in schoolyard cussin, I'd never really thought much about it. (Memorable still is an incident in which, at about age eleven, I drew a firmly clasped newspaper between a surprised classmate's legs, and she rolled eyes at me, guffawed, and barked, "Georgie! You black bastood!") But now I was—or had so been born—a veritable "black bastard." What did that mean?

I began to feel an alienation. I'd been born "George Elliott *Johnson*": my first and middle names had been chosen by Gerry to match her own initials, i.e. Geraldine Elizabeth. But "George" (Greek for *farmer*) was also selected to honour my matrilineal great-grandfather, George Johnson, still living when I was born, and to ensure the carrying on of his name, a commission that had first fallen upon my mother's first cousin, George Albert Hamilton, but who had been convicted of murder and executed, aged twenty-three—along with his brother Rufus James, aged twenty-two—in Fredericton, NB, in 1949, when my mom was only ten. (I only found out about my killer cousins when my mom, ill with dementia, blurted out the truth to me in 1995.) "Elliott" (derived from Hebrew—Elijah—for *man of God*) was selected whimsically because, while pregnant, Gerry had developed a yen for the TV crime drama *The Untouchables*, starring Robert Stack as *Eliot* Ness.*

(By the way, "Clarke" descends from Old French for *clerk* or *cleric*. Combine my names and you reconnoitre a writer/scholar attracted to the religious "pasture," but also romanticizing the pastoral. Furthermore, in poetry, *verse* is derived from the Latin for "turn," which referred originally to the turnabout a farmer would make in ploughing to one end of a furrow, then working back in reverse direction on the next . . . Check: a poet "ploughs" lines across the page or screen . . .)

I still loved my father—and my mother. But I began to feel that my birth had wedded people who didn't suit each other. I was my father's son by blood, but was I by *brand*? Well, yes, but only *via* a legal name-change. But was I *really* a Clarke? Indeed, now I understood why I'd always felt closer to my mom and her parents and siblings than to my father and his single mom (maybe widow) and siblings. Did anyone in his—Bill's—family shun me as a country-boy "bastood"? Was my mom considered second-rate to the spouses that my father's siblings loved and wed? What I did sense was a coolness—a chill—between the "high-falutin" Clarke and White clans in contrast to the salt-o-the-earth Johnsons, even if, on paper, the Johnsons were more prosperous than most Clarkes, and never felt they should kowtow to the Whites.

By my later teens, I began to think of myself as a displaced African, as "black," and so the Johnsons—countrified and partly Indigenous—began to represent "authentic" blackness to me, while the Clarkes and Whites seemed white "wanna-bes," putting on airs and denying commonality and solidarity with other black people. I know that portrait of them is unfair, and it was exacerbated by my feeling close to the Johnsons and distant from my patrilineal relatives. Yet, I was also ignorant of the barriers that the Whites and the Clarkes had had to

---

* I'm often asked whether my middle name is connected to the politico Pierre Elliott Trudeau or the writer George Eliot (Mary Evans). I do now close the book—pun intended—on the question!

surmount, the pressures upon them to always be upright (morally) so as to "uplift the race," and how the stresses and strains of having to be superhuman achievers to "prove" black equality with relatively insignificant white folk had corrupted family feeling and corroded family bonds.

The irony of being black strivers—and achievers—is that we have to keep proving—to Caucasians who are demonstrably our inferiors (in talent, intelligence, aptitude, athleticism, morality, and occasionally even income)—that we merit equal treatment as citizens. That is one of the most galling consequences of the practice of *"White Supremacy,"* which is itself such a falsehood that it can only be sustained by systemic discrimination. Yet, black achievers and strivers do overcome—due to their innate superiority; yet, their success is too often individual, so they become symbols, role-models, exemplary "exceptions."

Sometimes, the individual attainment translates into a family legacy, so that offspring also overcome, and become exceptional, further glorifying their surname which might even now represent a dynasty. Seldom, however, does individual—or even familial—triumph translate into communal betterment. The lesson is clear. Barack Obama was elected president of the United States, and will radiate eternal glory as an exemplary individual (who was, incidentally, vastly superior to most of his presidential predecessors and definitely to his immediate successor); yet, the personal triumph could not—and did not—"advance the race" (to use an old-fashioned phrase). No, it's Rosa Parks and Martin Luther King, Angela Davis and Malcolm X, whose individual struggles raise up the whole of the people, whether they ever receive a Nobel Prize or a perch in a hall (or mausoleum) of statuary.

viii.

Whatever the disclosures of my own true roots, my own black beginnings, I was still just a minor, as a mid-teen, and still distressed by my parents' slo-mo breakup. My brothers and I were living with our mom and R. J. in West End Halifax, while stopping at our dad's after school, awaiting transport home. In the winter of 1974, my mother's finances had begun to sour. She stood tearfully in the doorway of our rented home while a sheriff and tow-truck driver hauled away—repossessed for non-payment—the 1972 olive-green Comet that had announced her proud independence—at last—from Bill.

Soon, we'd had to move from the spacious, prestigious, West End starter-mansion closer to downtown Halifax—to 2340 Hunter Street, a dwelling radically *déclassé* and *dégoutant* in contrast to the former address. We'd plummeted from plummy to slummy: Gerry had to dial the landlord incessantly to fix various utilities. At one point, the toilet emptied solid-waste-studded bilge into the bathtub; bedbugs crept and fleas leapt (both bloodsuckers quite happy with our offerings); the furnace emitted lukewarm heat (quilts and space-heaters were mandatory). We'd had a fireplace on Chebucto Road; but the Hunter Street abode was a fire-trap. The stove worked by kerosene, and it seemed always my chore to ensure that the oil canister was topped up and piping kerosene to the smelly burners. To light one, you had to set afire a length of twisted newspaper and drop it in the open hole, then step back in case the igniting kerosene sent flames growling, leaping, and clawing at your face.

(Another sign of decline? I'd had my own room at 2357 Maynard, a blessing for being the first-born. Out on Chebucto Road, all three of us sons bedded down in a large room, with never any sense of crowding— or being cramped. However, at Hunter St., my brother Billy—the youngest—was favoured with his own room, while I had to share a space with Bryant. It wasn't uncomfortable, but I had lost the sense of protected and cultivated dignity that privacy permits.)

On Chebucto Road, no neighbour was neighbourly; they were a) standoffish or b) racist. The saving grace of Hunter Street was that our neighbours—white—had kids the same ages as my brothers and me, and the same class background, and we chummed around a lot, playing games in evening twilight, hide-n-go-seek, *et cetera*, with brown boys latching—playfully—or semi-seriously—on blonde gals, while the streetlamps shone down transcendent incandescence.

I think there was a storefront church—with a minuscule congregation—on our street, which held evening services. (On the northwest corner of Hunter stood the Olympic Gardens Dance Hall, which was still "Olympic," but now given over to bingo and used-stuff bazaars.) One night that spring when we were all out running and pursuing and snagging windbreakers or releasing coat fringes as our much-sought-after blonde prey scampered or skipped or wriggled free, a middle-aged gent, exiting the presumably holy site, stopped me, under a streetlight, and intoned, "You have the light of God in your face." It was my smile that had radiated—beamed—that light; due to my radio-sermon-wrought, apocalyptic Christianity, inspired by the Armstrongs, *père et fils*, I thought that there could be something to the stranger's comment.

Lookit! At age ten or eleven, I'd aspired conscientiously to be a saint. I kinda liked the idea of being able to levitate, heal wounds (except for my own stigmata, which would be essential for establishing my sainthood), and call down (or up) hellfire and lotsa brimstone for bullies. I'd been reading all the Catholic-inspired saints' bios available to me in the North Branch Library. (I read the Holy Bible wholly— *thrice*—between the ages of thirteen and twenty-one.) I was very partial to Saint Therese of the Roses, Saint Francis of Assisi, Joan of Arc, Saint Patrick, and adopted my own diet of fish-sticks and water to try to pine away, waste away, and achieve an ethereal body and/or stunning stigmata. But my apprenticeship to sainthood ended when my father noticed that I was refusing to eat and chided me for taking the idea of fasting too far.

Soon, I embarrassed my mother and shocked the Cornwallis Street Baptist Church when, at age thirteen, as the comestibles and *digéstifs* made their rounds thanks to white-gloved deacons wafting about steel platters, I reached out and snatched a piece of cubed white-bread and a shot-glass of grape juice to take Easter communion, which I thought

I could take *because I believed*. As a hush fell over the congregation and a deacon intoned sombrely, "He can't have that," my mother saved the day by murmuring—sternly—"Oh, let him have it! It's not harming anything!" I hadn't realized that only the fully water-immersed—baptized saints—could join communion in our Baptist church. I was chagrined, but Gerry had had my back, and the deacons backed down, and I consumed my grape juice and white bread, though the act had become sacrilegious humiliation rather than a gesture of obeisant humility: I'd ended up a minor Martin Luther rather than a junior Martin Luther King.

ix.

No matter the springtime jive and japes, our matriarchal relocation to down-at-the-heel Hunter Street from well-heeled Chebucto Road, my parents' dissolution frothed and fizzed. Almost as soon as we settled into our decrepit edifice, a stranger rapped, dropped the D-I-V-O-R-C-E decree papers through our mail slot and slunk off. I went to the door, opened it and saw a camel-hair-coated back humping away, heard boots thumping down the front-door steps, as the stumping dude scrammed back to his lair (whatever and wherever it was).

R. J. and Gerry were still a couple; I mean, the twenty-ish student was still with us, but he was also seeing playmates who were classmates, at his own apartment, even if Gerry was an actual helpmate. For example, when R. J. sought a job as a waiter at the tony Halifax Club, and was convinced that racism had nixed his hiring, Gerry came to his physical aid, employing her Caucasian looks to apply for the same job, and succeeded. At that point, presented with *prima facie* proof of prejudice, the Halifax Club decided to offer R. J. compensation to dissuade him from taking his case to the Nova Scotia Human Rights Commission. So, R. J. took the cash, and took a job as a stevedore on the Halifax waterfront. In this lattercase, my mom seems to have come to his metaphysical aid. She reported that, on a night when hoisted cargo came loose, or broke from moorings, and the materials dashed earthward, missing R. J. narrowly—at that precise instant, his slight spectre appeared in my mother's bedroom, grinning, and then vanished. Despite such episodes, however, their relationship remained turbulent.

Moreover, my mom was finding it ever more difficult to balance the needs of three teen sons,* meet expenses of transportation and accommodation, and have leisure funds for herself (and R. J.). She had made a strategic error (as she soon recognized), when she had allegedly "abandoned" the marital domicile to Bill, and thus had forfeited all her sweat (and tearful) equity in our family home. The mid-1970s was still too-soon for equitable division of marital assets, and so Bill benefitted by keeping (and eventually selling) 2357 Maynard Street, while Gerry was forced into having to pay rent to landlords—though she was the one with the children (including, shortly, R. J.'s younger, teen brother who arrived from Jamaica and came under Gerry's care). Too, she was dislodged from the directorships of the daycares that she'd founded, was reduced to being just a staffer, directed by a woman she had directed, and thus suffering a psychological plunge in self-esteem as well as a precipitous slide in income.

Gerry then accepted to be a part-time secretary with the Canadian Navy at CFB Stadacona. However, her new job did not compensate for the income lost when she lost her daycare directorships. So, suddenly she was—we were all—at the mercy of Bill Clarke's alimony and child-support payments as a priceless subsidy of household income. That was

---

* Some help was afforded her and us by the Black Education Fund, a provincial-government grant directed to parents of registered black school children, paid once a year (if I recall properly) at about $40 per child, to help keep us in clothes, shoes, pens, and pencils, so we'd stay in school. Disparaged as "the nigger fund," it constituted hard-won, state reparations for 150 years of segregated schooling in Nova Scotia. By the early 1980s, the program shifted to support first-year and sophomore "Indigenous Black" university students. It still exists in this form.

a parlous situation, for Bill—normally self-righteously punctilious and proper—expressed his displeasure regarding Gerry's relationship with R. J. by being stingy and irregular with his payments, thus vitiating the judicial stipulations. My mother's dwindling resources soon went to spurring on the bickering of lawyers whose victories were pyrrhic and ephemeral. Yet, due to her disintegrating hips (because of her lifelong limp), Gerry's health was deteriorating, and she had to be hospitalized—in 1976—for hip replacement surgery. That necessitated the move—by my brothers and I—back to live with Bill.

However, by summer 1976, Bill headed a new family. Once my parents separated for good, in spring 1973, 2357 Maynard Street became a Dinky-type, Playboy mansion. My father's second wife, Pammy, complained that she'd had to "fight my way through a host of floozies" to become mistress of the domain. There was irrefutable evidence for her testimony: in early 1974, Bill impregnated our once-maid, Brigitte, who gave birth to my half-sister in September 1974. Following his patented bull-head and iron-heart, Bill had then gone to court and seized his daughter from the custody of her "unfit mother"—Brigitte—and then had wed Pammy (who had been, like Brigitte, a bar-maid, but whose homeland was New Brunswick, not Québec). True to my quixotic effort to keep my family "unified," I attended the wedding (presided over by my track coach, Rev. Rod MacAulay), which took place at 2357 Maynard, in the living room, in early 1975. Pammy and Bill then raised his daughter as if she were also Pammy's.

Thus, between 1974 and 1979, when I left Halifax to attend university, my mother, brothers, and I celebrated Christmas in a different house annually. Xmas 1974 was distinctly surreal because Bill and Pammy came to visit us at 2340 Hunter Street, and Gerry and R. J. entertained the about-to-be-married couple. It was weird to see both my parents smoking (both had inveighed against the "sin" throughout my childhood) and making nicey-nice with each other's diametrically opposite partners. There was R. J. jesting respectfully with Bill; Pammy being cordial to Gerry; Bill being polite to Gerry; R. J. being pleasant to

Pammy. My brothers and I milled about, smiling, trying to salvage Xmas okayness—if not jollity—out of the derangement of what had once been a disciplined and formal (extremely strict) household. The trauma of that moment, for me, lay in trying to decipher what was genuine and what was fake (or forced), and what it all meant.

x.

Divorce, for Gerry, marked the beginning of a fiscal crisis that she could seldom mitigate. Lawyers only intermittently succeeded in wresting funds from Bill; insurance companies spurned costs pertaining to her immobilizing hip surgeries. Lenders took her to court for missing loan payments; she was branded publicly as a bankrupt. These stresses were exacerbated by boyfriends who were playboys and lovers who were ingrates.

Following her split with R. J. (pursuant to his spring 1975 one-man-commando-raid on her bedroom), Gerry accepted one other black university student as a lover, namely, L'Abbé—who was African, from Ghana or Nigeria, and whose record collection—kept in a red-plastic milk-carton crate—was polyrhythmic romps. R. J. had been into James Brown and Miles Davis, but L'Abbé preferred Parliament-Funkadelic (who kinda fused Brown and Davis). Gerry also dated—off-and-on— one Africadian writer (G.), plus a West Indian railway porter (who poured his dollars stereotypically into a white Caddy pimpmobile, cool-dude duds, and, unstereotypically, into a Sherlock Holmes-style pipe), and an Africadian small-businessman, who was married—but—to his mind and loins quite unsatisfactorily.

Still, Gerry's last lovers—in the late 1970s and through the 1980s—were basically common-law husbands. "Hank" was utterly a no-nonsense, black, working stiff, a soldier *cum* truck driver for the Canadian Army. His voice was gruff; his hands were huge; yet he was a gentle giant, as far as I could tell, and he seemed to love Gerry, his "fancy lady," and she enjoyed being doted upon; to be both loved and fawned over. So, goodbye James Brown and hello George

Jones—Country-n-Western—along with truck loads of bacon, fried hotdogs, molasses, beans, ketchup, fried mackerel, beer, red wine, rum-n-coke, cigarettes, and sherry. Hank was a big guy with a big laugh; he seemed perpetually good-spirited. When tipsy, he maintained a dramatically uneven gait—like a boxer bobbing in a singsong way. My mom and he shared his trailer in the historic Africadian community of Cherry Brook, about ten miles from Halifax.

Gerry adored Hank's earthy, good-humoured simplicity and he loved her glamour. Imagine Charley Pride and Elizabeth Taylor as a couple: that was them. The one huge problem was—his hankering for spirits. Gerry's love was no cure, and he drank himself into a coma over one unholy, October weekend in 1978 when he would not tell her where he was. While still conscious, he was vomiting and evacuating blood. (At Hank's funeral, the presiding minister, Rev. Skeir, suggested that, dying of a massive heart attack as he sat up in his hospital bed, Hank had taken that posture because he could see Christ coming for him, beckoning to him, through his hospital-room ceiling.) Because they were together a couple of years, Gerry added Hank's surname to hers, though she did so inconsistently.

Her last love, after Hank, is not a gent I view objectively. Her last fellow used her financially, used her to fund his business, and used her to raise his kids. (He was a widower, and brought Gerry into his household just over a year after his wife's death in a car accident.) I deem her last chum—Bison—purely despicable, regardless of his smoking pipes, his Conway Twitty-addiction, his rum-n-coke, his "Keats" India Pale Ale.

Gee wiz! Gerry had used her property in Three Mile Plains to secure a loan to purchase Bison a truck. She lived with him for a decade and raised his young and motherless children. However, the loan was never paid off, and a lien got placed against the property; worse, once Bison realized that Gerry had begun to suffer from early-onset senility, he trucked her (in the vehicle that she'd arranged the purchase of) to an apartment, dumped her there with her extricated furnishings (more fluff than functional), and vamoosed. Her sister—my Aunt Joan—recovered her; took her to her home; and nursed her for a decade until she passed away in August 2000, aged only 61.

Even though I knew she was mortally ill, her death still shattered my heart like a thunderbolt. Fitting it was that she passed away on the fifty-fifth anniversary of Hiroshima's atomic incineration. I elected her plot, selected her white, pink-tinged casket, and then erected a tall headstone, whose legend reads, "Her beauty was a perfume / Making oxygen itself redundant."

But no epitaph can sound my mother's raucous, rowdy, irreverent, cantankerous, "country," earthy, African, black—even *black comic*—laughter, so untameable as liquor got into the blood, a mirth so powerful it could shatter glass and buckle steel. I can still see her sitting before the TV soap operas that she loved: *Coronation Street* and *Another World* and *Santa Barbara*, her right foot bobbing as she consumed Red Rose tea and Carnation milk, plus raisin-bread toast with slabs of butter. Born in the same year as debuted *The Wizard of Oz* and *Citizen Kane* and *Gone with the Wind*, she idolized only Judy Garland—another blanching, brunette knockout, though she was equally proud of her "Shirley Temple" curls. Proud was she always of her selection to serve as a "princess," elected by the Halifax Coloured Citizens' Improvement League—in the later 1950s, to sit atop the hood of an open convertible, each gloved hand deigning to dispense a royal wave. Proud was she of her mixed-race pulchritude—to be a—*the*—Beauty of Three Mile Plains, to make white men pant and black men pray, even if she had the challenge of a limp—a "handicap" that could not cap or hinder her indomitable *Elegance*. Know what? She skittered high heels—pumps—across the smoothest floors, pampered herself, lavished perfume on the undeserving air. Bespoke poetry through carmine, plush lips; offered speech as uplifting and brilliant as the sparkling lacquered effects of Champagne! (Years after her vanishing, an Indo-Canadian family, the Joshis, contacted me, seeking her. Why? Decades before, she had dearly befriended the immigrant couple.) Glad was she to give social Darwinists nightmares because she couldn't be slotted into one of their restrictive, racist categories. Nor let anyone try to "keep her down"! Her smile was telegenic, but her anger conjured fiery glares and scorched-earth language. (Once, Ladies Auxiliary harpies dared stop on her Dartmouth doorstep to tell her that she was smiling upon the wrong men—their husbands—and she shook her jumpy locks and guffawed at em, called em scruffy, hideous, jealous, unimaginative, and hellish, a pack of sweaty, stinking hypocrites, their scriptures just so much break-wind *bavardage*.*) Upon her friends—and children, she expended enormous cheer; was vehemently cordial. (She made a pillow for me—at my request—when I was 4 or 5 years, and I still have it, use it—striving to keep it clean—and I do ask that when the day comes, when I'm laid out—white robed—in my "long home," do rest my head upon it: I will not slumber luxuriously without that cushion!) She was a *tour de force* of Verve, a supreme Empress of Suave. Why wasn't she always blizzarded, buffeted, by kisses? She merited that homage! No matter for who Ellington claimed he wrote "Sophisticated Lady," it had to've been for her. That title was hers. Unmistakeably. And modelled on Maria Montessori, colleged by Barbara Clark, Geraldine Elizabeth Clarke founded *three* daycares.[†]

(Early on in her decline, but still possessing wit, Gerry had a last encounter with Bill, for he arrived, as a taxi driver, to ferry she and her gal-pals to some Halifax address. She told me that when she saw her ex-husband, she put her face in her hands and shook her head, all her great curls tossing, and laughed and laughed. He, for his part, was, apparently, the acme of politesse.)

---

* Sometimes, ashy people gotta be pissed on—royally.

† The Centre for Exceptional Children, which she founded in 1970, operates now as the Alexandra Children's Centre, located in North End Halifax.

William Andrew White, Jr.—not yet "Rev. Capt. Dr."—at Wayland Seminary, Washington (DC), 1897. Vividly dead-centre in the photo, his glance directed left (our right), he exudes already way too much charisma—plus gravitas—for any mere camera lens to capture.

Nettie Jean Clarke on her appointment as Commissioner (of Oaths) for the Supreme Court of Nova Scotia in 1975.

Portia May White in the Karsh Pantheon. Likely shot in Ottawa (ON), 1946.

Glamorous, Elegant, Justified: Geraldine Elizabeth Johnson, later 1950s, likely at Windsor (NS) Academy *or* at Nova Scotia Teachers' College, Truro (NS).

Robert Havelock Johnson & Jean Leota (*née* Croxen) Johnson. At the homestead, Newport Station (NS), circa 1968.

For Better and/or for Worse: Geraldine Elizabeth Johnson and William Lloyd Clarke, wedding, June 1960.

A Nat King Cole kinda "Soul Man": Bill Clarke & BMW "machine" and buddy, sometime in the mid-1950s, somewhere in the Maritimes.

Commencing The Long March! Georgie, aged 1, at
Newport Station (NS), 1961.

The Clarke tyke-triumvirate and mom, Geraldine, on
their world tour at Expo 67, Montréal (QC), 1967.

On the [Haligonian] Waterfront: Bryant, foster sisters
Leelee and Darlene, George, 1969.

All aboard to Winnipeg! Billy, George, cuz Scoop Johnson,
Bryant, Halifax (NS) train station, 1969.

Bill Clarke with Labour College profs at Université de Montréal (QC), summer 1969. His highest grades were in Trade Unionism and Political Science.

Gerry Clarke attending Early Childhood Education classes at the University of Ottawa, summer 1969.

CROSSBARS WERE NEVER the softest of seats but two wheels almost always have been quicker than two feet as young Eric Mendes finds after hitching a ride from neighbor George Clark. Both boys live on Fuller Terrace, Halifax. (Wamboldt-Waterfield)

Wamboldt-Waterfield of *The Halifax Herald* Ltd was "motivatin" (Chuck Berry) round North End Halifax (NS), when he stopped his car, and asked to snap this snap of George and cuz Eric Mendes, "innovatin" bout "the hood," spring 1974.

Grade 9 "Africa Cool": Genesis of a poet. Bloomfield Junior High School, Halifax (NS), spring 1975.

First, Queen Elizabeth High School, and then Queen's University! Mom Gerry and Georgie, Halifax (NS), June 1978. Photog'd together again when GEC graduated from Queen's University—Kingston (ON)—in 1993, Ph.D. in hand.

Direct pointing to reality? GEC at Halifax Harbour (NS), May 1980.

Taking Mount Royal by Strategy! GEC *et* Dionne Brand à Montréal (QC), attending the first National Black Arts Conference— just days after the first Québec Sovereignty Referendum, May 1980.

Capriciously fashionable as Lenin-on-Capri (1908 & 1910): GEC kickin back with Lenin's *What Is to be Done?* Backyard of 24 Mountain Avenue, Dartmouth (NS), June 1980.

The Long March *via* Newport Station (NS): GEC with Mao bio (and peasant-class hosses awaitin liberatin).

from pupil and proletarian to

activist and intellectual

i.

While my parents were heatedly separating—glacially divorcing—and
I was tongue-tied about my secret feelings for Sibyl, for Alma, for Mona,
there was one grade nine event, in fall 1974, that began to see me retire
my shy nerd, Einstein wanna-be, or would-be "saint" (though likely on
the salty, earthy side) identities. What lifted me out of my doldrums was
my participation—over six weeks—in the junior-high and high-school
student drama company Mind the Flowerpots, under the direction of
David Renton, a dapper and intense Brit, a silver-haired fox, natty in
bow ties and spiffy in sports jackets, but a compact-sized, singular guerilla of theatre. He sought to turn the plaid-staid Nova Scotian art scene
upside-down by organizing teens into a cadre of committed actors.
Somewhat a dandy, but no fop, he was Trotsky according to Ionesco, or
Beckett allied with Brecht. (Indeed, we performed a scene from *Waiting
for Godot*.)

We were a radical cell of *agents* provocateurs, not just a theatre
troupe. It was our mission to subvert morals and suborn the saintly. I
think we were roughly twenty-five kids (and adults—our group included
eighteen-year-olds), but I was the sole black and the sole North Ender.

Officially, I was an "Assistant Stage Manager," but I also got to dance, and that meant learning to Charleston and—gasp—to waltz, which also entailed holdin my lady dance partners real tight. One gal even kissed me—blush—and I suddenly felt cool and sophisticated. Our company visited every Halifax-area school, striking the set, staging the shows, making our own props, drinking too much cold black coffee (yucky fake-cream blobs bobbing in the midst), the older kids puffing joints, some of em makin out unreservedly, but all of us *in service to art*—to theatre.

David saw us as upstart, tyro theatre-folk. So, we were virtual adults, and exceptional, because we were making art—and entertainment, and saying, in essence, we'd live and die for applause alone, that we needed nothing else. At the end of those six weeks, we put on our show—for parents, siblings, and friends—on Neptune Theatre's stage— the same stage my father had strutted eight years before, playing the role of a cop in *The Physicist*.

Bill didn't attend our final performance, though my mother did. What was most vital for me—being fourteen and finally kissable—was that the troupe members all liked me—and I them; although some were to-the-manor-born, I never felt "less than" or "not-as-good-as" anyone. Excitingly, when our "happy few" played the integrated—black/brown/ white—working-class schools of the North End, *I was the star* (despite my bit parts); and when my peers at Bloomfield chanted "Georgie" as I did the Charleston, I did register extra bravura in my step and extra brio in my swivelling hips.

That experience, of living in (and with) a theatre company for six weeks, got me out of my North End comfort zones and intro'd me to other brainy, artsy teens, who didn't think it was weird to read a lot, to exercise the body sensually—*via* yoga—in trusting concert with others, to do music or dance, or construct theatre sets and memorize lines. I can't recall now our various ethnicities because, well, it just didn't matter. Some of us were Scottish, some Jewish; I was Africadian—and "cool" and "different"—and not a bad fellow to kiss! *At last!*

ii.

I went on to complete grade nine at Bloomfield, partly by writing a five-hundred-page science project report on "How to Build an Atomic Weapon," in which I fantasized the destruction of Halifax by a device secreted in a dumpster. I received full marks for that project—consisting of many scribblers rife with photocopies of missiles and bombs and blasts and schematic diagrams of my own device and the dumpster container, and boasting my first neologism, "hurriquake" (a combo of *hurricane* and *earthquake*) to define the double-whammy effect of atomic detonations: to both destroy *via* a pressure-wave of wind and to tremble the earth.

I wouldn't have realized it then, but my "explosive" project was likely a projection of my angst over my parents' divorce. Even worse was the truth that my father could spurn his first family while creating a new one; or that my mother would accept a lover—R. J.—who was suave and hip, but lacked exceedingly the panache and gravitas of Bill. Raised on reports of the Halifax Explosion and well-read in the atomic bombing of Hiroshima, I suspect that my epic science project was an attempt to allegorize the detonation (or devastation) of my birth family and home.

There was a tradition of mounting a grade nine graduating-class trip. So, in 1975, thanks to fundraisers and various grants, the school was able to fly roughly twenty of us—including adult chaperones—to Ottawa, the nation's capital, for a week in May. We stayed in student residence at the University of Ottawa, and toured the science museum, the Centre Block parliament building with its Peace Tower, plus Rideau Hall. At the latter, my classmates and I did meet His Excellency Jules Léger, the Governor-General—the reigning, vice-regal appointee— while investigating the rooms and the grounds. That same day, if I recall, we missed having an audience with Prime Minister Pierre Trudeau because he was called away from 24 Sussex Drive on business. However, we stopped outside the residence's driveway gate as it opened and his limo appeared, and he scrupled to power down the back, passenger- side window, lean his head out, and wish us a pleasant visit and apologize for not being able to meet with us. I was so shy to be in his bobble-head presence that I half-sidled behind a taller boy. But I'll always respect him for that welcome to us, a bunch of schoolkids—not yet able to vote.

We dropped by the US Embassy in the wake of the Mayaguez Incident, and I stopped at the Department of National Defence, excited to pick up the annual report of the Canadian Forces (featuring the 1974 peacekeeping dispatch to Cyprus). However, the moustached officer who descended an escalator to deliver the report seemed to lose all keenness in the charitable mission when he saw that the recipient was "Coloured." (I can't prove that my tint injured his comportment; maybe he'd just had a bad snack. Still, once he saw that dorky I would take hold of this report, he seemed to lose his vigour, as if my very face were a kick in the groin.)

A different, yet also likely racialized moment, awaited me in the parliamentary restaurant, where a member of the Senate of Canada had invited our class to dine as his guests. As I was trying to select both cold salmon and hot roast beef for my plate (double-dipping that a parliamentary waitress nixed—I ended up with the bony fish), I looked up and spied the former prime minister (1957-1963), the white-haired Rt. Hon. John George Diefenbaker, staring fixedly at me, two blue eyes to two brown eyes. The instant seemed discomfitingly elongated; so, shortly, I dropped my eyes, sat my butt down, and attended to my salmon.

In the decades since, I've tried to understand its meaning: surely I was not the first African-Canadian that Dief the Chief had ever encountered. (There were plenty of African-American homesteaders—and voters—in his central Saskatchewan constituency, plus black porters on the overnight trains between Prince Albert and Montréal, plus black showgirls he'd sip ginger ale with while stopped over in Hochelaga.) No, I now think that my distinct Windsor Plains physiognomy reminded Dief (who likely knew that we were a class of Nova Scotians come to Ottawa) of the brothers Rufus and George Hamilton,

Afro-Métis like me, who had been among the last murderers hanged in New Brunswick, in 1949, and who were my second cousins (but about whom I knew nothing until twenty years later.[*]) I was not to be so scrutinized by a prime minister until I was introduced to the House of Commons as Canada's seventh Parliamentary Poet Laureate—in 2016—and Bill Clarke's first-born son exchanged nods with Pierre Trudeau's first-born son.

That same spring of 1975, I was designated the recipient of Bloomfield Junior High's Murray Studley Award, presented to the student best exhibiting qualities of Manliness and Good Sportsmanship. The award was a boon, but I was most honoured to ferry it homeward because it had also been received by Bill Clarke (in 1950, when he'd turned fifteen). He dropped by the Hunter St. digs, and I pointed out the plaque to him, with both our names emblazoned thereupon, and he regarded it admiringly. I guess he felt some pride in the fact that I had garnered it (in the next generation), or that I'd walked in his footsteps and those of his brother, my uncle Gerald, yet another recipient of the Studley Award. Keeping it all in the family, as it were.

iii.

The summer of 1976 was notable, not only because I was back with Bill, with Pammy serving as stepmom, a role I rejected no matter how many cheeseburgers and ketchup-bludgeoned fries she slid before my

---

* While we were having toast and tea in my Aunt Joan's kitchen, in May 1995, Gerry blurted this declaration: "You know you had two cousins who were hanged!" Her dementia hindered her saying more, but I instantly undertook research that resulted in authoring *Execution Poems* (2000) and a novel, *George & Rue* (2005). True to form, when Bill saw I'd writ works about criminals, he left me his 1959 *Diary*, to urge my penning work about him, and I did: *The Motorcyclist* (2015). I returned to the Clarke/White lineage in issuing a book-length poem in the voice of Great-Aunt Portia: *Portia White: A Portrait in Words* (2019). That I'm related both to victors and villains is a typical bequest of the Transatlantic Slave Trade. (Thanks a bunch, *Europa!*)

brothers and me, but because—perhaps at my mom's and/or my Aunt Joan's urgings, my Uncle Rex—Tyrone—originally of Jamaica—took me on as his help, for $1/hour ($40/week). We rolled bout in his brand-new, 1976 Summer (Montréal) Olympics Special Edition, white-exterior Chevy pick-up truck, with a red interior, red hood, and an upper-body red racing-border wrapping the rectangular vehicle. Either I'd walk a few blocks from 2357 Maynard Street up to 2629 Fuller Terrace, or my uncle would motor by and pick me up. In any event, I was out with him weekdays, nine-to-five, with an hour's break for lunch; and we also did some Saturday jobs. He was a general contractor: toting garbage to the dump, stripping, then buffing and shellacking wood floors, or painting this and rewiring that. He'd climb a ladder into an attic or descend steps into a basement, his flashlight bobbing or lancing.

One of his contracts was with Gulliver, a pudgy slum landlord. We'd clean apartments whose occupants had fled, unable to pay rent, or who had been evicted. These premises were nauseating in stench and surreal in filth. In one apartment, conditions were so bad, I found maggots writhing away *inside* a lightbulb, not content to merely twist away merrily among a garbage-strewn floor, about which numerous flies buzzed, at times buzz-bombing their beloved (if bastard) offspring. In another apartment, my strapping six-foot-something uncle, all wiry, iron-coloured muscle, could not stoop to remove a dead rat, stinking, wedged beneath a bathtub. It became my task, and there wasn't much to it, except for having to drop to my belly, stare into the black beady eyes of the rotting, grey rodent, its head stuck in a death-trap, and then—without retching—haul the thing out in my gloved right hand and stick the stiff in a waiting garbage bag. Its gag-reflex-worthy ugliness is forever mausoleum'd in my memory, a remembrance that my uncle dodged.

Gulliver resided in the suburban West End of Halifax, in Rockingham (not too far removed from my boyhood home on St. Margaret's Bay Road), presided over a castle-like mansion (thanks to the slum rents), and, as befits such a pile, owned a swimming pool and maintained three distinct lawns that it was my job to mow (using a trio of mowers).

So expansive was the estate (with not a dead rat in sight), the job was an all-day contract. Uncle Rex would leave me on a Friday morning, ensure there was gas for the gas mower, and return to extract me bout 5 p.m. Over the next eight hours (with 30 mins off for lunch and two 15-min breaks elsewhere), I'd go round and round and round "in the circle game" (Joni Mitchell), scything the flying grass in "a widening gyre" (W. B. Yeats), scissoring near-hay to stubble, up hill and down dale, and around and around ("where he'll stop, nobody knows").*

At lunch, Gulliver was kind enough to call me into a sun room off his pool, and there I would wolf an assembly of cold cuts—salami, pepperoni, pastrami, Montréal smoked meat, and cheese, and then a bottle of Coca-Cola to swill and swish the protein bits down my throat. At day's end, that night, my dreams would feature pure patterns of concentric circle-grounded chlorophyll, the mowers going round and round and round the endless estate. Most excruciating for my sixteen-year-old self was Gulliver's equestrian-lean, sixteen-year-old daughter, who helmed her own sports car, and often did so with the top down, gold hair flying, and bikini—top-and-bottom—jittering. Perhaps she said hi once. Maybe. But I was the hired help, and I realized that her class far outclassed my ken. Besides, I couldn't even drive, let alone lay claim to a car, let alone a sports car.

My uncle was an old-school Jamaican, who liked Johnny Nash, Bob Marley (whom I also discovered in '76), and so he was "Sexy Rexy," and passing a girl on her bicycle prompted randy speculation about her *derrière*, its dimensions and its depths. Dear Reader, I condemn such frank sexism, unreservedly. And yet I also stole glances at those eye-level tushes, not tendered for ogling, but inevitable to sight, unless one prayed and averted one's eyes, which I did, more than once, but not, I have to confess, *all* the time.

---

* Ironically, the source of my mind-numbing, "go-round-in-circles" (Billy Preston) tortuous (if not torturous) labour was black! The inventor of the lawnmower—in 1898—was an African-American, namely, John A. Burr.

Out of my $40 per week, I'd buy blue jeans, embroidered denim shirts, and records. I was edging away from Elton John but hadn't yet reached Bob Dylan. So, the records were 45s—but not of contemporary songs. I focused on *what had been*—the 1960s. My sudden purchasing power let me buy items (including sci-fi paperbacks) that built self-awareness, that helped me establish an identity that was mine. Moreover, my physical tasks as a handyman's helper (while bankroller Gulliver fattened in the background) made me feel more adult, and my entrée into strangers' homes and apartments let me glimpse other people's lives (as I had done as a paperboy), i.e., their attractive or repellent ways of thinking, being, and doing.

I also benefitted from my exposure to my uncle's eccentric parley, which included his own neologism—*derassifyin(g)*, which means *excellent* or *delightful* or *satisfying*, and got applied to meals. On one long drive bout Halifax, he told me of his own divided boyhood home, a fate occasioned by his father falling in love with another woman; at which point, Rex elected to follow his own counsel. I couldn't know then that two years later, I'd seek my uncle's help to move me from my father's house, and that he'd use that same pickup truck to do so.

iv.

That same summer of '76, on Saturday nights, when Bill and Pammy were out clubbing, to down ale, fries, clams, or "wings" (either chicken or steak, but always with Houses of Parliament sauce as the piquant condiment), Bryant, Billy and I would catch a Hollywood horror flick, broadcast at midnight. In these B-movies, filmmakers would cast dusk, dawn, or forest shadows as "night," while the monsters or freaks were always conglomerations of leather and/or feathers and/or paint. The dialogue would alternate between smooching and screeching; the action was guys' failing fists and gals' flailing legs. The low-budget attempts at horror always depended upon hooey and hokum, thus eliciting snickers and guffaws.

Before the laughable trash appeared, we'd tune into the local cable—outta Bangor, Maine—farcical preface, namely *Dick Stacey's Country Jamboree*, whose emcee—Mr. Stacey—would sidle on, straight from his gas pumps, all puffy-faced, to interrogate viewers, "Do these hands smell gassy?" An exasperating query, that. But such was the kick-off for a raucous amateur hour of C-n-W quackery and God-forsaken gospel. Faces: inbred, lopsided, haggard. Dungarees, overalls, leather, denim, gingham, checks and plaid, boots, loafers, and pumps. Lotsa backwoods, boogaloo yodellers, yokels manglin mandolins, geezers bawlin over banjos, and rednecks chompin harmonicas, polka-dotted dames swishin and prancin, but the whole, unholy squad buzz-sawin through "songs" til there be nothin left of em but the vapor trails of cigarettes and the silent punctuation of flies droppin dead. Yelps, screeches, caterwauling!

Unwilling to tolerate these assaults on our senses, nor these insults to intelligence, my brothers and I would mute the TV and plunk a Parliament-Funkadelic record on Bill's Clairtone stereo. Now the Maine clodhoppers would mimic high-steppin funksters, and the back-o-God pickers and strummers would be smokily demanding, "We want the funk! Give up the funk!" The surreal synchronicity of the dowdy fiddlers and hoe-downin guitarists performing George Clinton and James Brown rhythms had my brothers and I hooting and hollering and tee-heeing at the mash-up that constituted absolutely no meeting of equals.

One other point of congruency for my brothers and buddies was the tradition of the all-night horror-movie extravaganzas that our Gottingen Street theatres would program several times a year. On such nights, for $5, you got to watch a succession of B-movies, 9 p.m. to 5 a.m. Thus, a row of Coloured guys would end up sitting behind a row of Coloured gals, and teasing, joking, and laughing would ensue. (To this day, black theatre and cinema audiences, everywhere, will talk back to actors and comment loudly on events on stage or on screen, crediting that communal dialogue enhances the drama.) The films were often British or Italian (dubbed), and so along with the ketchup blood, there'd be—gosh—brazen nudity and raunchy bedroom romps, all emblazoning tales of mad scientists and sadists, Dracula spin-offs and Frankenstein cast-offs. Too soon would 5 a.m. arrive, and we'd have to turn our once-hypnotized peepers to the grey dawn flushing away faded night, and our little mob of *faux* and *fausse* dates would splinter as we filtered our way through the North End streets to our separate abodes.

v.

By fifteen, I'd begun calling myself "Africa Cool," and, at seventeen, "George Johnson." It seemed right; it was the name I was born under and the clan I felt closest to: never the Whites and not-too-much the Clarkes.

Between eighteen and twenty, I dubbed myself "Nahum Shaka" and "Natt Moziah Shaka." (I published my debut poems under these names.) Even though the latter surnames arose out of black nationalist cultural beliefs, the outer initials—"N" and "S"—were sleight-of-hand for "Nova Scotia(n)." (For the record, "Nattt" referred to Nat Turner, the slave insurrectionist; Moziah was a shout out to Marcus Moziah Garvey, the Pan-Africanist leader; and Shaka referred to the warrior Zulu leader!*)

These rebrandings, as it were, had much to do with my coming under the tutelage of Africadian actor, playwright and poet Walter Borden (who was an "Afrocentrist" long before hip-hop began to venerate pharaohs and pyramids), and then his backers and friends, namely, Rocky and Joan Jones.

I met Walt in 1976 while playing a comic role in a yuletide production of *Puss in Boots*, directed by David Renton. Walt was the star (the iconic feline). I was spellbound by his actor's velvety voice and precise

---

* My latest—and last—pseudonym is "X. States," which is both a salute to Malcolm X and a shorthand for "ex-," so that my name should be read as meaning "out of the States"—i.e. the US. But "States" is also a signal, Africadian surname of unknown origins.

and capacious vocabulary. Not to mention his inventory of memorized poetry—his own—a mix of strident militancy, Africadian down-home registers, and a patented Beat union of skid-row Vancouver East and of Beatnik Greenwich Village. He'd spent time in both, learning to be an actor, and to live more freely as a gay man, after abandoning the repressive state that was Nova Scotia when he started out as a teacher in the early 1960s.

Crucially, Walt was "black like me," and like me, a light-complected Africadian, but also very pro-Black, and that "tude" was righteous. Eighteen-years-my-senior, Walt knew lots about art and protest and politics and intellectual journalism. He was also the first Africadian I'd ever seen identified in the pages of the Halifax press as that spectacularly peculiar being, a *poet*. In fact, he'd won an Honourable Mention in the 1976 provincial writing competition, and so, there he was, with an outsized James Brown-fro, bow tie, smoker's jacket, lookin like an Academy Award, red-carpet bard. He was an (unpublished) black poet, *but a poet*, an actor, an editor!

Following that on-stage time together, Walt became my mentor—1978-79—cramming my ears and head with Egyptology and sliding his Queer, Afrocentric poetry and Steve-Biko-like Black Consciousness editorials before my avid eyes. And I admired his once-New Yorker life; his having quit a gig as a Nova Scotian teacher to become a live-by-your-wits actor in Manhattan theatre. (Walt was doing, in fact, what Bill Clarke had nixed: to be an artist—that precarious personage—as opposed to choosing the safer, conventional path of being a family man.)

The editor of the BUF—the Black United Front of Nova Scotia (a now-defunct, government-funded Africadian advocacy agency)—newspaper, *Grasp*, Walt echoed scholars who swore that ancient Greece was an outpost of Egyptian and Ethiopian thought (as it likely was) and that whatever Plato/Socrates and Homer had to say was echoing the psychology and philosophy voiced in works like Aesop's (i.e. "the Ethiope's") fables. (Yep, although Eurocentrics hate the truth, the first civilizations were Negro, and the proof is everywhere. Not only did Black Africans tame horses and invent embalming, paper, ink, clocks, calendars, forged iron, sailboats, and other technologies, they also were the first theologians—and, thus, philosophers, so that all the later monotheisms are indebted to Negro thought.) An adept of "Dr. Ben" Jochannan and his research, Walt rapped that Beethoven was as black as Nefertiti, plus that astonishingly accomplished black civilizations had been systematically whitewashed out of historical memory.

Come the summer of 1978, I'd visit him at his waterfront office where he was a staffer—really, the house intellectual—for BUF, and I'd scoot to the Bluenose II Restaurant to buy us both banana-cream pie and coffee, and I'd sit, yes, at his feet, while he delivered monologues—between cigarette puffs—expounding on everything: black history, politics, the need for revolutionary (violent) action, the texts of James Baldwin and Lorraine Hansberry (the African-American writers he admired); or he'd spin tales of black resistance to white racism.

Walt reinforced these teachings through his editorship of *Grasp*. The news stories were editorials; the editorials were essays. Under Walt, the paper was a detailed syllabus for a Harvard Black Studies course. But Walt was also one of those community intellectuals who could be found holding forth in a café, cigarettes wisping, a tower of Baldwin tomes at his elbow. That summer, I was virtually his shadow as well as go-fer, but I learned, under his guidance, not only history, but poise; not only literature, but style.

Later summer '78, Walt gave a talk for the BUF at a fancy-pants joint in waterfront Halifax. Elegant in a violet smoker's jacket, Walt's speech content is long-forgotten, but not his cigarette smoke inching up—cobra-like—toward a stratosphere beyond the ceiling. He'd be fired—for insubordination—soon after. I saw his strut—to the restaurant podium—as that of a would-be guerilla, ready to be violent, possibly. (In those days, Rocky Jones's Transition-Year Program students at Dalhousie University would chant, "If society won't turn aroun / Burn the motherfucker down!") But Walt's lover was white, and so, given the day's heteronormative black politics, he could not be publicly a "leader." His Queerness set him apart from straight Scotians, even if they thrilled to his jottings, his oratory, and his board-treading.

(How magical, years later, when Walt played "Pablo" in productions of *Whylah Falls: The Play*! And I returned the favour, writing intros for—and teaching—his fine one-man show, *Tightrope Time* [1986]; and I interviewed him when he became one of the first Black Canadians to star in Stratford Festival plays. When Walt won appointment to the Order of Nova Scotia in 2014, the provincial government jetted me to Halifax to recite my tribute, which was hearty and sonorous, given my gratitude for his teachings and preachings.)

My protégé relationship to Walt brought me—forcefully—back into the demesne of the Joneses, whose Black Panther poster in the foyer of their then-home had startled me when I'd been their twelve-year-old paperboy. I can't say precisely how I came back into their bailiwick, their sphere of influence, their gravitational pull, but my brother Bryant had been—and still was—dating their daughter, Tracey, and I'd written a few love poems for Tracey that I gifted Bryant to utilize. (I'm sure he didn't need any help from me for his sweet-talkin, but I felt inspired to aid his romance by inking a few lyrical ballads for his delivery!)

Walter was related to Rocky and lived at his home, on and off, as circumstances required (when he was between acting gigs or other jobs). The Jones household was more a commune than a house, anyway, with various Rocky pals—poker-players (gamblers), hunters, sport fishers, Dalhousie students, profs, ambidextrous leftists, good-time hangers-on; and Joan's own crew—social workers and sisters (Rocky's and her own) constantly visiting. I joined the freewheeling, non-stop seminary, visiting Walt there, and participating in the rollicking, wafting cigarette-and-wine-glass, political and cultural analyses, all witty, uninhibited, *relevant*. Too, the children—Tracey and adopted—were always about, with chums, and it seemed there were always lectures—no, symposia—bursting out in every nook, plus curry on the stove, wine in the fridge or on the table, music blasting, political raps exploding from tape recorders, lotsa chat, endless laughter, gossip-as-tall-tales, a carnivalesque pedagogy whirling and swirling about. There was always the scent of curry, but also aromas of coconut, wicker, a Cuban atmosphere—not of rum or cigars—but of revolutionary dreams chastened by Halifax's salty breezes and briny coastline.

Joan and Burnley "Rocky" Jones were not just a power couple, but a Black Power couple, who'd inspired much 1960s black radicalism (irrefutably necessary and positively consequential) in Halifax and elsewhere. They fought all three levels of government relentlessly to ensure that Scotians got treated as citizens, not as ex-slaves or practically slaves. They created a playground—the "Tot Lot"—for inner-city youth; they warred gainst slum landlords and racist cops; they struggled to see Black culture and history implanted in school curricula. By hanging out with Walt in the sunroom-style living room of the Jones's demi-mansion, I could also reconnoitre the admirable Jones library and recordings, housed in a ground-floor den.

Yep, my up-front status as a Borden/Jones protégé gave me access to their treasury of Black Arts and Black Power literature, the bards of *Négritude*: speeches by Malcolm X and Stokely Carmichael (later Kwame Ture), poetry by Gwendolyn Brooks, Ntozake Shange, LeRoi Jones (Amiri Baraka), novels by Richard Wright and Toni Morrison and Ralph Ellison; record albums by the Last Poets, the Fugs, and Dylan. (I admit that a Dylan album and pamphlet of Malcolm's speeches that I "borrowed" are—ahem—still in my possession!) Friendship with Rocky and Walt brought me a bumper-crop of books to peruse, including Ralph Ellison's *Invisible Man*. Its opening gobsmacked me: A "spook" tussling with white male muscle, throwing his own black—"ectoplasmic"—punches. I read Martin Luther King, but preferred X. Days and nights at the Jones household began to fill the holes in my education—or "miseducation" (my indoctrination in the myths and protocols of *White Supremacy*)—in the Nova Scotia school system.

Now, becoming the young adult that I was, I came to know of Rocky as a firebrand, black revolutionary of the 1960s, which explained his heading up the only Canadian chapter, in Halifax, of the Black Panther Party for Self-Defense. Radically, Rocky had invited two card-carrying Panthers to Halifax in 1968, and that single action resulted in more progressive change—given government fears of a black revolutionary cell coalescing—than Africadia had ever seen hitherto. Moreover, Rocky and Joan had established Kwaacha House, a drop-in "freedom school" of sorts for black—and white—youth to rap about issues of race and to explore mutual recognition. Rocky'd also helped to organize the Black United Front of Nova Scotia (the agency for which Walt had worked and for which I worked in 1985-86), the Nova Scotia Human Rights Commission, the Transition Year Program at Dalhousie (copied by the University of Toronto), and many temporary coalitions around one form of anti-racism or pro-equality struggle or another.

Rocky's rhetoric was Malcolm X—black pride, black history, plus fire and brimstone summoned to blister Babylon. But his practice was more congruent with M. L. King: Protest, threats of protests, and then negotiations to seize concessions from government and business. A sharp, grassroots thinker (he advised Alexa McDonough—my ex-kindergarten teacher—when she led the provincial NDP), Rocky's rhetorical talents were A-1, and he had an instinct for urging and directing dissent. Over six feet tall, Rocky exuded charisma, and thus, was a lady's man (much to Joan's chagrin, and they later divorced, in the 1980s, but remained close friends).

Joan was quieter: Rocky was the spokesman, but she was the strategist and the home-front organizer (so to speak). Due to her grand corona of an afro, her slender build, and indomitable spirit, Joan resembled Angela Davis, the proud Black Panther supporter and Communist doctorate in philosophy. Because she was lithe in form, electrifying in presence, Joan's vests and leather jackets even seemed to be themselves aglow, infused with some inner illumination. Rocky manned barricades, but Joan just barrelled right over them, and suffered no fools—black, brown, or white; man, woman, or child; and not in any way, shape, or form. Moreover, Rocky and Joan had been friends with Trinidadian-American Black Power activist Stokely Carmichael and his wife, the South African singer and anti-apartheid activist Miriam Makeba (to whose voice R. J. had intro'd my brothers and me). When the entertainer, actor, and *socialist* Harry Belafonte played Halifax in April 1978, Rocky ushered him to his place, and he sat cross-legged on the living room floor, encircled by Rocky's students from the Transition Year Program, tucking into Joan's curry and discussing Black Liberation movements worldwide. The Jones household was practically a university outreach service, and many were the nights when I resided in their library, reading African-American writers or listening to their Dylan records, then falling asleep, only rousing myself at 6 or 7 a.m. to walk back to Bill's house where I was again living (December '77 to September '78).

It was Rocky and Joan who pushed me to hie my hiney to university, an option that scared me. I doubted I had either the moolah or the mind to survive the still white-old-boy-staffed Ivory Tower, nor did I wish to remain in Halifax. I preferred a school distant from boyhood neighbourhoods: I wanted to try new places and spy new faces. But how could I afford it? And where to go? Rocky solved the first problem: "You're going to the University of Waterloo, because Canada's foremost expert in black history teaches there!" (He was describing Dr. James St. Germain Walker.*) Joan solved the second problem: I'd been working as a grocery clerk (a job my mother arranged) since March 1978, but Joan hired me in a program that she headed, namely, Community Employment Strategies (CES) to work as a Tutor and Counsellor in the same North End grade schools that I'd attended as

---

* I did go to Waterloo, but, because I ended up in English Co-op, I never got to take a history course with Jim! However, Jim and I spurred Rocky to speak and record his autobiography (2007-13), which Jim edited, and was published posthumously in 2015 as *Burnley "Rocky" Jones: Revolutionary*. That project brought our trio together severally.

a boy. Starting in October 1978, my pay escalated from $120 to $150 per week, while my rent for my rooming-house room was only $35 per week. I could save enough now for at least one year of board and tuition. And I had to save some money—because Joan was certain that I'd go. More certain than anyone else in my life! More certain than I.

But Joan also taught me to be proud of my brains, to never hide "brilliance" due to shyness. Because I was taking a night school class in Political Science (to maintain the habit of study), Joan advised, "Always put your hand up when you know the answer." (That's wisdom I've passed on to my daughter.) When I'd express worry and reservations about attending university, Joan would glare at me and shout, "Don't gimme that white-Hippy-dippy shit! YOU are GOING to GO to university!" Though Rocky owned the "scary" radical rep, Joan's tongue was sharper, her thought more sure, and there was just no successful counter-argument to her opinions and judgments.

vi.

While working for Joan out of her downtown offices, I made the bizarre, definitely teen decision to join the Ku Klux Klan. My Africadian—originally Cape Bretoner—co-worker Karen (so skinny, so slender, so svelte—as twiggy as the cigarettes she inhaled incessantly—as reedy-voiced as a cracked clarinet, as potty-mouthed in vocabulary as a sailor, as Catholic and as raunchy as a defrocked priest)—returned from lunch in that same October with one of the KKK calling cards that had been circulated to Gottingen Street businesses. A restauranteur—scoffing at it—had handed Karen a card. She passed it—a Louisiana address emblazoned thereupon—to me. So, I sidled before one of Joan's IBM Selectric typewriters and, using the office address as my own, tapped out a membership inquiry letter and posted it to one of David Duke's would-be sophisticated Louisiana digs.

A week or so later, I received two brown 9 x 12 envelopes, within a day or two of each other. One envelope arrived from Louisiana and was fat with KKK paraphernalia: tabloid newspapers, a T-shirt, bumper-stickers, and other obscenities, vomiting much Negrophobic and anti-Semitic natter. That was easy to laugh off. But the second envelope was worrisome: it came from nearby Sackville, New Brunswick, and included a letter from a dude who wanted to come to Halifax to meet me. Well, I wasn't laughing about that.

I told Joan or Rocky or both bout my teenage "prank," and, then, I was in the midst of a meeting of a powerhouse of Africadian politicos: the ex-prizefighter—and now Sergeant at Arms of the Nova Scotia legislature—Delmore "Buddy" Daye; George McCurdy (uncle to future MP Howard McCurdy), then the director of the Nova Scotia Human Rights Commission; Art Criss / Hamid Rasheed, the director of the BUF; and Rocky. All were gathered, myself at the centre, to decide what to do about my accidental catch of a clutch of Atlantic Canadian Klansmen.

They decided that the Mounties would mount a "sting" operation, to ascertain the Klan's regional strength, and who were members, and then intimidate em into ceasing and desisting from all activities. And that's what happened. I wasn't privy to the details of the sting, but I heard later that an undercover Mountie had befriended a Sackville Klansman, feigned interest in the cause, and, once accepted into the clandestine body, threatened all its Maritime members with prosecution (I suppose for being members of a subversive organization).

Late that autumn, I'd learned that the East Coast Klan was three or four dudes, and the (dandruff) flake who'd written to me, seeking my companionship, turned out to be a hairdresser. Perhaps he would have wielded his hair dryer as a terrorist weapon . . .

vii.

My teenage self-rebrandings and cultural spelunkings moved me further and further away from the orbit of—I thought—the "white-identified" Whites and Clarkes. My self-stylings were meant to repudiate the false consciousness—bourgeois, integrationist, highfalutin, pacifist ("turn-the-other-cheek"), and *noblesse oblige* attitudes—that I associated with the patrilineal genealogy. That's not to say that my mom—or the Johnsons—were Afrocentrist or Black Nationalist. They weren't. But they were comfortable with our roots culture, our pungent vernacular, welcomed curry and rice, were palsy-walsy with whites but never acted as if they thought whites were better than black people, and were ecumenical in music, savouring folk, Country-n-Western, Rhythm-n-Blues, and soul, and both danced to and played these songs/records interchangeably. A Three Mile Plains Africadian—like my mom—could have Patsy Cline follow Sam Cooke, or set Phoebe Snow on the turntable right after Hank Snow (still, she'd prefer the frank eroticism of R-n-B to the yodels and fiddles of C-n-W; yessum, she'd elect bedroom squeals over snake-handlers' squeaks). I thought my father's lineage too stiff-upper-lip, too starched, to ever be able to shake and shimmy, to growl and cuss. I still admired Portia White: she was the premiere *artiste* of Africadia. But Malcolm X was now more vital for my consciousness than my Great-Aunt's Command Performance for the #1 WASP in Canada, i.e., Her Majesty . . .

Thus, my adolescence didn't only usher in the usual awkward discovery of sexuality, but also my essays to comprehend myself as a brown-skinned black (young) man in a white-majority society that feared and disdained us, short-changed and harassed us, marginalized and criminalized us. In that process of becoming "young, gifted and black," if the Johnsons were not central, the Whites/Clarkes were irrelevant—or so I judged. (In time, I would see that their history of extraordinary accomplishment in spite of our oppression as black people had revolutionary significance. But as a teen, I tended to ignore familial history in preference to enlisting with urgency-inspired, activist circles.)

My own formation of a black identity had everything to do with adopting Walt's teachings, heeding Joan's praise of black academic success, and listening to Rocky's records and reading through his (or their) library, plus almost everything that the North Branch Library had on African-American struggle. I went from having once tried to be a pallid, "Catholic" saint (based on my reading) to trying to be as black and "bad" and smart and hip as Malcolm—the black saint, radical thinker, and political martyr (thanks to my reading).

I look back on my life now, and I know that those years, 1977-79, thanks to the teachings of Joan and Rocky and Walt, helped to determine my orientations as a young adult scholar and writer. There are others I need to mention here—Sylvia Hamilton and Bev Greenlaw, and Jackie Barkley—and I will. But I need to backtrack again.

viii.

One April morning in 1978, I was sitting in my father's kitchen, spooning cereal and preparing for school, when the phone rang: it was Rocky. He had an extra ticket for a flight to Toronto. I was eighteen, an adult, according to Revenue Canada and to the law, but I still asked Bill's permission to leave—to skip school—and fly to Toronto with Rocky and his daughter, Tracey. Well, about thirty minutes later, Rocky pulled up in his red Jeep, and then we were up, up, and away—to Toronto the Good, Hogtown, the Big Smoke, the Big Crab Apple . . . Not used to travel, I didn't pack proper clothes to address the April chill. Rocky didn't hesitate: just took off his own jacket and put it around my skinny shoulders. His mantle upon my back. The man was unfailingly generous—always. (The jacket was grey or beige with small black checks. I wore it proudly for years—slowly growing into it as my political consciousness too-slowly expanded.)

Once we landed and eventually took a subway somewhere, I revealed myself to be a Haligonian hick by boarding the subway car and hollering, "Hey, everyone, I'm from Nova Scotia!" Was I ever properly silenced by the stony looks the other subway riders hurled my way! If they'd thought, "Here's another half-ass, Haligonian half-breed, come to suck up our welfare and/or bum," I couldn't have blamed them. (A couple years later, as I exited the humongous discount bazaar of Honest Ed's, at Bathurst and Bloor, with a backpack stuffed with eternally creased polyester pants and tinfoil-fragile cutlery, an older black woman, spying my delight with my shoddy, shabby purchases, yelled, "You must be from Nova Scotia!" Yep!)

Rocky had flown us—Tracey and I—to Toronto to participate in a meeting of the Black Youth Community Action Project (BYCAP), which was stewarded by Dudley Laws. Laws was a black elder who sported a Black Panther-style black beret right rakishly (and who organized the Black Action Defence Committee, in the early 1980s, to protest white cop aggression—often lethal—against unarmed black Torontonians). He had the smooth, suave, licorice complexion of R. J., and also hailed from Jamaica. But Laws was tutored in Malcolm X, not *Penthouse*; was devoted to *Liberation*, not partying. He spoke softly, but radiated grace—charisma as a cognate of charm under pressure. BYCAP—with the support of Laws and a bespectacled, tan-complected elder who seemed to speak through his teeth—namely, Ed Clarke, of the Black Resource Information Centre—was, that April weekend, holding a youth conference.

I think we landed on a Thursday. That night, there was a welcome supper—rice-and-peas, curried chicken, hot sauce. The inspirational fare included poet Dionne Brand, then twenty-five to my eighteen, reciting her Dub-styled poetry alongside drummers—just like those that I'd almost memorized from Rocky's *The Last Poets* LP. I was floored by her massive, beautiful, florid fro—and her huge, astonishingly ami-cable smile. Were we introduced? Or was I bold enough (having already yelled out my origins across a subway car), to just go up to her and announce, "I'm a poet too"?

But Dionne was already an established bard of shout-down-Babylon truths, and I was a seaside bumpkin, an East Coast tyro, just startin out on my ragamuffin, R-n-B way. Anyway, Dionne was gracious—or took pity on me—and shook my hand. Soon, we were pen pals, and she'd drop me a postcard from Havana or Amsterdam.

(Then, sometimes, shuttling between Halifax and Waterloo—once I became a student there, I'd get stuck in Toronto for a night. No problem! Dionne let me crash on her floor a few times, even once when she was away. I met her again in Montréal in May 1980 when we both attended the first national Black Artists Conference, convened at McGill University.*)

The next day convened the youth conference. After auditing a lot of fervent, Carib-accented rebel talk, I just proclaimed to the few dozen delegates, "The young man from Nova Scotia would like to speak." And I spoke! Some chutzpah, some cojones! I don't recall what I said, but my peroration met with generous applause.

I soon made my way to Third World Books, that shrine to Black literature. I didn't have much money, but the priceless works went dirt-cheap. A few "Red" pamphlets and Black poetry booklets were a buck each. Everything I bought was treasure: Carolyn Rodgers (the stone-soul boss), Dudley Randall (who got me readin Pushkin), Angela Jackson (southern-fried eroticism), all titles from Third World Press (Chicago) or Paul Breman (London). Now I had drums in my ears, poems in my head, folks trying to initiate a Black culture and consciousness revolution in Toronto, only a decade "late" after the US movements. (Yet, they were right-on-time for Canada; I mean, what Canadians could possibly be ready for—in this *de facto* Red Tory state.†)

---

* How strange: to be a bunch of black anglos, in Montréal, right after the first Québec Sovereignty referendum. The Oui and Non posters were still up; passions were still high. But I got to meet, not only Dionne, but, for the first time, Austin Clarke, Reshard Gool, Lorris Elliott, and other black writers and scholars, plus black artists from Nova Scotia and black dancers from Vancouver, all of us at McGill (a slave master-founded university) in the balmy month of May.

† Established by conquered French royalists and English Loyalists fleeing the muskets of Yankee rabble, Canada evolved a political culture favouring "social solidarity" over "individual rights." A "Red Tory" is a conservative who don't trust the "free market" to "do the right thing," and prefers that the Queen's gloved left hand stop Adam Smith's "invisible" hand from t'iefin.

One of our meetings that weekend occurred in the Universal Negro Improvement Association (UNIA) Hall, on College, about halfway between Spadina and Bathurst. I eyed the gold-tasselled, roped-off, crimson-velvet chair that had once cradled the tush of Marcus Moziah Garvey (whose middle name I'd pinched for my triple-barrelled *nom-de-plume*), and who had helmed the UNIA—the greatest global organization of black people that has ever existed. (Harlem was the HQ, but branches could be found in Europe, Canada, the Caribbean, and Africa.) When no one was about, I plunked my own bottom on His Excellency's sanctified seat, but experienced neither epiphany nor blasphemy—just a sense of history.

That weekend also intro'd me to the Underground Railroad soul-food restaurant (home of barbecued ribs and sweet potato pie—which I wouldn't fork again until living in North Carolina in the mid-1990s), and to Fran's (where I was partial to rice pudding). The cookery in Toronto's air, around Kensington Market and Spadina and Bathurst, was competitive with the seaside aromas of Halifax: every breath was to trek Marco Polo's Silk Road; or to anchor in a Caribbean Isle, leeward or windward; or to shuttle through Europe, from Brit-theme pubs to Iron Curtain vodka. Resonant were East Indian and West Indian mash-ups of curry and samosas and doubles; plus the Aeolian, Tyrrhenian, and Mediterranean, Black, and Aegean seas; plus the Tex-Mex/Cajun food/music corridor (Houston-New Orleans); plus the array of Argentinian beef and Brazilian hog; plus spicy dishes outta Szechuan or Vietnam (thanks to resettled, so-called Boat People). Anyway, Toronto's mutually consented-to *coitus* of cultures creates beautiful bastardizations or creolizations: a Greek *and* Chinese restaurant? An Italian *and* Jamaican restaurant? All's possible in this bastion of Apollonian multiculturalism: a feast for the belly—and a fiesta for the bedroom. (Multiculturalism mandates cosmopolitan canoodling. Amen!)

ix.

Touching down again in North End Halifax, I now blipped the radar of Sylvia Hamilton, who'd babysat me when I was a boy. Ten years my senior, she exhibited an uncompromising (and uncompromised) Hippy aesthetic, more Joan Armatrading than Joan Jones, or more Haight-Ashbury than Harlem. Her wardrobe was Earth-mama jazzy (plus beads, bangles, braids, bandana, and boots); her mood-altering substance of choice was, however, tea (herbal or black); her profession was teacher; her interests were broadcast journalism, feminism, and environmentalism interchangeably; Alice Walker was her New Testament and Zora Neale Hurston her Old.

Sylvia was an independent-minded, free-spirited intellectual. She couldn't care less if someone called her an Oreo or stuck-up because she had read Nikki Giovanni and *Giovanni's Room* and could quote Truffaut on Hitchcock. Nor did she allow anybody's sense of "blackness" or "womanhood" to determine how she should dress, whom she could love, how she could comport herself, where she could work, what her success should mean—that it was miraculous to be an *artiste* and unapologetically unconventional, *avant-garde*. She seemed to already be living luxuriously the ideal of committed freedom that Rocky and Joan were yet struggling to achieve. She was already, breathtakingly *there*—where Malcolm X meets Herbert Marcuse, Gloria Steinem meets Bessie Smith. So, she was her own person, in soul and substance, neither confined by stereotypes nor defined by Mr. X or Miss Manners. How enticing to witness, how entrancing to hear! (Like many oppressed peoples, Scotians can mistrust and distrust "the book-smart" for fear that anyone who excels in "the white man's schools, reading the white man's books" must be white-identified and self-hating. Sylvia turned those phobias upside down by asking, "Who does your illiteracy benefit?")

Being an activist, archivist, and artist, one interested in film screening the realities of Scotian women's lives, Sylvia insisted on these roles as necessary and transformative. Too, Sylvia's communal sensibility and social consciousness were familiar—as in familial. Like Gerry, Sylvia was involved in the Congress of Black Women of Canada; like Bill,* she'd done social work (*via* the BUF), and, like Walt, she'd taught—albeit in an alternative North End school called New Options. She admired Joan and Rocky, but preferred pragmatism over ideology. Sylvia was most akin to Walt (despite his pronounced Afrocentrism), for he was also a journalist—and an artist, and Queer; so he could sympathize with black women striving for their *Equality*. Thin and thoughtful, anxiously interrogative, Sylvia's sentences tended to end with a questioning accent and a wondering glance and fingers fidgeting with the astonished air, to try to solicit further reflection. She forbade all declarations uttered as if they were *Law*; but would probe and push, to forbid any facile answers.

Sylvia was also pre-eminent for me because, like me, she wore glasses and flashed prominent—but, unlike me, properly fitting—front teeth; and her hair reflected natural black styles. Thus, like Walt and the Joneses, and Terry Symonds (of the North Branch Library), Sylvia's staunch sense of self instructed me that one can be black and an activist, a scholar, "hip," and "rootsy," and an artist. I could do—be—all the above—even with my brain stuck on the liberatory ethics of the 1960s and my heart fixed on a Soul soundtrack (Chi-Lites, "Oh Girl," James Brown, "Bewildered," Phoebe Snow, "Poetry Man," and Bill Withers, "Ain't No Sunshine" . . .).

In spring '78, I ran into Sylvia upon leaving the North Branch Library, where I'd been doing some reading or rapping (maybe with Terry), and she accosted me and reminded me that she'd been my babysitter ("a long time ago in a galaxy far, far away"). She somehow knew—maybe

---

* From 1970–73, Bill was a part-time social worker with the Halifax Neighbourhood Centre (HNC). Inspired by Saul Alinsky (who also influenced Barack Obama), the HNC sought to organize North End Halifax unemployed, slum tenants, drop-outs, and the poor to find jobs, win housing improvements, and obtain a high school diploma.

from joint membership with Gerry in the Congress of Black Women—that I was attempting poetry. She welcomed poems for an anthology that she was compiling, entitled "Black Kids, Write On!" The proposed title was endearing, partly because I didn't see myself as a kid anymore (being eighteen, if not yet a high-school grad).* Now, a new mentor-protégé relationship began, and I was grateful that a black woman in my community was taking seriously my pretensions to be a poet.

After I started to work for Joan Jones, I had a key to her Community Employment Strategies (CES) office (and thus access to an IBM Selectric typewriter). I also had my own digs about five or six or seven blocks away from the CES property at Falkland and Gottingen (where a cop had forced me to abandon a grocery cart four years before†), but it was often lethally frigid during the winter months, and I dreaded making the twenty-to-thirty minute trek home from the office, come end of day. So, I'd knock—bam loudly—on Sylvia's door along the way, and she and her beau—Bev Greenlaw (who happened to be white)—would let me crash at their place, under heaped quilts, on the floor, with a cat highsteppin about.

However, sleep would be staved off until Sylvia and Bev (also an intellectual, savvy basketball coach, and a community-minded, but quiet activist) would spin some bluesy discs, boil some tea (I think that Bev would share some beer with me), and we'd—our trio—discuss EVERYTHING (caps are mandatory): community politics, pop charts, international politics, Black writing. I gotta tell you, it was a big education for me to be in a black—and white—household where *Black Scholar* was even bathroom reading and the turntable would let Billie

---

* Yet, being sixty years old as I write these words, I gotta admit that anyone younger than forty looks quite juvenile in my eyes now.

† Perhaps now it has rusted down to a tetanus-positive assembly of steely spaghetti? If so, I hope it will be gifted to that deleterious peace officer as a keepsake for his years of harassment of black kids.

Holiday exclaim, the North Preston Baptist Youth Choir proclaim, and talk move flexibly—diagonally—among concerns about Jimmy Carter and Prez Ronnie "Ray-Gun," or praise of Toni Morrison, or critiques of Pierre Trudeau. (Dear Reader: note that you have just witnessed Morrison and Trudeau being mentioned in the same sentence; that's the difference that being Africadian makes.) Bev and Sylvia would indulge my predilections—until contradictions arose. So, I'd praise Declan MacManus—"Elvis Costello"—and then Bev would report that Declan had called Ray Charles "a nigger" and James Brown "a jive-ass nigger." How quickly the would-be transcendent artists or politicos would thus collapse! Busted!

In March 1979, Sylvia arranged for me to jet to Winnipeg for a Caribbean Writers Festival, organized by Ralph James (a university scientist)—and other Winnipeggers. Dr. James billeted me at his place, and gave me a copy of *Canada In Us Now* (billed as the *first* African-Canadian literary anthology, though it was the third*), edited by Harold Head, and including Austin Clarke, Dionne Brand, and one African-Nova Scotian poet—Ms. Gloria Wesley-Daye. That was my first time encountering an Africadian poet—in print. Not only that, but Gloria was beautiful—as lovely as Dionne—but also of my "hood." Her existence validated my own—I mean, in the sense that now I suspected that I might also publish—author—poetry, not just scribble lines.

Most memorably, during that grey, dreary March weekend in Winnipeg in 1979, I was able to share my truly first "adult" poem that I *imagined* was consequential: "Watercolour for Negro Expatriates in France." That writers like Sam Selvon, a Caribbean-Canadian author who used Creolized English in his work, were present at that confab, verified my talent, gave me confidence that I could proceed. I recall murmurs of approval, if not windfalls of applause; yet, still, I returned to Nova Scotia a confirmed poet—with a poem that could appear in any

---

* Camille Haynes edited the first, *Black Chat* (Montréal, 1972) and Liz Cromwell edited the second, *One Out of Many* (Toronto, 1975).

anthology in English, with *no one* being able to say that it did not belong. (I dare ya!)

In autumn '78, Sylvia joined a (hitherto white) feminist group, "Reel Life," in filming the first Central Planning Committee (CPC) conference of Scotian youth in Halifax, as we sought to form a provincial Black Youth Organization (BYO). (The BYCAP meeting in Toronto that April 1978 had given me the idea.) On those black-and-white tapes, I am a spindly, grey-complected figure in a grey-flannel suit, gesticulating on some political point, when, in my heart, I just really wanted to recite poetry. (Why the tension between the pursuits of poetry and activism? I feared the second interest would overwhelm the first, so that the *griot* becomes a sloganeer.) Our provincial parley—in November '78—took place at Bloomfield Junior High, where I'd been enrolled grades seven to nine. How weird to be back there—three years later—as a would-be weekend revolutionary!*

From '78 to '80, Sylvia would invite me to accompany her to vaguely leftist films—such as Martin Ritt's *Norma Rae* (1979) and Stanley Kubrick's *Dr. Strangelove* (1964). This was part of her education in film, but of mine in social responsibility in art. These films established that our politics—progressive—could be filtered (enhanced) through celluloid. Yet, these narratives also taught that projecting a social conscience doesn't necessitate barking propaganda.

Later, Sylvia managed to blend her leftist, womanist (black feminist), and historical interests in the films that she made, including *Black Mother Black Daughter* (1989), treating Africadian women's history, a TV-doc on the Jones clan (including Rocky), and a full-length doc on none other than Portia White (*Portia White: Think On Me* [2000]).

---

* When I was fourteen and fifteen, in Bloomfield, the character of J. J. (played by Jimmie Walker) from the hit TV sitcom, *Good Times* (1974-79), plagued me awfully because some white folks swore that dorky I resembled the buffoonish personage and expected me to repeat his signal expression, "Dy-no-mite!" But I loathed—even as a mid-teen—the blackface-style simpleton. How much better to be back at Bloomfield as a Black Panther acolyte than as a supposed twin of a minstrel clown!

Sylvia's film subjects were also my inspirations, my models, as was she herself.* (Thus, Sylvia scribed the intro to my debut poetry collection, *Saltwater Spirituals and Deeper Blues* [1983], and she called me, in September 1993, to tell me that the ancestors would uphold me, the next day, when I'd defend my doctoral dissertation at Queen's University.) Always has Sylvia been a guiding presence.

A couple of times, Calvin Gough, a Scotian teacher, joined Sylvia and I at film screenings. Once, Calvin brought along a gal pal who was beige, bespectacled, and acerbically snooty; she seemed to deem Africadia equivalent to a failed state. When Calvin reported that they'd broken up, it seemed an obvious liberation. In any event, Calvin—bearded and bespectacled—had an ironic laugh that was gargantuan, frequently rolled out to accent some deadly serious pronouncement on the extreme urgency for (armed-if-necessary) revolution. Calvin's political tutor was an Asian gent who had fled apartheid South Africa. He was a vivid, fire-breathing Communist in his own living room; but was self-preservingly mum whenever Calvin attacked the racism infecting their school—and got attacked in turn.

Despite his thunderclap guffaws, Calvin's absorption of history's revelations had rendered him implacably bitter, for he could see betrayal of himself, betrayals of black people, all around, all the time. Nor was he wrong. Yet, his inability to convince others of the deliberate nature of our oppression was grandly frustrating. Where Joan or Sylvia would display nervous energy, Calvin was always tense—explosive—his anger gauge set at a hair-trigger. No matter his intense outrage at

---

* Sylvia, Walt, and Rocky, and I got to share in honours that were partly a result of the activism and artistry that they exemplified for me. Sylvia, Walt, and I received the Portia White Award for Artistic Excellence, and Rocky and Walt and I were inducted into the Order of Nova Scotia; then Sylvia, Rocky, and I all received honorary doctorates, while Walt and I were also inducted into the Order of Canada. Moreover, all of us are related to either the Olivers or the Whites, those Africadian families of indubitable and inimitable accomplishment. But we were the protesters (and born strugglers), not—automatically—the strivers...

our marginalization and our brainwashing by White Supremacist teachers and textbooks, he was, in practice, a staunch pacifist, a truth that heightened his scornful laughter and increased his verbal rages.

x.

A few members of Dave Renton's Mind the Flowerpots drama troupe also attended Queen Elizabeth High, and we chummed around, for we shared the university-prep Honours English courses. However, when I visited them, in the South End, I went to their homes; when they taxi'd to the North End, we congregated at a pizza parlour in the section of Gottingen Street that had been bestowed with a bland and gentrifying name, "Novalea* Drive." (Given its pretentious effort to slough off its umbilical connection to rough-n-tumble Gottingen Street, it should have been called "Novel Drivel" instead.)

Then, in my last year of high school, in winter '78, a shocking thing occurred: there was a house party on Cogswell Street—one of the borders between North and South End—wherein South End whites danced with North End blacks. Utterly unchaperoned. It was the single occasion in high school that there occurred greasy-spoon—so to speak—and silver-spoon integration, and the music on tap was black. On that sub-zero March night, present were approximately two-dozen party-goers. It was all secretive (by word-o-mouth invite only), but a chance—finally—for black and white teens to clench and kiss, apart from the censorious eyes and thou-shalt-not lips of white parents and authorities. Excitingly, we were breaking *apartheid* taboos imposed to ensure that opportunities would shower white offspring, while servitude posts would bedevil blacks.

Usually, classes and races self-segregated subtly according to QEHS door locations. The "north" door was the portal for working-class and/or black youth; it gave direct access to shop classes such as

---

* If you hear an echo of Lucy Maud Montgomery's "Avonlea," your inner-ear is not imbalanced.

auto repair and stenography; it was also the door for Special Ed ingress.

Opposite to the north was the "south" door, which was, along with the "gym" door, the site of snobs and/or jocks meriting hero-worship. Many had done grade school privately at parental expense, but had been switched to public high school to be "finished"—groomed for university—at taxpayer expense. Their futures assured, they kicked around in deck shoes, sweaters, polo shirts, and if any skin showed, often it was tanned, fresh from Florida or Bermuda. They were chauffeured to school, or wheeled their own wheels (a point also true of North End or West End white guys, purring muscle cars and eager to quit school and start full-time, closed-shop, unionized jobs). Apart from their physical occupation of the south door, the upper-class pupils didn't flaunt their status because they didn't have to. They were the automatic elite, and the rest of us pecked for crumbs in their sunlight-eclipsing shadows.

In the middle of the school was the main door: no one who really fit anywhere else would hang out there; but that door also allowed access to the smokers' "pit," so called because it was sunk into the floor like a shallow swimming pool. Directly opposite the main door was the gym (and auditorium) door; this door was the most "integrated" of all because jocks—black, white, and brown football and basketball players—all hung out together, talkin shared jive and chattin up gals passin by. These were the cool guys, the "in" crowd, and none else were welcome.

Now's the time to review the English teachers who moved me through the curriculum from Grades 10 to 12. Carole Gibbons was English—from England—I believe, and taught us poetry that included song lyrics; took us to see Hamlet at Neptune Theatre [in which the prince appeared briefly but memorably—literally—bare-assed], but also a Newfoundland play, featuring Gordon Pinsent, during which a lad-and-lady copulate in the lower berth of a bunk bed [which had me thinking that this was a Newfoundland tradition]. Miss Gibbons also took us to see Alden Nowlan's script adaptation of Shelley's *Frankenstein*—at Dalhousie University—just before Halloween 1975.

She had a sharp-point nose, black spectacles, shoulder-length wavy, amber hair, and favoured blouses and floor-length skirts. She encouraged my poetry writing, and later told me that I should "prostitute" my talents in advertising, because I'd invented copy for an ad campaign— as a class project—for "Soft Seduction" perfume. Miss Gibbons returned to England in 1977 to take up a post at a private school.

My grade eleven English teacher Fred Holtz was affable, amiable, progressive, funky, cool, unassuming, and all of the above, simultaneously, everyday and even after-school. He drove a yellow VW bug, and he and his wife would often give me and my brothers a lift after school to a staircase leading uphill to our then-home in Cowie Hill, Spryfield. His wife was a pioneer environmentalist with the Ecology Action Centre, and both were ban-the-bomb, pro-feminist, anti-racist, good-hearted, decent-treatment-oriented citizens. In the classroom, Mr. Holtz was tweedy, soft-spoken, almost always willing to educate via jest, and freewheeling, reserving Fridays as the day when class members could bring in our own music (tapes) to play, or serenade everyone with Leonard Cohen selections on guitar, or recite our own poetry. He had me memorize and recite lines from Othello (of course, I was the green-eyed Moor); but he also wrote me a poem, which I still have, a short, Beat lyric extolling me as being "a cool cat."

Barry Fox—excuse me, *Doctor* Barry Fox, P.-H.-D.—was the head of our high school Department of English—and his "Dr. Ph.D."—was further accented by his handlebar moustache, the ends of which he would twirl round his fingers—while his own kinda British inflection could remind us that colonials like ourselves were usually best off as cannon-fodder. I think he felt that he was upholding standards in the face of a Tommy Douglas liberalism that had degenerated into a disco-era libertinism. Yet, when Gerry was at rest in a Windsor, NS, funeral home, in August 2000, it was Dr. Fox who drove quite a distance to express his personal condolences.

I gotta mention my French teacher—Miss Hattie: a petite, slender brunette, pure nervous energy, who cruised in the only Citroën convertible—fire-engine-red—in Nova Scotia. Although I was only a "B" student at French, she welcomed my interest in *symboliste* poets, and accepted to read scads of my tyro poetry imitating the precursors of surrealism.

The class-and-race cleavages in QEHS exploded openly during my editorship of our newspaper—my first foray into journalism. The Student Council appointed me the editor for my senior year, 1977-78, when I'd begun consorting with Rocky and Joan and Walt and Sylvia.

Thus, with a micro-squad of volunteers, I began to put together—in the school basement—bi-monthly issues of what had to be called *The Subterranean Times*. This "newspaper" was 8½ x 14 paper, photocopied and stapled, lengthwise, eight pages, run off on Joan Jones's Xerox machine at her office—which had been my mom's office—at 5557 Cunard Street. One of my helpers was her daughter, Tracey, and we'd gather after-hours to blast copies off the machine—almost passing out from the stench of ammonia. I think we only ran off about 100 copies per issue, and they cost a dime—but there was no way to collect the coins. So, they were anarchistic, anachronistically (back-to-the-1960s) "free."

Due to my Black Power and Hippy Libertine *ideals* (gleaned from all my 1960s-oriented "retro" reading*), the "newspaper" throbbed with Dylan riffs and fumed with Malcolm X allusions. It had a decidedly Rimbaldian beat, a Baudelairean bent, and a Muddy Waters *cum* Allen Ginsberg howl, plus groovily dirty-minded illustrations. I rampaged through the don't-give-a-damn anything-goes-ism of Dylan's *Tarantula* (1966) and his liner notes to *Bringing It All Back Home* (1965) and

---

* I've often thought I was born a decade (too) late because *I still believe* the Hippies and the pacifists and the Free Speech Movement, the Beats and the Panthers, the Back-to-Nature dreamers and the Jesus Freaks (a people's Christianity closer to Christiania, Copenhagen, than to colleged theologians), the feminists and the gays, were all correct; and in their romantic rectitude, *humane*, Walt Whitman prefacing Dylan, *Hair*, then "the Age of Aquarius." All of it glorious! Scrumptious! Neither Marx nor McCarthy, but Marcuse!

Highway 61 Revisited (1965)—to try to mimic what I saw as a zany and rambunctious, madcap, slapstick series of unexpected mash-ups, juxtapositions. To be cool, to feel cool, smashing together pop culture and black culture and Brit Lit (canonical) references. There were sports articles, news stories (including a review of an adult movie that a volunteer snuck into a cinema to catch), and illustrations. Of course, I was also trying to imitate the dense, fat, thick, slabs of Afrocentric prose that Walter had in his *Grasp* (pun intended). But I was inking, really, paper equivalent to sheets of unlined foolscap, and so my columns had to be skinny, ragged right in margins, gangly and scrawny and scraggly!

My style guides were Kerouac's *Mexico City Blues* and *The Penguin Book of Surrealist Verse*: weird, elliptical statements rendered resolutely in initial-minuscule letters. I'm sure I banged out—literally—a bunch of the pieces on Bill Clarke's 1977 Xmas gift to me—a plastic, turquoise-and-cream, entry-level Olivetti typewriter. I even enlisted my father's cartoon art for an issue or two because of my boyhood memories of watching him paint fetching pastoral scenes on glass. Everything would eventually get churned into columns (three per page) on an IBM Selectric typewriter—with those seductive, Georgian-round, interchangeable ball-heads.

The final issue brought the wrath of the South Enders down upon my head. It featured a notorious editorial by a Greco-Canuck student who complained about well-off brats—WASP spawn—dominating the school as their preserve and sidelining everyone who had less cash, or who lacked a British accent, or who had too much melanin. Well, our ruling-class preppies complained that we'd chastised their hardworking parents, whose savvy and industry had made them our betters, and whose taxes funded our parents' welfare and Unemployment Insurance cheques. We were—in their eyes—ungrateful snivellers, jealous about their superiority. These retorts were broadcast school-wide because a South Ender commandeered the P.A. system to castigate the article and its author. I demanded to have—and received—equal time to blast back, sending my voice crackling over every classroom speaker, while also feeling my own blood thunder. How heady is that mix of adrenalin and outrage that fuels so much social protest!

Well, I did view the South End retort as foul play: to castigate the writer, a North Ender (like me) and immigrant youth, and, though white, rejected by the paleface plutocrats, for not being born into lucre, but being born to "money-grubbing" entrepreneurs. My buddy editorialist had merely exposed the school's class/racial polarities which were starkly obvious (indeed, fistfights would ensue if the wrong person showed up at the south door). (Rocky's sister, Janice, had interviewed black students—I was one—for a Halifax School Board study, which did report our alienation—no surprise—from the school, and for the usual reasons: lack of black content in curricula, plus teachers acting in ways tacitly or explicitly racist.*)

My editorialist had exposed the hypocrisy of Canadian social "peace": so long as the oppressor seems "cordial," and the oppressed react courteously in expressing grievance, irritants can continue and even increase in harm, until the oppressed demand justice and the oppressor takes offense that "good intentions" are being rebuffed and a good name slandered. Way too often do Canucks pooh-pooh injustice: we deny the obvious and blame the victim and talk about "persons of goodwill . . . improving understanding," pass out honorary doctorates, appointments, encomia, and emoluments, but change *zilch*.

My crowning riposte to the South Enders was effected on graduation night. Though the principal—Dr. George Butler (who had once suggested that I could be a philosopher)—nixed my request to deliver the speech, I spoke anyhow, an extemporaneous valedictory address. I wore a dashiki that I'd borrowed from Walt, an afro nicely coiffed by

---

* Visiting QEHS to talk to black students, Walt was accosted in the hallway by a guidance counsellor, who asked, "What can I do for you boys?" Walt was thirty-six; I was eighteen; thanks to Walt's upbraiding, the counsellor was soon red-faced and blubbering an apology. Still, in discussing my future, the same guidance counsellor said, "We can't afford to waste you." My reply: "So you waste everyone else?"

Tracey, and my mom and her beau (Hank) were in the audience; Bill was also present—but poignantly incognito (as I'd later learn*). I strode to centre stage as my name was called, received my diploma, then turned and faced the audience, and said, "It is time to ensure that more black pupils get to graduate from this school!" Then, I strode off the stage to applause, while Dr. Butler half-scowled, half-grimaced.

Did my father credit his parenting of me was now "fulfilled"? I'd achieved one milestone that he'd set for his sons: to complete high school. Was it enough? I did score a Social Studies scholarship (value $300) to apply to university tuition, but he expressed no interest in that possibility for me. I was so lucky that the Joneses (and my mom, as much as she was able) did.

xi.

After reading *The Autobiography of Malcolm X*, including his screed—or invective—against black people straightening their hair, I decided to try the procedure. To find out what it was like—and also to establish my own independent thought. It was Tracey Jones who put the hot comb through my curls (or naps) and singed my scalp and temples a couple of times. But superb was the result: Cascades of long, black hair framing my face and flowing past my shoulders. How peculiar to turn my head and feel my hair laggingly follow! Tracey straightened it thrice—including for my final high-school prom (I was dashing in a white tux and that big, black hair cascading). But, soon enough, I returned to my roots (pun intended), and have borne the same basic helmet of an afro ever since. (I might try dreadlocks though, one day, God willing!)

---

* His second wife, Pammy, divulged that Bill'd attended, but hadn't wanted me to know. Perhaps he didn't want to take the chance of running into my mom (in case I'd've tried to yoke them into a photo-op). Or maybe Bill was trying to decide when to tell me to leave (his) home (i.e., throw me out), just as he'd always said he would, for I was now eighteen and had completed high school.

So, summer '78, I did let my afro explode wildly while wearing white painter pants and a blue (actual) Chinese Communist uniform that the International Education Centre (IEC) at Halifax-based Saint Mary's University (SMU) had permitted me to take. I even had the dark-blue cap with a bright-red star on the front, but didn't wear it much because it intruded on my fro. I encased my feet in steel-toed workboots, thinking that would be a hipster and revolutionary-ready look.

But, being a grocery store clerk, for eight hours a day, five or six days a week, I developed pain in my toes. My father sent me to his doctor to get checked out. Well, instead of telling me to change my footwear or change my job or reduce my hours, the doc proposed that I have an operation to remove the bones in my toes. I had enough smarts to ask how that might affect my ability to run (I was still into track-and-field). His answer? "Your toes would flop around." "No thanks!"

Some folks say the MD was kidding, but I didn't find a flicker of humour in what he said or how he said it. I think he sought to hobble me for life—for whatever glory or lucre that would've brought him. Why he would have done so, if he was serious in his recommendation (and he must have been, because he prescribed no painkillers), I suppose it would have been a reflection of the racism that has led—deliberately—to allowing African-American men, syphilis-afflicted, to receive *no* treatment so that laboratory physicians could study the progress of the disease.[*] In truth there is a genocidal history of North American doctors sterilizing black women, or using black and/or Indigenous peoples as guinea pigs for experiments ranging from the effects of LSD (see Dorothy Proctor, *Chameleon* [1995]) to the impact of nutrition deficiency.[†] (In 2020, when an Indigenous woman in a Québec hospital recorded herself dying, while being denied treatment and being peppered with racial slurs from medical staff, Canucks were scandalized. But such has been the experience of

---

[*] See, for instance, https://en.wikipedia.org/wiki/Tuskegee_Syphilis_Study.

[†] See, for instance, https://www.ncbi.nlm.nih.gov/pmc/articles/PMC3941673/.

Black *and* Indigenous people on both sides of the 49th Parallel. Fact!*)

I was growing suspicious anyway of all white authority, and that stance was cemented by my friendship with Danny—an Africadian, outta Scotia, but a Montréalais. He was back in Nova Scotia, summer '78, and he was—with me—a disciple of Malcolm X. We had the same complexion, similar coronas of hair (his somehow Byronic, and mine more like Panther George Jackson's); we wore the same white pants, and both fantasized about fomenting "good trouble" (to quote John Lewis)—anti-racist radicalism in the streets of Halifax and Montréal.

Danny would talk about "throwing down" and mime a machine-gunner. It's not that we wanted to hurt anyone. No! But our passion was the obliteration of the stupidity of racism. Our rhetorical feroc-ity was egged on by an African-American Vietnam War vet, married to one of Danny's Haligonian relatives. Dude was a dark stringbean and emitted a Mississippi drawl, most pronounced when castigating "peckerwoooods" and "craaackers" (who, for him, included white Bluenosers, as if he knew that some flour-power Nova Scotians were actual spawn of Dixie). The vet limped due to a war injury; so he drew ephemeral health from long hauls on spliffs and wielded a tree branch for a cane. His favourite seat was a tree stump, uprooted from some-where and plunked down in his living room. I think Danny admired his military background and his militant rhetoric, but his Yank cousin-in-law's Molotov-cocktail-tossing days were long gone.

Danny and I hung out a lot. Then his girlfriend phoned from Montréal to say that she was pregnant with his babe, and he dis-appeared immediately back to Hochelaga, impending fatherhood trumping any notion of revolution. Danny was nervous about taking on the responsibility, but he did not hesitate, even though he was only eighteen—just like me.

---

* https://hms.harvard.edu/magazine/racism-medicine/field-correction?utm_source=SilverpopMailing&utm_medium=email&utm_campaign=Daily%20Gazette%2020210127%20(1).

(When my daughter's mom-to-be called me, almost twenty years later, to tell me that she was expecting, I was less prepared—less mature—than was Danny, although he had only just legally become a man. Despite my intelligence, I was still determining my identity as a son, and I was fearful of fatherhood, afraid I'd repeat the violence I had witnessed as a child.)

xii.

That same summer, sporting that wild afro, I was seated on the No. 7 bus, at rush hour, travelling on Robie Street, away from the leafy South End to the working-class and immigrant and Royal Canuck Navy neighbourhoods of the North End. A Friday. Soon, an elderly white woman, in a head scarf and an old dress, boarded, seated her ass cross from me, eyed me coldly, and began speaking loudly, in an Eastern European accent, about the presence of an ape and a baboon and a nigger on the bus. I look around, to see who she is ranting about, and then I realize, it's *me*. Instantly, a well-dressed, white, professional man stood, and intoned, in a strong, CBC Radio-stentorian voice, "This is Canada. We don't tolerate that sort of thing here." Other passengers applauded, the bus driver swung to the curb, directed the woman to leave: she did. I thanked both the man and the bus driver for their action. I had just experienced a terrific example of white courtesy taking umbrage against white discourtesy: although, really, all we'd collectively done was put an aged—maybe disoriented—lady off the bus. In what way was this action "radical"?

Another reflection of the impotence of white umbrage at white racism that goes "beyond the pale" (pun intended) ... Shortly after my high school graduation, in late June 1978, Rocky invited me to appear on a four-episode CBC-TV documentary series on Africadian history and culture. Titled *Black Insights*, and co-hosted by Africadian beauty queen and activist Sharon Ross, I joined Tracey Jones for the segment on "Education." However, when I arrived for the interview, at 5 p.m.,

I had no problem gaining entrée to the CBC building. A security guard buzzed the door open, and without really even looking at my brown face, or requesting my name or i.d., told me where I could find the broom and the mop. Was he shocked to learn that I was present as a "talking head"! My point? White Canuck politesse, courtesy, and charity cannot repeal their entrenched privilege that relegates black and brown people—automatically—to the political margins and socio-economic doldrums.

But incidents such as these and Danny's influence weren't the only catalyst of revolutionary fervour. No! I also found myself regaled by argumentative, spirited, and didactic conversation with Jackie Barkley. Like Rocky and Joan and Sylvia, Jackie had interacted with me, briefly, when I was a boy. But that summer, she re-emerged as another central mentor.

American-born, Jackie had come to Halifax with her husband, hired to direct the Halifax Neighbourhood Centre (HNC), circa 1970-73, where Bill Clarke also laboured as a social worker (during days, while still doing a railway night-shift). The HNC was a government-funded effort to ameliorate the lives of the North End poor whose penury got blamed on addictions, illiteracy, or dysfunctional families, or an amalgam of all the above rather than on deliberate structures of inequality. The idea was to save the suffering, one soul (or household head) at a time.

[Exercising typical do-gooderism, my father decided to hire a white drunk, Leo, to do household carpentry. The intervention was charitable; the intentions laudable. But Leo would go proudly sober to lunch, then return just as heroically intoxicated (if he returned); yet still attempt to drive nails into wood. Well, nails got bent and wood got battered. I think that Bill Clarke experiment lasted about two weeks before the social worker decided that the alcoholic was more determined a drinker than he was a committed carpenter. My father's reformism had been altruistic, but unrealistic, given Leo's inability to cease hammering booze and thus stop screwing up nails.]

Jackie and her husband had dined with my parents at 2357 Maynard St. in 1970, and she remembered the occasion. Between 1970 and '78, she divorced her husband (who had come out as gay), converted from Catholicism to Communism, and took up teaching and later social work. A slender brunette with coruscating eyes, an ever-present cigarette, and a vocabulary that could combine "surplus value" and "a lot of fuckin shit" in one sentence, she'd first come to acknowledge oppression while a student at the Catholic University of America, witnessing the National Guard called out to quell riots in Washington, DC, all cherry blossoms, flames, and tear gas, in the wake of M. L. King's assassination in April 1968. Then a young housewife in Halifax, she found herself weeping, alone in her home, not because of post-partum depression, but because her personhood was being limited to the constricting roles of wife and mother. She started to study feminism, class struggle, anti-racism, and evolved a razor-sharp analysis of all social evils. Her intensity combined Joan of Arc's combativeness and Frida Kahlo's devotion.

In summer '78, Jackie infiltrated a meeting of the Nova Scotia Youth Multicultural Movement (NSYMM), the outgrowth of a summer job that SMU had granted me (likely at the urging of Rocky, who knew Dr. Bridglal "Bridge" Pachai, my boss, also a historian of Africa and African-Nova Scotia, and the IEC director). Jackie had intended to take over the meeting to promote Marxism, and had angered me by "communalizing" *my* plate of french fries, snatching several for herself while declaring them to be "public property." Though she was my elder by a decade, I also found her fetching: I liked the sight of her small fists pounding tables. However, it was hard to enjoy a beer with her, for she'd point out that we were consuming—metaphorically—the sweat of exploited workers.

(Thanks to my involvement with the NSYMM, I made it onto the radar of the federal Liberal Party—then in its fifth year [the expiry date] of its government. So, I jetted to Ottawa in October 1978 and attended a youth multiculturalism conference on Parliament Hill. I made my "parliamentary debut" in a speech in a Centre Block committee room. The following March of '79, a bunch of us black youth, participating in another conference, in Dartmouth, NS, encountered so much racism we stood against a back wall and began—spontaneously—to sing spirituals—in spirited protest of our marginalization, much to the chagrin of "ethnic" whites who couldn't understand how their behaviour and attitudes had disgruntled—disenchanted—us.)

My friendship with Jackie brought me into the orbit of members of "her" party—the Marxist-Leninist Organization of Canada (MLOC), which was Montréal-based, like most Halifax "Red" groups. Though I never joined any, I was a Fellow Traveller—literally—for I attended an MLOC convention in Montréal in May 1979, accompanying three other guys in a car-ride up and back, almost choking to death due to one dude's infernal puffing of a pungent, acrid, stinking cigar— likely a stench one must confront in Hell itself—throughout the trip. What a relief to sit beside a window and crank it down enough to gasp fresh air. Another benefit: I wrote, on the return, "love poem/ song regarding weymouth falls."

In June 1979, Rocky prompted me to join him in Toronto for a meeting of the National Black Coalition of Canada (NBCC), an organization that he'd helped to found in 1969. It was moribund, so this meeting was intended to pump fresh life into the organization, stricken by division between Caribbean-born and Canadian-born blacks, but also by squabbles over funding and allegations of fraud—or mismanagement. The meeting opened with speeches by the leading black political activists from across the country—from all political stripes. There was Lincoln Alexander, the newly minted Minister of Labour in the cabinet of the brand-new Tory prime minister, Joe Clark; there was Jean Alfred, a Parti Québécois Member of the National Assembly (who dumbfounded everyone by declaring, "I'm not interested in black liberation; I want independence for Québec"); there was Rosemary Brown, who'd almost defeated Ed Broadbent in her 1975 bid to lead the federal New Democratic Party; there was Rocky—who'd seek election to the Nova

Scotia legislature in 1980 (but lose); and there was Dr. Howard McCurdy, a city councillor from Windsor, Ontario who, following a fist-fight, emerged as vice-president of the NBCC. (Eight years later, Howard would became another mentor for me: 1987-91, I was his go-to, media-relations guy while he was a Member of Parliament, 1984-93.)

Whatever the excitements and lessons of such travels, as a black youth in a hyper-policed "ghetto," the precinct of slum landlords, black kids being streamed into might-as-well-drop-out courses, with rotten food on grocery store shelves (including *apartheid*-sanctions-busting tinned fruit from South Africa), the one explanation for these inter-locking oppressions was the idea of class struggle, with ruling-class racism pitting unionized white workers against unskilled black labour. However, like us all, I'd been propagandized to reject Communism out-of-hand. Truthfully, I'd never want to live in a society that would police my reading or determine what I could write or publish. I'm too much of a liberal to accept anyone's dictatorship. Yet, my study and experi-ences were leading me inexorably—guided also by Walt, Joan, Rocky, Jackie, and even unaffiliated Sylvia and Bev—to the conclusion that an authentic democracy must fiercely tax the wealthy and energetically redistribute income (*via* social spending*).

In late August '79, the night before I left Halifax for the University of Waterloo, Jackie dined with me in a Chinese restaurant and gave me a passel of books that I still own, including Mao's *Four Essays on Philosophy*. She was worried that university would corrupt me into seeking bourgeois success over supporting people's struggles. Luckily, Mao teaches, "What is correct invariably develops in the course of struggle with what is wrong. The true, the good and the beautiful always

---

* Those who believe that governments should never spend the people's money on people's needs should be permitted to take all of their capital—converted to gold if they like—and go and live on a deserted island to grow or catch their own food, weave and mend their own clothes, and do everything else they need to do—for themselves: No employees, no servants, no troops. Ultimately, their survival would depend upon their evolving a system of sharing duties and goods.

exist by contrast with the false, the evil and the ugly, and grow in struggle with the latter." One comes to know truth through struggle. Cf. Malcolm X.

xiii.

The radically uplifting possibilities afforded by education were emphasized, one spring eve of '79, when I encountered, Flora, a hood gal who'd shared several elementary classes with me. I'd lost touch with her when I changed schools in 1971, leaving Alexandra for Joe Howe School in grade six. For sure, I'd never forgotten my first day at Alexandra in spring 1966 because, sitting beside Flora, as a six-year-old, I'd said something disparaging that she'd resented, and mute and swift was her retaliation: she'd planted her long fingernails on my shorts-exposed lower thighs and scraped out ten ruddy gouges. (I didn't complain because, well, I knew that I deserved it, and my reward for whatever it was I'd said that upset her is this memory.) Now, thirteen years later, we were both nineteen, and she was tall, lithe, dark, entrancing, with her afro suppressed in a bandana.

One of us suggested that we talk-and-walk (have a rap-chat), and I led her from the North End (the "Got-a-gun" Street of Tony's Donair) to "Dixie"—the "near south"—i.e., Spring Garden Road (the tony shopping street). There Flora stopped me—shocked me—by saying she'd never been there before. *What?!!* Her revelation floored me, for, even if my brothers and our chums were resolutely proles, we'd never hesitated to ride our bikes everywhere or walk our feet off, perambulating thoroughly the narrow, oval peninsula (shaped like the head of a Tyrannosaurus rex) that is Halifax. Yet, here Flora was, a grown (young) woman, insisting that she'd never been out of, roughly, a seven-block-square portion of the North End of our compact, sea-cinched city. I couldn't understand how she could have permitted herself to be held hostage—to be contained—by some perimeter that must have ended at Citadel Hill, the Commons, the (Old) Bridge, and maybe Fort Needham.

To have all one's world limited to those few blocks—a horizon of beer bottles and diddle mags, of fish-n-chips and syringes, of cigarettes and handcuffs! I presumed to operationalize my neighbourhood nickname: "Perfessor." I felt driven to pass on my knowledge of Halifax and our black history, and so, I escorted her deeper into the shadowy, leafy, thickly dark, no-streetlamp-lit South End of mansions, to encourage in her what Sylvia and Joan had and Jackie had urged for me: to ponder and question.

We breathed together in that dark-green night like conspirators, like insurgents. Strolling through those naturally—star-lit—illuminated streets, Flora revealed to me also that she was a sex worker. Another stunning revelation. Here was proof that racism immobilizes us—in terms of income or status, while sexism encases us in stereotypes, exploitative relationships, and even imprisons us in households. I couldn't think of any response but the Marxism that I was learning from Jackie and the various Québec-based Communist cadres then-active in Halifax. However, none of that suited Flora—not really, and not myself either. What I thought most useful was that we just keep walking and talking, and we did, all over the South End—in its most tree-dense, dark-shadowed, grassy inlets, and landscaped outlets. And then we parted. Maybe with a chaste kiss.

I met Flora again, fourteen years later, when I was picking up my doctorate at Queen's University at Kingston-on-the-Lake. She'd quit Halifax and was now a dietitian—and an artist—in Kingston; that was in 1993. In 2003, she called me to let me know that she was now a social worker. She told me that our walk-and-talk that night, back in '79, had spurred her to further her education and even try her hand at art. Her story assures me that my mother's kindergarten insistence on Barb Clark's freedom of thought (creativity) and Maria Montessori's freedom of mobility (independence) constitute, in part, "pedagogy of the oppressed" (Paulo Freire). Likewise, Bill Clarke's insistence that we go everywhere we could go that was public property, that we walk and cycle and skate, that we assume self-starting locomotion (as he had in his motorcycling bachelorhood), that such was the *sine qua non* of personal liberty, was also what I'd sought to impart to Flora all those four-decades-plus ago.

xiv.

Never have I forgotten my roots, my origins, my Windsor Plains and North End beginnings. In 2005, an African-Canadian scholar descended upon my University of Toronto office to inform me that my scholarship is so much piffle, because it doesn't help "a brother walkin up and down Gottingen Street find a job." I leaned back in *my* chair, behind *my* desk, and let out a big belly laugh, not in his face, but defiantly in his direction. I confessed that he was right: excepting the now-and-then successful letter-of-reference, not one word I've ever written can likely find anyone a job. But I went further. I asserted that the point of my scholarship is to correct (or attack) *racist* scholarship, which demeans my people—the Africadians, the Afro-Métis. I agreed that my work could not much aid the job-hunting, Gottingen St.-wandering bro or sis.

Then, I related this anecdote: when I wrote my doctoral dissertation (in one month) and graduated from Queen's University, in October 1993, I had no job offers, no prospects. Even so, Haligonian North Enders decided to big-up my "achievement" as if I were an Olympic athlete. All round the North End, posters got stapled to lampposts, "Come and Meet Dr. George Elliott Clarke": I was the first Africadian to *earn*—yes!—a doctorate since theologian Peter Paris had taken his from the University of Chicago, by the later 1960s. However, Dr. Paris was from New Glasgow, NS; while I was from "the hood." So, though I still lacked a teaching post, I flew from Ottawa to Halifax, to be fêted, on a bitterly cold January Saturday night, at the North Branch Library (where my mom had taken me to get my first library card a quarter-century before), by a hundred-strong audience, including poets, dancers, and singers.

The reason? It wasn't only *my* doctorate: my success belonged equally to the community that raised and challenged and inspired me. Rocky Jones was there—and spoke; Sylvia Hamilton was there—and spoke. Jackie Barkley was there—and spoke. Others prayed and sang. I spoke; I recited poetry. It was an Apollonian moment. My Ph.D. was being celebrated by my community, and never have they ceased to call me "Dr. Clarke," even when I say, "it's Georgie."

love & poetry

Before thinking of attempting poetry, I first tried song-writing: I couldn't sing and couldn't read music and didn't play any instruments, but still wanted to be close to song. So, I turned to penning plausible lyrics instead. Maybe the reason why I picked up a set of pencil-thin, coloured markers, on Dominion Day, 1975, at age fifteen, to begin to write lyrics, was because I could still see my father, hunched over a table, painting some scene. Maybe I was attracted to trying to accompany music because of my knowledge of the career of Great-Aunt Portia. When I graduated from using coloured markers to employing a fountain pen, it was one of Bill Clarke's (which I still own). Likewise, his *Roget's Thesaurus* came into my possession just as I began to explore the vivid properties of synonyms and antonyms.

I happened upon song-writing as my chosen "art" due to my father's adoration of Elton John and Cat Stevens, but also my mother's tutelage in letters, her own mania for surrounding me with books, and—righteously—the awarding to me of that initial library card as an eight-year-old. Furthermore, while I gleaned much from dedicated study of the lyrics of Bernie Taupin (John's lyricist), Stevens, Leonard Cohen, Joni Mitchell, and Lennon & McCartney in those tyro song-writing efforts, I also must acknowledge many basement spins of

Bruce Springsteen's *Born to Run* (1975) LP, cranked at full teen-must-upset-mom volume. This antic also demanded concomitant poring over of Springsteen's urban, gritty, unrepentantly Rock-n-Roll, anthemic lyrics bout mean streets, mean ladies, mean lads, vrooming chrome, and gloomily flesh-enclosed blades. I loved his portraiture of ghetto brawls and lurid poolhalls. To me, he could've been singin bout—writin bout—good ole "Got-a-gun" Street and us "boyz in da hood." Springsteen's booming vocals—all brio and black-leather bravado—were music to my ears, yes, but his words were liquor—oiling my echoing lungs as I ventriloquized his urban angst . . .

My choice to try to become a self-conscious songwriter that July 1, 1975—and to begin with scribblers and coloured markers—was the result of those childhood parameters that were so beautifully wide, though Bill was so narrow-minded in disciplining our behaviour and Gerry was penny-pinched into subservience. Yet, as I began to use my bed as desk, to imagine four different "song" scenarios per day, I was replaying both my father's assembly-line approach to painting and my mother's interest in art as a means to stimulate intellectual inquiry.

When I knelt on the floor beside my bed in that lousy Hunter Street abode (somehow colonized by feisty bedbugs just to spice up its dilapidated misery) that July day, and began to scribble out four "songs" (a practice I would continue daily for four years), I had the angels of family history for guidance and the demons of racist intolerance to confront—although I was only vaguely aware of "race," generally, until entering Queen Elizabeth High in September 1975. After all, high school is where the separations of class and race and ethnicity and language intensify because there is the promise—or threat—of coupling and family formation, and many parents sweat to (pre-)select the sort of person they would like their son or daughter to wed.

At this juncture, I was becoming more sophisticated in my songwriting. Through reading books on the subject, I learned that I should really be a poet, and I moved up from Taupin and Springsteen to Dylan, whose outsider persona, cruel singing voice, and bizarro world-view

appealed mightily to me. Like countless other "Bobcats"—Dylan fans—
I cottoned on to Dylan Thomas because of the similarities in their
names, and that drew me into symbolist, surrealist, modernist, Beat,
Black Mountain, Anglo-Canuck, and Black Arts poetry. (These connec-
tions were furthered by my impassioned scrutiny of the anthology
Grandfather Rock [1972], whose editor, David Morse, sets side by side,
for instance, a poem by Wilfred Owen and a pop lyric by Leonard
Cohen, or a poem by Amy Lowell and a lyric by Judy Collins, and so on.)

I was, among my peers, perverse, to be "digging" Dylan and dissing
disco. But I was also reading Atwood alongside Blake, Cohen alongside
Dante, Eliot alongside Ferlinghetti, Ginsberg alongside Hayden . . .
Leafing *The Flowers of Evil* took me to *Leaves of Grass*; *American Negro
Poetry* complemented *The Jewish Poets of Spain*. Just as my parents'
musical and literary tastes were a callaloo, a melange, a stew, half-
curry, half-pepper, or half-sugar, half-salt, so were my own tastes a mix
of disparate icons and idols. But my base was Dylan.

Many of the poetry books—paperbacks—that I relished, Halifax's
Red Herring Co-op Bookstore vended. Verily, I cleaned that academy
of social activism out of their New Directions Pound, Baudelaire,
Rimbaud; their Penguin Books Verlaine, Marcuse, Marx and Engels;
their Third World Press Gwendolyn Brooks, Carolyn M. Rodgers, and
Dudley Randall. The store location was downtown, on Barrington
Street—steps from the city hall, steps from the provincial legislature,
steps from the navy brass and the suit-and-tie honchos, steps from the
swishy yachters. But everything I bought and read was about my life
in and around Gottingen Street (German in name, but black in soul)—
and the site of the dispossessed of Africville and sailors cut adrift and
the laid-off on pogey—and the Salvation Army holy rollers. I mean, the
poems revealed we were underclass; the poems exposed our over-
seers. I'd clop up the wooden staircase to Red Herring, always with an
expectation that I would learn more, know more, enjoy words more,
and become more enlightened. I'd clop back down the steps holding
a treasury of intellectual and artistic weapons. How beautiful: to have

Trotsky's writing on "the Negro Question" and Tia Maria in my glass; to admire Huey P. Newton holding a rifle and Leonard Cohen holding forth, crooning "Suzanne." Pound was purchased and Shange got sold: I was the master of none and the thrall of all.

In fall 1976, I homed in on Pound's translation of Rihaku (or Li Po), and his—as Pound titled it—"The River-Merchant's Wife: A Letter." That poem shouted at me as if it was Huddie Ledbetter (Leadbelly) his-damn-self, cryin Mississippi blues outta T'Ang Dynasty China. "Mississippi (Long March) Goddam"—Nina Simone—indeed! How prescient it was of my loneliness and yearning—a millennium-plus before my birth! Damn! I signed as "Johnson Clarke" the fly-leaf of that 1966 Louis Dudek-assembled, unsurpassed anthology of Brit, Canuckistan, and Yank poets (that I'd plucked out of Alexandra School discard trash), namely, *Poetry of Our Time.*

ii.

As grade eleven commenced, I came slowly to know that my locker was near Una's. We shared at least one class: Honours English, and I found myself won by her laughter, somehow far more forthcoming than was her smile, while her eyes were dark stars. She was white, a sombre-haired brunette, a combo that recollects my mother, maybe subconsciously, but I began to pay her some attention. Never glamorous, her look was preppy—a white blouse under a sweater— and the predominant colour was a grave brown, a style signifying the dowdy. For one thing, her feet were oh-so-sensible, clad in Clarks Wallabee wedge-toed shoes: a man's shoe, but suiting Una's no-nonsense, stolid-but-not-plodding, one-step-forward sensibil- ity. But her laughter was her glitz, her spangles, blitzing the air and one's ears. It denied the ordinary and suggested the extraordinary. Meeting at our lockers or in class, we began to chat, to exchange quips and art: her drawings, my poems. I sensed a mutual liking that was promising . . .

While I was acting in David Renton's 1976 Xmas play, *Puss in Boots* (starring Walt Borden), Una materialized—with family or friends, and she may have appeared twice, and she gifted me a self-made Xmas card containing a tipped-in drawing she'd done, picturing me as one of T. S. Eliot's "Practical Cats." Then, drawn to her dark brown eyes, I did hear—or feel—my heart thumping away, and the sound was amplified when, walking her toward her home, a light snow freckled and speckled the top of her hatless hair. I felt that I could like—maybe love—her because of her devotion to art (shades of Bill) and her superficial resemblance to Gerry. Then too, in conversation, her face was wide open with mirth, with laughter that came geysering up and rollicking out, while her eyes lanced the air with light, disputing the dullness of her clothes and disrupting her aura of being well-policed. I was the cause of such thrilling amusement, I knew, and then when her lips opened to let out her glee, they became shivering, wet apple parings, but soft, promisingly appetizing to kiss.

On the second and last eve that she watched me act, Una seemed inordinately quiet, extra muted, and alarmingly shy. Back again toward her home, we trekked the gloomy, dismal, Gothic South End. I was warm in my camel-hair coat, but shivering within because I knew that I'd ask her now to kiss, to let us be gal and pal. She suspected—knew—my interest, and our stroll was muffled by a steady snowfall, as we inched inexorably toward her tony abode. I found courage—to tell her my feelings—to expose that young, still-half-boyish heart; and then, about a block from her house; under a streetlamp, in the deep South End, near a bridge that I'd crossed with Bill when he taught me about death in relation to JFK's passing, Una whispered, whimpered, that she'd been afraid that I'd ask for that kiss. Her eyes loosed tears as snow sifted into her hair: No. We couldn't kiss; I was black; her father was adamant. I felt confused—and sucker-punched.

I realized then that all those stories about working hard, studying, staying out of trouble, being polite and courteous—all those lessons that Bill Clarke had drilled into my brothers and me—were worthless:

we could be fine, upstanding, young men, excelling in athletics, excelling in art, excelling in invention, and we would still be poor, dumb, criminal niggers in the eyes of the rich, white world. How naïve I'd been to think that I was any different from other black and brown people (especially Indigenous), so marginalized, so beleaguered, so downpressed, so harassed, so over-policed and undervalued. How could I have not recognized that, since Columbus got lost and booted ashore in the Americas, the white attitude toward black and brown people is, primarily, we exist to be their servants, entertainers, and enablers? After our usefulness is exhausted, or after our goods are looted, our duty is to disappear, without fuss. If we complain or resist, we meet insult, assault, jail, and/or execution. I could admire Einstein all I liked; I could quote Eliot all I liked; I could go to church and vote for Tories. But any white person could still reject me—as a lover, friend, colleague—peremptorily—based on a skin-deep-level of analysis and dismissal.

(Yet, that dismissal is based on more than hair or skin or the shapes of noses or lips; it's an attempt to disown the history of exploitation and oppression; to pretend that it's only a matter of people "failing" to understand each other; or that it's only a question of "likes" and "dislikes." The fact of slavery and of colonial exploitation is covered up by a pretense of legality—of constitutional euphemisms—that pretense that everyone is equal, when in truth, black and brown people are forced into subsidiary and abject positions that only a few, now-and-then, may escape, but only to end up isolated from suffering brethren and sistren.)

My heart was thudding like a sledgehammer. Snowflakes melted on Una's teary eyelids. Our single kiss—in the mansioned and demi-castled South End, snowflakes swirling round—was cinnamon—salty-sweet. There was a red light flashing overhead—for a four-way stop—where I kissed her—where we kissed, sighing, she. And then she was gone—her Wallabee-shod feet ferrying her home to her hollow mansion.

My reaction was distraught—all distressed pulse and discombobulated heart. Instead of being a cavalier poet, I was a black man carrying a cancerous DNA. Maybe I wasn't so upset over Una's rejection? True: the romance of it infused my teen-poet-self with inspirational distress. (Yet, in my turmoil, I'd smashed a school bathroom mirror, cutting a hand, using the blood to draft Una an unsent poem. In that mirror, I viewed a splintered, Byronic figure.)

Shortly, I left Una poems at her locker; she'd retrieve them and cry. We took different dates to our February prom night—a Friday—cheekby-jowl to Valentine's Day. Yet, I didn't struggle for Una. I didn't contest her father's nullification. I didn't love her; or not enough.

iii.

But I was sixteen "going on seventeen," and despite my *Sturm und Drang* moodiness, self-lacerating blues over Una, I began to walk-ntalk with Molly, a green-eyed blonde (a *live* ringer for the jazz-phrased, wispy-voiced singer Rickie Lee Jones), part-Acadian, who had been assigned a *fausse* Irish cognomen and surname. (Her Anglo-Irish name was meant to pass muster on the school roll-call; her post-colonial name was meant to disguise her Francophone heritage, to preserve her from Anglo-Protestant derogation . . .) Molly also studied Honours English, and was, like Una, an artist. Pallid-complected and blue-denim-apparel'd, Molly partook of my class position too. Una alighted in school from a gold Cadillac (though her dad was rumoured to purloin toilet paper from a supply room, for his salary was not— alas—mansion-quality), but Molly stepped from a bus.

Una's art was fine-tooled, precise in figure and line and form, and agreeable in colour. In the art shows, she brooked high praise and took first prize. She was destined—clearly—for a high-paid post as a commercial artist; she'd deliver deftly whatever a client would ask. In contrast, Molly's pens and brushes were fountains; just flowing lines, playing off whatever mood controlled her eyes and unscrolled her hand across a sheet or canvas. Una's works were stellar, but as soulless as blueprints; Molly's were gritty, explosive images, coarse as Tijuana bibles, for her impulse was realism, anti-painterly, anti-picturesque. She condemned such "art" as "chintzy," just *Kitsch*. Una was—perhaps—a South End trophy for this North End kid. If her walk was a shuffle, with her aspect often eyeing the ground, her house was a mansion and she could ski ritzy slopes at Xmas or jet back from March Break with a Miami Beach tan. But Molly worked part-time in a bookstore and a burger joint. Her vacations would be provincial bus trips, no landings in some temporary Shangri-La. Her tans arose only from summer sun-bathing.

(In later decades, Molly was a jewellery maker, a journalist, a gardener, a puppeteer, and a chef. What became of Una, I can't say. But Molly was always the true *artiste*.)

I never met Molly's dad. Divorced, he lived a ways away; so he was remote to her life. A Francophone Catholic, he'd been a soldier in Her Majesty's quite Anglo and pure Protestant and right prejudiced Canadian Forces. He gambled that his children would be best off if they could pass as Anglo, whether or not they remained Catholics. Soon, Molly reported that he was unhappy about our "going together," but she was making her decisions, not he.

According to Molly, her mom—an Anglo native of Northern Ontario brush—had split from her hubby as soon as she'd found his tinkling trophy of a belly-dancer hip scarf that he'd brought back from Egypt after a stint there as a Canadian (Suez Canal) peacekeeper. The hip scarf was a G-string, and Molly's mom required no further proof of infidelity. In this way, too, Molly and I identified a defining experience: parents split due to adultery.

Due to her patrilineal ethnicity, Molly showed keen facility in French, a subject that I was still puzzling through in grade eleven, when we became friends. I was reading intensely the French symbolist poets—Rimbaud, Baudelaire, Verlaine, Apollinaire—as prefaces to surrealism. So, *oui*, I eyed our class's premier French speaker. But Molly was also devoted to art—painting and drawing—and my canvassing of reproductions of works by Picasso, Monet, Modigliani, Dali, Gauguin, Hopper, Warhol, and the painter Rousseau (who Molly also admired— alongside Van Gogh, El Greco, and Colville), urged me to ogle her canvases and sketches. Unconventional in dress—being a belated Hippy (like *moi*)—modelling painter's pants, baggy sweaters, eye-watering sheer blouses, plus sandals or boots—Molly seemed a glad non-conformist—like me—to our Honours English, Honours History, and French classes. An army brat, crypto-Catholic, and a West Ender, neither tweedy nor tartaned, nor *Vogue*-sex kittenish, she was also a loner.

Inadvertently erotic (to my teen gaze) in a moody—*muse de l'existentialisme*—manner, Molly's gait was a loping slouch, conveying a jaunty, exhilarating (I felt) twist in her hips. Her gestures were jerky, unsure, and when her hands flew up as she spoke, with her fingers outspread, fluttering, it was like half of her was avian and the other half feline. We both indulged—were allied by—our sense of estrange-ment from our privileged peers.

But Molly was also pissed off by the South Enders's rejection of her art as being too "unprofessional" (unorthodox), while Una's was the cat's meow. Her aesthetic was challenging, but Una's was Establishment.

My juvenile poetry attracted disparagement too. My grade twelve English teacher, Dr. Fox, alleged I had a "construction worker's attitude to writing poetry": he loathed my tendency to force words and phrases together; my blue-collar brawn swatting aside airy-fairy inspiration . . . or maybe I was applying Bill Clarke's damn-it-all-to-Hell-and-just jam-shit-together collage technique? Maybe my work shadows my father's arty craft, or—best—crafty art. It's the Black North Atlantic *Aesthetic*— to "nigger-rig" (Scotian slang for *engineer* [v.]) functional *Beauty* outta nothin. Our stained glass is blood-stained glass; our jazz is garbage-can-lids pummelled *Götterdämmerung*-style with sticks; or it's two spoons beaten against a thigh. Moreover, just as my poetics were shaped—warped—by reading Dame Atwood and Mr. X back to back, so were they twisted—contorted—by juxtaposing George Clinton *and* George Grant.)*

Bringing Molly to meet my parents was telling. My father's white wife, Pammy, loved Neil Diamond's "Girl, You'll Be a Woman Soon," and I played it—that song full of trepidation and lust—for Molly when she dropped by my father's, where I was—again—briefly in summer '77. My dad was cordial; but Pammy cottoned to Molly: they were two blondes with black men, despite the generational difference. We saw Nettie at a grocery store, and she smiled sweetly and asked me to bring Molly over. I was flabbergasted: I was her grandson, but she'd *never* invited me to visit her home— just to visit! Now, because I had a white girlfriend, I was welcome.

I did not take up Nettie's invitation. I didn't feel that I needed to bring Molly to my grandma's home to be deemed a respectable relative. I was still an outsider to that family—just as my father believed he himself was. Nor did I understand, then, that *whiteness* seemed to mean, for Nettie, accession to bourgeois status and power. (This is often the temptation of members of an underclass: to think that the standards of "superiors" are somehow untainted by the prejudices and power-plays that foster their positions.)

For her part, Gerry was kind to Molly, though she preferred that I date black girls. Still, she found ways to let Molly and I be alone together in her home, and we made cheerful use of the chesterfield before I'd have to giddily—gleefully—walk my gal home, happy with my soggy sweat; happy with her hugs and sloppy kisses; happy in rain or starlight. (Often intimacies had to be outdoors; I wasn't skilled enough to lie my way into a motel. Nor could either of us drive. Gerry

---

* Still, it took me a long time to accept my "voice," to blast out poems without waitin for white folks to grant their "okey-dokey." Happily, later critics opined that my verses exude "vigorous plainness" (*The* John Fraser) or "vernacular formalism" (Kevin McNeilly) or "maximalism" (M. Travis Lane) or "coarse beauty" (Marco Katz Montiel) or "unapologetic . . . polyphony and hybridity" (Jon Paul Fiorentino) or "majestic euphony" (Terrance Hayes); or they are "Compendious and baroque" (Fiona Sampson) or "Poundian melopoeia at its finest" (Marjorie Perloff). *Et cetera. . . .*

bought me a black Pontiac Beaumont 1968 model, but I had to let her return it to the Africadian dealer. I just wasn't ready to learn to drive.*)

My Aunt Joan was cool toward Molly. Then again, Molly'd gone to retrieve condoms and other birth-control items (and info) from a clinic where my aunt worked. Given our youth, Molly's mama coaxed her (us) to avoid producing a "brown papoose."

That same year, 1977, Molly told me about Brigitte Leduc's *The Bastard* (*La bâtarde*), which I didn't read then. Partly out of curiosity—and remembering Molly's fervent recommendation, I read it in September 1994, and was hooked. The autobiographical account of a homely, father-less, wistful French girl, wanting desperately to be loved, reminded me of Molly's fretting over her looks (lovely as they were), and her popularity (unquestioned among our artsy fringe). Still, I, too, felt I could identify with Leduc's loneliness, her grasping for ego satisfactions, her search for love, affection, sex, companionship plus orgasm.

The Bastard is also deep purple in synesthesiac detail, so that its prose melts (or curdles) into poetry. Leduc's every heartbeat seems to be breast-beating, a tom-tom, no tinny thrumming. Her autobio can't be passively read; rather, one throbs in its clawing clasp. You want to hold her, to tell her she's okay, that her big nose is kissable, and that Schiaparelli mini-skirts and Mary Quant boots only magnify figure. (Hey! Bro & sis Canucks, to understand our Nobel Laureate Alice Munro, ya better take Leduc as her preface and mentor.)

Molly pushed at me a library of recommendations, while I played us tapes of Bruce Springsteen ("New York City Serenade"), Yvonne Elliman ("Hello Stranger"), and Jefferson Starship ("Miracles"—the long version with the naughty reference to cunnilingus). En route to our coupledom, I penned a long poem (a full scribbler) on Gary Gilmore's execution by firing squad in Utah on January 17, 1977, a nice start to Jimmy Carter's disappointing presidency.

---

* Tarnation! In 1968, only 708 Beaumont SD hardtops were created for the Canadian market, making the auto both relatively rare and highly collectible.

Molly's older bro fashioned us a sauce of ketchup and Coca-Cola so that we could chow down on Meteghan (NS) mussels. We went to beaches and drank red wine and ate pie. She danced in moonlight, on those beaches, her hair looking like fire under the full moon. She wore green shawls in the cool spring, that also made her yellow hair look incendiary. She jigged atop fortress ruins; she fed a red apple to a black horse, her own hair such a brilliant contrast to its sable mane. We lunched in a ladies' dress shop that also boasted a soda fountain. We rode the bus to Three Mile Plains, or to Meteghan. We kissed in fields. We visited with seniors in residences overlooking graveyards. We practiced speaking French, but I was better at the kissing. We ate rapure pie and lobster and drank Manischewitz Concord wine. All her cool, all her changeable self, all was the soul of April (and I still treasure those 30 days, yearn for them all year, every year, because our love began in that holy month). I read Willy Blake but Molly talked up Mikey Ondaatje's *Coming Through Slaughter*. She made me a T-shirt celebrating my summer job with the Halifax Housing Authority (HHA), my one macho activity that summer of '77: hanging out with my greaser boss, Cookie, and helping the gang pick up garbage, maggots flying through the air, before we'd crack open beer and admire our work-shed's wallpaper, just *Hustler* centrefolds— so nasty and gritty—stapled to the pine-plank wall. (Just as my mom— and Aunt Joan—had arranged my summer job in '76, working with my Uncle Rex, Gerry had found out that the HHA was hiring summer workers, and got me to sign up for the gig.)

So, there we were, Molly and me, two proles in love, that spring, then summer, April to August, then harvest to Halloween. But I was insecure. Wasn't I too nerdy to be fetching? I had a library card instead of a tinted-window car. I second-guessed our love, thinking that a revolutionary romance had to be black-black. I saw Molly—idiotically— as being white, even though she was an excellent "mate"—match—for me because she was, like me, a Hippy ten-years-late, a flower-power daughter of the Age of Aquarius. But my identity was still shaky.

When she busted up with me—way too soon—that autumn of 1977, my solace was Dylan & Derek & The Dominos. Period. A lot of cater-wauling into the ether.

Sung by Dylan himself with all the original dread and anger with which he wrote em, any saccharine content in his tunes just drains away, and the acidic content swamps, searing through the eardrums and surging into the pulse of blood—just like the poison that Claudius pours into the "porches" of King Hamlet's ears. Too soon, miserable, out-of-sorts, abandoned, I'd go down into the basement of my Aunt Joan's home (I dubbed it "Big Grey" in homage to the Band's Big Pink), plug in turntable and speakers, and let loose, wailing my loss, bemoaning my rotten lot, with antennae-attuned cockroaches scattering whenever I turned on a light.

iv.

After my Molly breakup, I dated Deandra, a young black woman. Though I still loved Molly, Deandra was—problematically—in love with me. We hearkened to the same Africadian culture plus the same complexion. She was lusciously sweet, plushly perfumed, but her interests failed to interest me. Yet Deandra was a songstress—with merited local acclaim: her voice dominated every gathering where she'd sing, and she headlined every black community invite or poster. (Black people—Africadians included—feel collectively empowered to critique entertainers, boxers, and preachers; and so, for the community to assess Deandra as *excellent* meant that she was stellar.) I admired her—but admiration can't pass for erotic passion.

I was as unfeeling toward her as Molly seemed to be toward me. My mom and my Aunt Joan pushed me toward Deandra, this hood darlin. But our conversations were limited by both her halting laughter and the chewing gum she enjoyed as opposed to the wine that I wanted.

Because neighbourhood folks saw us dating, some presumed that I was Deandra's guy. But I really wasn't, and I resented their yoking together of we two opposites. She was peppermint, and I was caramel, and the twain did not suit. Then again, anyone can love anyone—for any reason; but, for no reason at all, the tendered love need not be reciprocated. Then, too, I didn't want to repeat what I perceived to have been Bill Clarke's error: to conform to convention rather than be outlandish. (And yet, in my two marriages, I chose wives who desired to be middle-class, conventional, much to my—and our—later, awful discord.) Deandra seemed cloying and smothering, just too much sugar. Molly represented challenge and excitement.

V.

To explain my pain respecting Molly's defection, I began to interrogate—for the first time—studies of *Race* and *Sex*. Thus, I bought a copy of Frantz Fanon's *Black Skin, White Masks* (English translation, 1967): Fanon's advice to writer Jean Veneuse? Be a man (not a "Negro") and express his love for a woman (not a "Caucasian")!

Yep, that drastic autumn of a shattered heart precipitated my plunge into Black Studies. Simultaneously, my mother's migration to Cherry Brook to live with Hank meant that I had to return to Bill's roof, in December '77.

Now, I took a creative writing course, Monday nights, January-April 1978, for "Adult Education," presided over by Sylvia Gunnery, who decided that I had talent, and introduced me to her Dalhousie University English prof, Richard Raymond. As he read through my verses, that April '78, I sat beside his desk, leafing through the *Norton Anthology*, while the sun came pouring through his windows like Cohen's "Suzanne"-style honey. The Bible-paper-thin pages fluttered in my hand as I leafed canonized poems while awaiting Dick Raymond's response. Soon, he turned, peered at me, and harrumphed, "You are a poet: get used to these!" He pulled from his desk a *Dalhousie Review* rejection slip!

Through all my identikit role-modelling, a Malcolm X Maoist

one day and a Dylanesque dilettante the next, a Trudeauvian non-conformist at morn and a Baptist Marxist at eve, I was still uncertain who I was—as a black intellectual youth, still in love with a woman who was also an intellectual and an *artiste*, but who happened to be white. I was still wanting Molly; and, to know what our relationship should be—if it could be rebooted. I turned to a trove of surrealist, symbolist, Beat, and Black Arts poets. I put Robert Hayden in the same bookcase as Wang Wei; I laid Sylvia Plath down beside Elizabeth Barrett Browning; I guessed that Dante and Garcia Lorca made a fine couple. I placed Shakespeare (Bard of Avon and Windsor) beside Elizabeth Bishop (the ex-Nova Scotian) . . .

(In summer 1977, I'd first begun to craft my own version of Pound's *The Cantos*: an idea of apocalypse, drafted by assembling rambunctiously ill-fitting verse forms, cantankerous rhetoric, and scummy, slummy images; by summer 1980, I was reading *The Cantos*—with its scurrilous attacks on bankers—while in line-ups at Royal Bank of Canada branches.)

Again I took up Cleaver, leafed through X, pored over LeRoi Jones's incendiary 1964 play, *Dutchman*. Who could explain best my amatory mishaps, my fuck-ups?

vi.

Fresh out of high school, I quit my father's house, in September '78, and took up residence on Belle Aire Terrace, in a shoebox-room (at the head of a shotgun-hallway) at eye-level with the streetlamp outside. Here's where I began to formulate a voice that was my own, not beholden anymore only to those I'd revered. I traipsed in and out of Red Herring Books; I went to record stores where "something was happening" (Dylan): "integrated" disco was about to be dismissed by white Punk and black Rap. Rick Dees vs. Dire Straits vs. "Rapper's Delight." (Or the MLOC vs. ABBA?) I turned to jazz—Coltrane, Davis, Mingus: My elegant solution for all cultural contretemps.

Suddenly, I knew it possible, in a poem, to talk about autumn leaves strafing a street; to liken the moon to a chubby Goebbels; to hear windows—wind-shaken—sounding like tambourines; to compare a telephone to a black skull; to describe loins as the pubic trunk; to bemoan that Jesus figurines can be priced for clearance, from department-store shelves.

That autumn, writing as "Nahum Shaka," I now considered myself a poet—though I'd published nothing but a poem or two in the Queen Elizabeth High School annual anthology. However, pushed by Rocky and Joan, I was contemplating attending *some* university *somewhere*, to study English—to be a better poet. By December, having read what I'd read, including Baldwin's *Giovanni's Room* and Conrad Kent Rivers' "Four Sheets to the Wind and a One-Way Ticket to France," two Af-Am works presenting visions of Paris, I felt prepared to tackle a long poem on the subject of black artists who'd expatriated themselves to France.

Thus, after a day of reviewing the poetry that I favoured, I was game. On December 31, 1978, I took a bus from Halifax to Green Street, to Newport Station, to my maternal Nanny's house. It was New Year's Eve, but she lived alone with her grandson, Scoop, then fourteen or so, and she was appropriately uninterested in partying. She'd gone to bed by 11 p.m., when I began to write my poem while sitting up at her kitchen table, with the radio for company. "Watercolour for Negro Expatriates in France" took shape there, and took me two or three hours to write, from 11 p.m. of the old year to 2 a.m. of the new. How fitting that the home where I began my life on February 12, 1960, was also the place, almost nineteen years later, where I wrote the first poem that I knew that only a poet could write. I can't remember whether I had Tia Maria or Manischewitz Concord wine at my side. I'd've had Molly on my mind; I'd've remembered—and utilized—Walter Borden's analysis of *The Wiz* (1978)—the black version of *The Wizard of Oz* (1939), wherein he saw the Cowardly Lion, the Tin Man, and the

Scarecrow as types of black leaders, all perilously (if not treacherously) under-endowed in debilitating ways.

As my poem took shape, I was agog: Here was Richard Wright in Matisse-green parks; here was Josephine Baker on bebop phonographs; here were allusions to *Mary Poppins* (the movie) and Adam Strange (the comic-book superhero); here was Chagall's bowing Eiffel Tower; here was Paris's chain-smoking intelligentsia, all conjured by a North End Halifax kid who'd never yet been further east than Cape Breton Isle. I knew that, on January 1, 1979, I had written a poem that could be, should be, would be, published, and it was all mine—if an amalgam.

I entered it, along with some other poems, in the competition sponsored by the Writers' Federation of Nova Scotia. I "won" fourth place—Honourable Mention—and I'd like to think that "Watercolour" had shaken the judges. I remember dressing in black (and maybe another dashiki borrowed from Walt) and taking to the stage at the Neptune Theatre to receive my prize (a cheque for $25). It was winter, a Saturday night, and Gerry attended the ceremony. I had to rush from car to stage to car—to beat the freezing cold. (In 1981, I became, at twenty-one, the youngest person to ever win the Adult Poetry division of the NS competition. My mother attended that prize ceremony too, for which I showed up dressed all in white, with a beige scarf and beige "crayon" shoes. That evening, so spring/summer, warm, was again a Saturday.)

"Watercolour" got published eight months later, in *Caribe*, a black literary journal based in Winnipeg. But, unsatisfied by that publication, I mailed it to *The Fiddlehead*, whose editors rejected it, though lauding me as a "word-drunk poet." Finally, it got published—again—in *Scrivener*, in Montréal, in 1980; the editors were enthusiastic, ensuring that "Watercolour" was graced by De Chirico-like stick figures blowing horns and falling off a map of France in outline and in partial relief. Four decades later, that poem's still worthy.

Watercolour for Negro Expatriates in France

What are calendars to you?
And, indeed, what are atlases?
Time is cool jazz in Bretagne,
you, hidden in berets or eccentric scarves,
somewhere over the rainbow—
where you are tin-men requiring hearts,
lion-men demanding courage,
scarecrow-men needing minds all your own
after Du Bois made blackness respectable.
Geography is brown girls in Paris
in the spring by the restless Seine
flowing like blood in chic, African colonies;
Josephine Baker on your bebop phonographs
In the lonely, brave, old, rented rooms;
Gallic wine shocking you out of yourselves,
leaving you as abandoned
as obsolete locomotives whimpering Leadbelly blues
in lonesome Shantytown, U.S.A.

What are borders/frontiers to you?
In actual, seven-league sandals,
you ride Monet's shimmering waterlilies—
in your street-artist imaginations—
across the sky darkened,
here and there, by Nazi shadows,
Krupp thunderclouds,
and, in other places, by Americans
who remind you
that you are niggers
even if you have read Victor Hugo.

Night is winged Ethiopia in the distance,
rising on zeta beams of radio-free Europe,
bringing you in for touch-down at Orleans;
or it is strange, strychnine streetwalkers,
fleecing you for an authentic Negro poem
or rhythm and blues salutation.
This is your life—
lounging with Richard Wright in Matisse-green
parks, facing nightmares of contorted
lynchers every night. Every night.

    Scatalogical ragtime reggae haunts the caverns
of *le métro*. You pick up English-language
newspapers and *TIME* magazines,
learn that this one was arrested,
that one assassinated;
fear waking—like Gregor Samsa—
in the hands of a mob;
lust for a black Constance Chatterley,
not even knowing that
all Black people not residing in Africa
are kidnap victims.

    After all, how can you be an expatriate
of a country
that was never yours?

    Pastel paintings on Paris pavement,
wall-posters Beardsley-styled:
You pause and admire them all;
and France entrances you
with its kaleidoscope cafés,

chain-smoking intelligentsia,
absinthe and pernod poets. . . .
    Have you ever seen postcards
of Alabama or Auschwitz,
Mussolini or Mississippi?
    It is unsafe to wallow in Ulyssean dreams,
genetic theories, vignettes of Gertrude Stein,
Hemingway, other maudlin moderns,
while the godless globe
detonates its war-heart, loosing
goose-stepping geniuses
and dark, secret labs.

    Perhaps I suffer aphasia.
I know not how to talk to you.
I send you greetings of *l'Afrique*
and spirituals of catholic *Négritude.*
    Meanwhile, roses burst like red stars,
a flower explodes for a special sister.
You do not accept gravity in France
where everything floats on the premise
that the earth will rise to meet it
the next day;
where the Eiffel Tower bends over backwards
to insult the Statue of Liberty;
and a woman in the flesh of the moment
sprouts rainbow butterfly wings
and kisses a schizoid sculptor
lightly on his full ruby lips;
and an argument is dropped over cocoa
by manic mulatto musicians
who hear whispers of Eliot—

or Ellington—
in common prayers.

You have heard Ma Rainey, Bessie Smith.
You need no passports.
Your ticket is an all-night room
facing the ivory, voodoo moon,
full of Henri Rousseau lions and natives;
and your senses, inexplicably
homing in on gorgeous Ethiopia,
while Roman rumours of war
fly you home.

vii.

My involvement in assembling a Black Youth Organization of Nova Scotia (BYONS) compelled me and cadres to rent vans or cars and tour and get billeted in several dozen rural Black Scotian communities, and identify delegates to come to Halifax.

To explore the Annapolis Valley down to the District of Clare (where Molly and I had gone)—and enjoy all those vistas (the mud flats of the Avon River, the look-off at Blomidon, Paradise, the dykes and marshes twixt Bridgetown and Annapolis Royal, the Annapolis River tidal power plant, the long railway bridge crossing Bear River, the "Little Switzerland" aspect of Bear River, the vistas of white-coated churches plus black horses and green pastures, and other oases), the home-cooked meals (all those sweet meats, dainty pastries, tidbits, pancakes, fishcakes, johnnycakes, brown beans and black coffee, dark rum and white rum), and then glimpsing, ogling, eyeing, gazing hypnotized upon the dark and lovely, the tan and pretty, the cinnamon and sweet, the ebony and beautiful, luscious, precious, jolly, outspoken, Africadian gals— *young women*—hurrah—was mind-expanding, consciousness-raising, and scintillating. Finally, Molly began to recede in my heart as I encountered many young black—ideal—women.

In late October 1978, as the Jonestown massacre was unfolding in Guyana's jungle, I journeyed to Weymouth Falls, Nova Scotia, with Central Planning Committee (CPC) member Enus Crawford. It was his hometown—a black village founded by African-American Loyalists who'd ended up there in 1783. 'Twas a frigid eve, with a dot of white moon: your breath'd come out your mouth and hang in front of you like a minor Milky Way.

After having tea with Enus's grandmom, I retired to bed—a mountain of quilts; the scent of wood-smoke from the downstairs heater, wafting up, uplifted me: that aroma, the moon burning through the window, the ice-cold outside kept at bay by fireplace and quilt and tea. Weymouth Falls captivated me. (A year before, Enus had mystified me by declaring, "I'm not from Weymouth! That's a *white* town. I'm from Weymouth Falls!" I'd never heard an Africadian village so rhapsodized before; thus, I'd needed to see the place for myself.) The next morning, we called on Enus's ex-girlfriend and her siblings. After making our entrance into the warmth of that home, among the beauty of those sisters, I was entranced by Sassafras, whose skin was cinnamon peppered with freckles; whose voice was Country-n-Western husky; whose black hair was usually curled; whose obsidian eyes were glancing—chopping *et* charming.

(Sassafras dubbed herself "a bourgeois peasant" because she valued literacy, but shared a home with fish-plant, mink-farm, and lumbermill workers. Her approval of letters was rare, in rural Africadia. So, to meet a countryish "sister" like Sassafras, who was in favour of poetry and cinema and song-writing, intrigued me endlessly.)

Weymouth Falls—just the hilly look of the place—situated along the banks of the Sissiboo River—with its back-country life, reminded me so much of what I'd experienced as a boy and teen in Three Mile Plains. Yep, too many guys were drunks; too many moms were lonesome; jobs were intermittent. But parties sparked up with a two-four of beer, fried smelts, hash, bread and butter and brown beans, whenever a tune caught fire. Banjos, mandolins, guitars, fiddles, seemed to materialize instantly whenever a bottle was opened, and soon voices were wailing about Jesus' love and/or bedevilled love gone so bejesusly wrong.

Sassafras and I exchanged letters through the rest of 1978 and into 1979. Hers were always cordial, while mine hinted at wanting more. But I was shy—still. Each time we met, I'd feel awkward: she was so reserved, so laconic. Finally, in May 1979, I stood before her door, fragrant wild rose bushes flanking, and got out sumpin bout likin her. Did we kiss? If we did, furtive it was. (That very afternoon, her older brother had squared his fist in my face—teasingly, seriously—warning me, "Don't try nothin with my sister!")

It was late by the time I'd gathered the nerve to speak to her—too late to catch the bus from Weymouth back to Digby (where I was staying), a distance of 21 miles. Despite entreaties to stay the night, I was too much into my Maoist "Long March" mode of thought to accept. I set out—round 8 p.m.—to try to walk from Weymouth Falls to Digby.

The sky was overturned—churned white—by stars. They were everywhere—a solid, startling, sparkling mass that somehow salved my heart while my legs exercised a Bill Clarke-patented stride. I think I'd made it as far as Gilbert's Cove before a passerby returning from a Liberal Party shindig decided to try to win one more vote for the thirty-first federal election, only a couple of days away, by stopping for me and driving me on to Digby.

viii.

That spring unto summer of 1979, I wooed Sassafras by post—and other darlings of the Annapolis Valley (by stealth). Surprisingly, though, a different *bella* had her eye on me: my next love projected an *Ebony*-mag, *Jet*-mag, and *Soul Train* sex appeal that I could not resist. Yeah, I dreamt that she and I'd have spectacular adventures—maybe spark a veritable revolution!

Savannah had crossed my radar at a couple of CPC conferences in the winter, and she had told me, in front of my mom (so eager to see me date a black woman), that she was liking my skinny self in my tight black satin shirt and tight black polyester pants.

On a July Valley eve, Savannah was a whirligig of cigarette smoke, swirling blue-jean skirt, brown feet slapping sandals onto dusty floor, and sable eyes brimming lightning. Both fixated on me. Following my speech, she invited all us Fellow Travellers in-the-cause to her home, where we savoured blueberries and cream. Turned out that her dad was the town handyman and her mom a nurse: second cousins who'd married at eighteen. Their several daughters were stunning beauties; their son was awesomely handsome. Pops, who liked a pipe and a beer, had built his comfy home himself, and he was a maestro of country guitar.

Come 10 p.m., it was time for us—four CPC members—to boot back down the highway to Halifax. Just before we left, Savannah pressed a paper into my hand and asked me not to read it until I was home.

I honoured her request, and that was smart, for the note invited a new relationship. About half a page long, it confessed that Savannah'd been wanting to tell me—since the winter—that she was sweet on me. Well, I'd never thought that a bony shy-guy like me could ever have had a chance with a woman like her—who jocks would steamroll over other jocks to date. How could I—a non-dancer, bookish—land a skirt-twirlin, ABBA-dancin-queen, hot-child-in-the-city? (My pet name for her? "Babe.") To use 70s slang, she was fine-as-wine, a truly Jimi-Hendrix-style foxy lady. And her letter swore that she was *mine*. Part of my heart still belonged to Molly, but I was excited to contemplate this ultra-beautiful, super-sexy young black woman, despite my affection, also, for Sassafras. (Little did I know that I was repeating Bill Clarke's motorcycle-cyclical amours, a truth his 1959 *Diary* unfolded some three decades later.)

Two agonizing weeks crept by before I met Savannah again. From an Acadian Lines bus to Halifax, she descended—goddess—in a black-velvet pantsuit, black pumps, a beautiful afro, and a doll-like face with a playground-slide-shaped nose. I got a taxi, and she came with me.

Sassafras showed up the next morning, for what was to be the final CPC, Halifax conference, and was visibly sad that I'd settled on Savannah. She studied the two of us holding hands, and her face went blank. Later, she wrote me that she'd never deemed Savannah "a good girl," i.e., she was known to flirt and had no qualms about trying out different dudes. I did regret disappointing Sassafras, who projected honest, sweet, natch'al innocence; and I felt even more sorry that any choice to elect one person over another, in love or coupling, could cause rage and grief. Molly's defection had hurt me, just as my inability to love Deandra had anguished her. Now, here I was kissing Savannah, not Sassafras; but rueing any inadvertent heartbreak. Why is *Romance* so difficult? (Perhaps I could now understand my parents a tad better than I had.)

That summer of '79, disco ruled still, but was about to be sucker-punched by Punk and coco-butted by Rap. Donna Summer was heapin praise on the bad, bad girls the same way that Woody Guthrie used to praise the working-class. And I was completely into this "thing" with Savannah. Sultry mahogany was she—with onyx eyes, a nicely tossed fro at times pressed into whip-snapping, straight hair. She rocked that tight-fitting, black-velvet pant-suit; but she also slinked into a curve-hugging white-flowers-against-a-brown-background dress. She was a chain-smoker; but between puffs, Tia Maria was her poison—and mine too. Her step led back to Jean Toomer's *Cane*—dusky-sweet hickory-smoke, bergamot dashing the air.

Savannah's back-story was horrid, and, unfairly, it tainted her reputation (as Sassafras's reaction suggested). In her evil, vile—though bucolic—Gaspereau Valley town, Savannah had been lured into an auto dealership, on her fourteenth birthday, and raped repeatedly in a back room. Schemed up by a tag-team of lemon hucksters and redneck truckers, they thus showed a black girl-woman her worth—in their pinched, constricted, sexist and racist skulls.

(Savannah didn't call the cops. An investigation would have pitted her word versus that of the town's capitalist patriarchs, all worshippers in spanking white-washed churches—i.e., sepulchres. Better, she mused, to ignore the attack and own her life and future as best she could.)

Now, five years beyond that horrendous, criminal violation, she and I were lovers. The knowledge of that white-thug onslaught upon her brown-girl's self was awful to me to possess—as it was painful for her to confide. But her story confirmed our joint oppression as black/brown people, and I began to deem—dream—us as, not just lovers, but allies—in the style of Martin and Coretta King, Eldridge and Kathleen Cleaver, and Malcolm X and Betty Shabazz.

That political marriage of sorts didn't happen, but we did become literary companions. Savannah was eager to write poetry. She typed up a few poems that got published in a Black Canadian mag. Once, too, strolling through downtown Halifax, my right hand—curled around her shoulder—ended in a typewriter, bouncing gently on her bosom as we stepped. (I think I had a briefcase in my left hand). It was a drooling night—salty mist and rain—as we schlepped toward the ferry terminal to catch the Dartmouth boat.

(One of Rocky's Dalhousie U students, Kishie was another Africadian belle to whom I was amiable—and secretly hankering for—before commencing coupledom with Savannah. Afro-Métis, her copper tint and straight black hair reminded me of my Aunt Joan, as did her laugh, which either issued literally as a "tee-hee" or as titters that jittered her whole frame or as all-out, ear-walloping guffaws. In the winter of '79, we'd often write surrealist verses together—a line by her, then a line by me; but the exercise was also a kind of surreptitious dating though she had a black boyfriend whose nickname was "Jap"—due to his "Oriental" physiognomy. Our poetry duets didn't spark romance, but only feisty, truth-tellin Kishie could have turned me on my belly and paddled my bottom to say "Happy [nineteenth] Birthday," and then dish up Tia Maria and chocolate cake. When she met Savannah and saw that we were lovers, did Kishie betray a *soupçon* of jealousy by ask-ing, "How did a little girl like you get such big breasts?"*)

While Savannah and I were typing up poems together, we were relishing Angela Jackson's sultry poetry (1974's *Voo Doo/Love Magic*), while hearing Anita Ward cooing "Ring My Bell." I was with Savannah every chance that I had, in between fashioning peanut butter and banana sandwiches and filling tumblers with endless pours of milk at a Cobequid Valley summer camp where I was a counsellor for six weeks (last two weeks of July, and most of August).

The book Savannah loved that summer was Mark Twain's *The Adventures of Huckleberry Finn* (1884), a child-friendly version come to me as a Xmas '68 gift. The cover painting depicts straw-hatted Huck on a raft with torn-trousered Jim, who's just lucked out, hook-ing a fish, his mouth o'd in aw-shucks surprise, while Huck's face equals Santa Claus jollity. The image was as boyishly appealing as that of Little Black Sambo turning a troupe of tigers into hot butter streaming—steaming—down a mountain of "temptilatin" pancakes. Savannah had an aptitude for Twain's Mississippi/Missouri lingo and showed gumption in ploughing through it. Maybe because she was a "Valley Gal" (Gaspereau), Savannah was able to glean the text's achievement, while I was too citified to cotton to the banjo-licks and gheetar-twangs of the heroes' tobacco-spittin-interrupted locutions. Well, she ensconced herself on our palette, smoked *Export A*s, turned Twain's sheets, before or after we slid twixt sheets, her silver (poly-ester) panties shimmering—irradiating—our wan basement digs.

I was musing on Savannah and Three Mile Plains when I wrote another poem six years later, in Amsterdam, that I knew was significant:

---

* Kishie presided over my reunification with Sassafras the following year during a singular night that afforded me an unforgettable luxury: to sleep with four women! But the circumstances were economical, not erotic: Kishie had not paid a heating bill, and so when Sassafras and two of her sisters came to visit Kishie, who I was also visiting, in December 1980, the five of us—fully clothed—to stay warm—had to burrow deep under heaped quilts and snuggle up together..

an amalgam of Rita Dove and Alden Nowlan, Angela Jackson and A. Y. Jackson (of the Group of Seven), Jean Toomer and John Milton (blank verse blackened), Thomas Wolfe and Howlin' Wolf, and mandolins and locomotives (a lot of mixed motives) . . . A combo of decasyllabic beauty and *delirium tremens* pain . . .

Look Homeward, Exile

I can still see that soil crimsoned by butchered
Hog and imbrued with rye, lye, and homely
Spirituals everybody must know,
Still dream of folks who broke or cracked like shale:
Pushkin, who twisted his hands in boxing,
Marrocco, who ran girls like dogs and got stabbed,
Lavinia, her teeth decayed to black stumps,
Her lovemaking still in demand, spitting
Black phlegm, her pension after twenty towns,
And Toof, suckled on anger that no Baptist
Church could contain, who let wrinkled Eely
Seed her moist womb when she was just thirteen.
    And the tyrant sun that reared from barbed-wire
Spewed flame that charred the idiot crops
To Depression, and hurt my granddaddy
To bottle after bottle of sweet death,
His dreams beaten to one tremendous pulp,
Until his heart seized, choked; his love gave out.
    But Beauty survived, secreted
In freight trains snorting in their pens, in babes
Whose faces were coal-black mirrors, in strange
Strummers who plucked Ghanaian banjos, hummed
Blind blues—precise, rich needlepoint,
In sermons scorched with sulphur and brimstone,

And in my love's dark, Orient skin that smelled
Like orange peels and tasted like rum, good God!
    I remember my Creator in the old ways:
I sit in taverns and stare at my fists;
I knead earth into bread, spell water into wine.
Still, nothing warms my wintry exile—neither
Prayers nor fine love, neither votes nor hard drink:
For nothing heals those saints felled in green beds,
Whose loves are smashed by just one word or glance
Or pain—a screw jammed in thick, straining wood.

ix.

Late August, '79: time to head to the University of Waterloo (just as
Rocky had commanded); time to leave Savannah—and Gerry—beloved
mom—at the Halifax train station where Bill Clarke worked (but not
that day); time to take the Ocean Limited (James Brown's "Night Train")
up to Montréal, then on to Toronto; call up Dionne Brand and crash on
her apartment floor; and then train on west to Kitchener. My suitcase,
so to speak, was quixotic—a navy-blue duffle bag. It was as if I were
going to sea as opposed to school, but yet I managed to stuff that navy-
blue canvas cylinder—five feet long, one foot wide—with all that I felt I
needed—at least for the fall. (I would soon learn that cotton did not suit
a Grand Valley winter.) I continued to use that duffle bag—impractical
as it was—until at least 1982. It made sense that it was a sailor's suitcase, even though my "Ocean" conveyance was a train.

    Savannah and I pledged to wait for each other. I was gonna switch
to Acadia University to be closer to her; we picked out names for the
children we'd have ("David" and "Cassandra"); she'd stay in touch—
she'd write and call. I told Bill Clarke about my marriage plans, and he
barked, "You're nuts! Don't ever ask me for anything!"

    He needn't have worried: those tearful commitments twixt
Savannah and me hardly lasted ninety days. Yet, it's hard to ask any

nineteen-year-old to agree that three and a half months ain't a lifetime. Savannah could not say no to dances—and dates—and I found it impossible to persuade her—by pen or by phone (pricey long-distance) to wait til we could see each other again. My pleading and pestering only pleased Ma Bell, as the minutes ticked by—quick as a time-bomb count-down—and the expense of "sweet-nothings" skyrocketed.

Many a night I'd hike from my residence—EE in Village 2—up to Lake Columbia and squint my eyes until I could convince myself I was gazing upon the Atlantic. I was lonesome for Savannah, homesick for Nova Scotia. The result? I read every book about Nova Scotia and Black Nova Scotia that was available in the ten-storey white cube of the Dana Porter Arts Library.

The rich strangeness of that reading brought home (pun intended) to me the truth that Africadia is a Bible of incidents, love affairs, tragedies, comic episodes, travelogues, sermons, tall tales, folk songs, hymns, spirituals, jokes, recipes, mysteries, and trivia that is, in a word, epic—one awaiting its poet. It was startling to leaf a sociological study and read about Maynard Street (maybe even—disguised—2357 Maynard), or Creighton, or Gerrish, or Agricola; or to see Africville dissected by two sociologists; or to ponder *The Condition of the Negroes of Halifax City*; or to read, in *The History of Kings County, Nova Scotia*, the footnote that the grandfather of Thomas Chandler Haliburton, English Canada's greatest author of the nineteenth century, landed in Hantsport with household goods, including two Negro slaves. These books and pamphlets affirmed that I didn't have to look to Black America or Europe or Africa to nourish my Muse; that there was plenitude in Three Mile Plains and North End Halifax. I could put Leon Trotsky in conversation with William Andrew White; I could put Portia White in conversation with Duke Ellington (who used to visit his companion's family in Africville). My reading said that I came from a people and a place worth chronicling.

X.

My lifelines that autumn of '79 were cards and letters and a box of candy, potato chips, and homemade pound cake from Nanny Johnson, cards and calls from my mom, a few letters from Savannah (soon trickled to a stop), a loan of $75 (repaid) from my Uncle Sock, a gift of $100 from Bill (who made it concrete-clear that it was a one-off). My sole other solace was to trek to the library—the music library—to borrow headphones and rotate Joni Mitchell's *Hejira* chased by John Coltrane's *Afro Blue Impressions.*

December '79 was purely bleak, just unadulterated depression. Nanny Johnson passed away—the same day, incidentally—December 13—that sixteenth prime minister Joe Clark saw his government collapse (all seemed gloom everywhere). My shuddering, shivering, penurious train trip from Kitchener-Waterloo back to Halifax was desolation interspersed with despair. I'd loved my mother's mother; I'd loved Savannah enough to contemplate marriage; now Nanny Johnson was gone, and Savannah was saying "goodbye." I was bereft and betrayed; downbeat, downfallen, down-at-the-heel and down-at-the-mouth.

As quick as I could bustle off the train, I bussed to the Gaspereau Valley to reunite with Savannah; to recuperate—*maybe*—our summertime love. (I wore a white karate jacket, blue jeans, scarves, black army boots: yes, I froze.) Savannah was cordial to me as I tried to court her again; but that attitude was the same as being cold—as frigid as the December air.

I got up the next splintering, freezing, blue-black dawn, exited, strode to the diner/bus stop (not as iconic as what Marilyn Monroe made famous in the 1956 film), salty tears freezing as they icicled from my eyes, had blueberry pie and coffee, and then boarded the eastbound Acadian Lines bus. My mother's Xmas gift to me was T. S. Eliot's *The Waste Land.* Sure-as-shit, Eliot's "Burial of the Dead" nixed Peaches-n-Herb's R-n-B hit "Reunited."

At nanny's funeral, in Windsor, NS, I was a pallbearer. I surprised my Uncle Sock in rendering that service. To his morality, I was appearing "unseemly quick" in wanting to bury my grandmother. But I saw the duty as an act of devotion. Still, I wept so much that the chilly earth seemed like mud to my boots. It was a snowy, miserable, foggy, hostile afternoon. I wept for passed-away Nanny—for lost Savannah—and for very dismal me.

Well, my nurturing maternal grandmother followed my cold, distant, paternal grandmother in passing away that same year (1979): December for her; August for Nettie.

(Savannah had accompanied me to the hospital where Nettie lay dying that August. It was a poignant moment partly because Savannah and I were distantly related—fourth cousins—on my father's side. Yet so fractured had been my birth family by my parent's divorce that I received *no* invitation to attend Nettie's funeral at Cornwallis Street United Baptist Church. I did go, but ended up beside a local, Red Tory politico, flush-faced and jowly, who had once asked Savannah, behind my back, "How young were you when you started having sex?" So, it was a weird affair, that hot day, unexpected tears scalding my face, to look down from the church balcony at Bill, sitting in the front pew, near his mother's casket, and to feel so irreparably alienated from the Whites. Then again, we were the shadowy Clarkes—thanks to Nettie's shotgun-marriage to the long-vanished, Jamaican Clarke. We were matrilineal Whites, yes, but "black-sheep" Whites . . . still, in my affair with Savannah, I'd liked—a lot—that my gal was also related remotely to Portia's clan.)

It was only after Nettie had passed that I began to learn details about my father's childhood and the absence of my paternal grandfather, Norris Clarke, whom I'd never thought about as a boy. Because my mother's parents were loving and giving enough, and because Nettie had been so stern and standoffish (except for expressing interest in my white girlfriend), I didn't yearn for a connection to my father's father. I wasn't curious about who he was; then again, Bill Clarke had never mentioned him—nor did anyone else.

So, it was Savannah's breakup with me, and my attempt to understand it, that brought me to stand, the next spring, on the threshold of Gerry's bedroom and seek the facts about the Whites, about myself, and to learn how I transformed from a Johnson to a Clarke.

coming into intelligence

I was twenty, in spring 1980, when my mother, one night, as I stood silhouetted in the doorway of her bedroom, filled in the critical details about my great-grandfather, William Andrew White (WAW), and also helped me to better understand my father's frequent harshness toward us all. I wished that I had heard this intelligence sooner, but maybe I was only just mature enough now to be able to interpret it satisfactorily . . . For one thing, Nettie had passed on, and, as I would come to appreciate later, once Africadian elders passed, their secrets were almost instantly divulged.

My father's father—Norris Clarke—was a sailor, from Jamaica (according to the marriage certificate in my possession), whose legal bond to my paternal grandmother (Nettie) allowed his surname to anchor all of her children, including those she'd borne to other men. How shocked I was to learn that my dignified, reserved, and prideful patrilineal grandma had been, in her youth, a born-late flapper, who had fallen in love with—or simply made love with—some of the men—soldiers—her father—Rev. Capt. Dr. William Andrew White, B.A., D.Div.—had chaplained during the Great War. Indeed, as the first Black officer (non-commissioned) in the British armed forces, Cap White was the minister assigned to the segregated, No. 2 Construction

Battalion—"Canada's Black Battalion," whose men felled trees, built railway ties, and quarried stone, for ten-hour days, six days a week, all to construct infrastructure to support the western front allies and the Canadian Forestry Corps.

Though Nettie's children had various fathers, she'd wed Mr. Clarke—and he was also the biological sire of Bill and another sibling. In any event, whatever his feelings for his Africadian wife and his child and her children, Norris proved truer to the sea than to his spouse. He sailed away by World War II, never to be seen or heard from again, except for a 1941 postcard (now in my possession), written while he was aboard a troop ship—or a Merchant Marine vessel. My father grew up knowing only that his dad was a West Indian sailor who vanished during the Anti-Fascist War. Did Sailor Clarke return to the West Indies to start a new family? Did he perish in the Battle of the Atlantic? No matter, Bill grew up fatherless.

(Decades later, my father told me that other relatives had informed him that Cap White had arranged Nettie's marriage to Norris—in exchange for $200—a significant sum during the Depression—some land, and the assurance that, should he vamoose, no one would complain or go searching.* He would be free of any further obligations.)

As my mother relayed this basic info, the mysteries regarding my father and his ancestry began to come into focus. Gerry even deciphered the seemingly distant relations between Bill and his mom. She claimed Bill was, as a teen, so upset that Nettie had become the alleged mistress of BAH, O.B.E., head of the Halifax Coloured Citizens Improvement League (a cognomen that sounds like a colourized version of "Better Business Bureau"), that her puritanical son decided—unilaterally—to

---

* According to Nancy Oliver's research in the self-published, *He Was a Friend of Mine: Memories of David Oliver by Family and Friends* (2006, 2009), Canadian Pacific Railway (CPR) porters were welcome to bunk at WAW's Halifax home. Given that anti-Black immigration policies contradictorily extended West Indian railway employees eventual Canadian citizenship, it is possible that Nettie met "Mr. Clarke" as a railway porter—but one who also served as a sailor aboard one of the CPR "Lady Ships," cruising Canuck tourists to posh, CPR hotels in Bermuda and the Bahamas.

change the locks to his mother's premises. Bill wagered that, because his wages were paying some household bills, he held a veto over his mom's love life. A draconian attitude, yet pure Bill. I doubt that Nettie would have long stood his holier-than-thou stance, but his attempt to police her morals may have been the cause of what seemed to me—as a boy—to be their strained relations and her frosty attitude to her grandchildren (my brothers and me).*

Even more perturbingly Freudian, BAH managed the railways' black workers; thus, pillow talk likely bagged Bill his job, one that yielded the wherewithal to keep a bachelor pad, buy a motorcycle, and cut a rakish figure in his early twenties. That Bill's boss was also his mama's "friend" must have rankled my father—not that he could afford—literally—to say so. (In his 1959 *Diary*, Bill records a poignant episode: that autumn, while BAH was driving Bill and his gospel-quartet brethren to a church to perform for pay, the car incurred a flat just shy of the destination. Nixing the offers of his passengers to assist the repair, BAH shooed them off to sing while he remained outdoors, in a drenching, chilling tempest, to replace the wheel.)

Whatever the truth of his relationship with Nettie, Bill became the executor of her estate, following her 1979 demise, and so he held on to her private documents, such as her test scores from the provincial examination that she wrote in grade twelve. (Note that she achieved grade twelve—graduated from high school, unlike Bill.) She was accomplished in languages—English, French, German, Latin, Algebra (yes, a *lingua franca*)—and in music.

However, despite her intellect, Nettie had, by becoming an unwed mother—several times over—shamed her birth family, the Whites. Her chosen life scandalized her father and some siblings, for their task was to achieve, to accomplish, to triumph—so as to prove the worthiness of

---

* I imagine that this contretemps led Nettie to ask or tell Bill to quit her home by age eighteen (once he had completed his sole year of high school, i.e. grade ten). A quarter-century later, Bill echoed the same command (or demand) to me.

African peoples by excelling at whatever they chose to do in "the white man's world." Weren't the Whites descended from ex-Virginia (King and Queen County) slaves who'd been given their own land to farm following the US Civil War, and whose sons'd become schooled clergy, both in Canada and the United States? Thus, Nettie's indulgences, and her resulting children, must have nettled her esteemed pastor-father. For one thing, he was also, simultaneously, the Maximum Leader of all African-Canadians (particularly Christians), given his heading up of what was Canada's largest Negro population (until the 1960s); furthermore, his lieutenants during the Great War became—post-war—*the* local Coloured leaders cross the Dominion.

To be a wayward daughter of a forward-looking black preacher was bad enough, but Nettie's "selfish" behaviour could have also tainted the success of her sister, the diva, Portia. (Portia had also borne a child out of wedlock; yet, putting her career first, she gifted her infant to a childless Africadian couple. Says family lore, Portia told the pair, callously, "If you want him, you can have him," then handed over her son. Prized for her talent, Portia wasn't punished for having a "love-child," but Nettie was punished for having hers.)

I believe my father nurtured this narrative: that he and his Clarke siblings would have been heirs to a fate better than poverty had glory not been thwarted by Nettie's *ex-cathedra* sexuality or her secular individualism. Thus, not only was it necessary that the "Clarke" brand be imposed on all *via* an arranged marriage, but Nettie and innocent babes were then housed in a barn, while she, despite her scholastic success, had to make a living as a laundress: she scoured the uniforms of the sailors and soldiers that Portia sang before.

Another family story says my father and one of his half-brothers were placed, due to destitution, in the Nova Scotia Home for Coloured Children—an orphanage that their grandfather, WAW, had helped—ironically—to found. This story, if true, was also kept from my brothers and me when we were young. (It was not revealed until the Two Thousands that the orphanage sponsored a culture of child rape, torture, abuse. I pray that Bill and his brother were never subjected to such violence or violations.)

Thus, on that springtime eve in 1980, as my mom related to me long-suppressed stories, I was thankful—no, elated—to have some insight into potential reasons for Bill's bitterness, his acerbic attitudes *vis-à-vis* ourselves, his sons, during our boyhoods. But I was grateful, too, to glimpse, finally, Nettie's rebellious young womanhood; to know that she had been spurned—metaphysically slagged as the stereotypical "black sheep"—for claiming the same sexual liberty as gents—and even as had her sister. She suffered socio-economically for her flapper orientation by being tacitly shamed, married by arrangement, and then installed in a barn. But her children were also hurt—due to the alleged stigma of having no father-in-the-home,* a borrowed—or purchased—surname, poverty, an intellectual mama slaving as a laundress, an illustrious aunt who dropped by, now and then, dispensing toys and furs in a la-de-da style. What a sure-fire formula for producing Bill as a man of vehement contradictions, i.e., as a plausible *artiste*!

Even so, as my mother's revelations about the *real* Nettie entered into my consciousness (and my conscience), I found myself marvelling at this renegade bluestocking, who, in the 1930s, had decided to love whom she wanted, to be *a free woman* (a radical phrase in *any* language), no matter what others (including her powerful father) had to say. How astonishing that my rule-breaking paternal granny, so headstrong in her youth, could become so austere and dour—remote, unsmiling, stoic—a blueblood, black Bluenose *patrician* (defiantly no matron).

Although Nettie and offspring suffered penury and imposed shame, she still raised, of her eight children, an air force captain, Vancouver's

---

* Although many psychologists and sociologists condemn the one-parent family, it's still true that, due to first, slavery, then, economic marginalization, many African-heritage families in the so-called New World had to evolve *effective* single-parent-headed households, plus communal arrangements for child-rearing. Too, the child born-out-of-wedlock is usually accepted in African-heritage households.

first black policeman, a school principal *cum* community college principal, and one labourer-intellectual and BMW-class(y) motorcyclist, i.e., Bill. And she did it her way—the hard way—but still *her* way. She made her life for herself—irregardless (that's the essential word) of what churchgoers thought.

How much of my own literary talent (however limited) descends from that once-naughty missy who knew four European languages? Her intelligence nurtured my father's, but maybe her DNA renders me also a non-conformist, a misfit, one drawn to outré subjects and outlier authors.

My mother's revelation of Nettie's hitherto unspoken history was wholly unexpected, entirely a surprise. And yet, it humanized her. Now I could recognize Nettie as the forerunner of my own once-secular Christianity, my own "Baptist Marxism."

(Yet, reticence about biographical truth was a hallmark of older Africadians. Thus, when an Africadian elder passed away in 1993, Bill called me in Ottawa to ask if I had seen So-and-So's *Globe and Mail*-issued obituary. I said yes. He revealed then: "He was your Uncle X's father." As soon as the secret was dashed, I saw instantly the likeness between my uncle and his father, although his sire had appeared the epitome of rectitude, and had never given any hint, over many Sundays at church, of ever being related to Nettie or a son—in any way.)

Great-Aunt Portia also became more humanized when I heard gossip about how she'd commissioned a friend to help loot a liquor store during Halifax's VE-Day riot (triggered when the city fathers decided to close the liquor stores—just when folks wanted to exult in the Allied victory in Europe). But vain proved the friend's efforts. Yes, he'd returned from his booze-hound mission to Portia's thirsty digs with a box clinking promisingly like glass. However, once opened, the box was found to contain a teetotaller-suitable set of china.

(In *My Grandmother's Days*, a nostalgic account of Africadian life in the 1930s, Viola Parsons recalls that when Miss Portia White boarded with Viola's grandmother, she claimed "the best bedroom in the house." Well, "to the manor born . . .")

ii.

So, while I entered my teens feeling that the Clarke/White lineage had little to teach me about being black, a black youth, a black male in a society fearful of, suspicious of, despising of, and rejecting of, anyone and everyone who showed my complexion and shared my gender, I became aware by the age of twenty that my lineage of achievement, of intellectual acumen and artistic genius—the White line—had striven mightily to attain their position. They were—had been—in short, always black, always symbolic of the possibility of triumph (not just claiming "equality," but demonstrating *superior* acumen) for folks of African heritage.

In my thirties, I discovered that WAW had preached in Toronto in 1922 on Race Consciousness. He was no Uncle Tom. A startling forebear, he was a statesman of the pulpit.

In his missionary activities with the African Baptist Association on behalf of the Maritime Baptist Convention, WAW was soon smitten, at age thirty-two, by a lovely fifteen-year-old, Izie Dora White, who, by happenstance, shared his surname. Despite the seventeen-year age difference—August intruding on April as it were—Izie was equally smitten, and the girl became a wife. Her nomenclature only changed in the honorific, transforming from "Miss" to "Mrs." The sixth girl born to James and Alice White of Mill Village, NS, in 1890, Izie's bloodlines represented a blend of Caucasian, Mi'kmaq, and African. For his part, WAW's genetic heritage—according to White Family research—was of West African Ghanaian and Tikai Cameroonian heritage. Says family lore, so strong was their love, Cap White addressed a letter almost daily to Izie from France.* They had thirteen children together, though only eight survived into adulthood.

---

* In his 2017 article on WAW's war diaries, Gordon L. Heath affirms that White wrote to his wife, Izie, "27 out of 30 days in November 1917, 24 of 31 days in January 2018, 25 out of 30 days in March 2018, and 28 of 31 days in August 1918." His only fallow period occurred in February 1918, when he was able to visit England on leave for a few weeks, and then his correspondence to Izie fell "abnormally low at 13 days out of 28" (Heath).

Talented in playing piano, organ, and autoharp, Izie passed along musical talent to her children, principally Helena, Lorne, Portia, Yvonne, and Nettie. States her biographer, Nancy Oliver-Mackenzie, Izie also had "a deep sense of social and personal justice" and her home became a "hub of the Black neighbourhood."* I will speculate that these attributes were picked up as well by her children, with Bill III becoming the composer and House of Commons candidate, Jack the Ontario labour leader, and Lorne the jubilee singer and school principal.

WAW set a chivalric example regarding social justice. He broke up a riot at Jura, France, between black and white soldiers, by riding boldly his horse between the contending sides. Upon his death in 1936, his *alma mater*, Acadia University, honoured him specifically for this action, wherein he risked all—limb, life, and reputation as an effective and active Christian, to persuade those tempted to violence and hatred to repair to pacifist fraternizing. His heroism is remarkable, for a race riot among the Canadian troops, even if it had resulted in neither injury nor property damage, would still have proven as so much claptrap the then-triumphant Allies' propaganda about the Great War as having been a contest between civilization and barbarism.

In his 2017 article on WAW's war diaries, Gordon L. Heath pictures the incident thus:

On 7 January 1919, a black Sergeant major sought to arrest an insubordinate white soldier. Other white soldiers were infuriated with what they deemed to be impertinent behaviour, and quickly descended on a group of black soldiers. A brawl ensued, with rocks thrown and knives used. Injuries were bruises and cuts, but no deaths. White troops also raided some huts of black soldiers, and smashed windows and rifled their kits.

---

* I quote from her unpublished manuscript, "Stand Up and Cheer: Give Them an 'A.'"

I imagine my great-grandfather moving purposefully, astride his horse and stiff-backboned, dividing the hostile ranks, each side caveman-armed with sticks and stones—and blades, hurling found objects that had to be stooped for and snatched up, and screeching vicious, vile epithets. How he would have had to shout above the febrile divisions, to call all back to their senses, while also being bodily aware of his visible vulnerability (any well-aimed rock could have felled him from his steed). He would also have been conscious of the weird irony as a chaplain—a tribune for Christ—but also as an officer, a prosecutor of the War, of attempting to treat between soldiers whose training was to inflict crippling mortality rates upon the Enemy.

My great-grandfather returned from the war the *de facto* leader of African Canadians. Soon, he'd reunified the African Baptist Association, helped to establish the orphanage for "Coloured children" (into which his own grandsons were likely immured pursuant to his death in 1936), and also set up his own weekly sermon radio-broadcast. His golden voice and silver tongue—remarkable charisma and brain-and-heart-and-lungs combo of righteous rhetoric—permitted WAW to reach upwards of one million listeners, from Charlottetown, Prince Edward Island to Boston, Massachusetts.

Certainly, WAW seems to have been a man who was never content with a success or two, but strove to pile them up, one after the other, to set a redoubtable example for his children, and to nominate the White Family as being among the primary Blacks of most of twentieth-century Canada. Still, for most of his adult life, my father felt a measure of disrespect directed his way from his White-family relatives, as recompense for the headstrong ways of his once-wayward mom.

iii.

When I was eighteen, Bill complained that one of his uncles—a son of WAW—had not invited him to a cousin's wedding. He believed the slight was due to his mother's "outsider" status. His response?

"Son, I want you to receive the Order of Canada!" Given my circumstances on that autumn Saturday in '78, the bidding was memorable because it was so preposterous. We were in his basement, clinking beers and listening to Bob Marley records—the profits of my joe-job.

I'd stopped by for a visit, and was living in a miniscule room in a rooming house at 2634 Belle Aire Terrace, near where my father had grown up—impoverished—some thirty to forty years before. When my Uncle Rex trucked me to my cramped, single room (#1), my worldly goods included a set of 45s in a painter's box, an LP collection, a single bookshelf of paperback poetry (primarily Penguin and New Directions) and books of Bob Dylan's collected lyrics and an early 1970s copy of *Tarantula*.

That bachelor roomette could hardly squeeze in a cat—or a rat— let alone an eighteen-year-old with a milk-crate squaring circular LPs and that painter's box squaring circular 45s. I had to stuff my paperbacks in the oven (shades of Bradbury's *Fahrenheit 451*) and on a desk-top bookcase that had to perch atop the fridge. My stereo occupied the tiny desk that I sat before on a bar stool—because it fit. My clothes bureau was half in, half out the open-door closet. A streetlamp voyeured into my one window. A black lady *de nuit* occupied the much larger room adjacent to mine on the second and top floor of the house. Down the hallway was a rheumy-eyed smoker and drinker, who always reeked awfully of tobacco and aftershave—a nauseating concoction—and who always left his cigarette ashes in the shared-bathroom's sink, offering a vicious spectacle and a depressing aroma.

Yes, my father's summons to me to be triumphant enough—at something—to earn recognition from the State—the Queen—was a bizarre idea. Being a more-or-less minimum-waged grocery clerk (duties: stock the shelves and bag the groceries: I was—deliberately— never taught to work the cash register), I don't think I could have taken my father's desire too seriously. Although Rocky and Joan were encouraging me to barge into the Ivory Tower, I was iffy about that avenue of potential ascension. Yet, I did take Bill's comment to heart.

Certainly, I'd always sought high marks in school to earn his regard; now, as a young man, maybe I knew unconsciously that there was still more to which I could aspire—to secure his admiration . . .

Sadly, my father was deceased when I entered the Order of Nova Scotia in 2006 and then the Order of Canada in 2008. However, he was living when I received the Governor-General's Award for Poetry in 2001. That moment must have gratified him, then a Haligonian taxi driver. Indeed, I later learned that, when my father motored down a neighbourhood street, black folks stepped off the sidewalk, holding up the front page of one of the two daily newspapers, each bearing my face and that of the radiant Adrienne Clarkson, the Governor-General, to laud my laurels as a community triumph *and* a vindication of our own—the North End Clarkes'—proximity to royalty.

iv.

In one remarkable public-service act, White served as the pastor-comforter to the last black hanged in Halifax, in January 1935—namely, Daniel Sampson, who had also served in the No. 2 Construction Battalion. This role also required some courage, for Sampson stood accused—and convicted—of having stabbed to death two white, Irish-Canadian boys—Edward and Bramwell Heffernan, brothers, aged but eight and ten—in the summer of '33 for having called him a nigger. Some white citizens were so outraged by Sampson's alleged crime that they swore he'd be lynched if he weren't speedily hanged; but Black Canadians doubted the feeble-minded man's presumed guilt.

It took two trials and two appeals, including a last-ditch appeal to the Supreme Court of Canada (which divided 5-4 on the question of whether proven racial bias on the part of Sampson's jurors should invalidate his conviction), before Sampson's hanging was permitted to proceed. Sampson perished just a few months before my father's birth in May.

I wonder about WAW's attitude and aspect in that moment, considering that he was helping on to the other world a mentally challenged war vet for whom there was compelling evidence of an orchestrated, Crown campaign to hang im high—in a judicial lynching. I wonder how he felt as he assisted Sampson up the regulation thirteen steps to the gallows platform; I wonder how he felt to be reciting Psalm 137 or maybe I Corinthians 13 or some other standard text of the African Baptist Church as he rendered Sampson his last worldly comfort. I wonder how it felt to maybe sing or hum the spiritual "Were You There When They Crucified My Lord?"—perhaps with Sampson chiming in, their voices fogging in the winter chill, the cold that must have penetrated the room.

And yet I'm sure that WAW would have understood that he wasn't Othello, doing the state "some service"; for he'd already done so, in France. Perhaps he saw his role on that January day as the plain nationalization of his local pastorate—i.e., that his presence incarnated the dissent of African Canada from what his people saw as an abuse of police power, as a misuse of civic authority. WAW stood beside Sampson on the gallows to represent the higher principle of *Justice*, even if it *seemed* to the jailers and the hangman that he was acquiescent to the execution.

When folks tell me today that "We love your voice" or "You speak well" or "You should be a musician," I'm reminded of the genealogical inheritance—"the family business"—the gifts of cadence and phrasing and rhythm and rhetoric, but also of study and dream, analysis and vision, of song and music, so operative to the Whites. And all these talents descend to me—to us—from a man born only nine years after the US Civil War freed his parents. (I am thus, on my father's side, only the fourth generation born *outside* of American slavery.) WAW brought a tradition of perseverance and industry to Nova Scotia and Canada, when he arrived as a young man outta Virginia at the very end of the Victorian Era.

WAW had been so front-and-centre as a war vet, as a social-justice advocate, as a radio preacher, as a national African-Canadian leader, that his receipt of an honorary doctorate from Acadia University in

May 1936 marked, once again, a first: he became the first African-Canadian to receive the distinguished degree, allowing him to add a third honorific to his name: "Dr.," and another suffix—"D.Div."

But he was to die that same year, at age sixty-two. The last proud moment in his life was his return to sweet-home Richmond, Virginia, to see, one last time, his American siblings and relatives. To go from Acadia's apple blossoms to Richmond's magnolias; to go from the Latin-dubbed province of Nova Scotia to the Latin-dubbed state of Virginia, where a Latin teacher had helped to propel him north, from the Old Dominion to the Dominion of Canada, in 1900.

When his funeral was held in Halifax, on September 12, 1936, the Cornwallis Street (African United) Baptist Church could not contain multitudes; the funeral cortege departing the church for the cemetery passed before thousands of mourners, black and white; prominent churchmen attended the service as did the King's representative, the Lieutenant-Governor of Nova Scotia. Five years later, stained-glass windows were installed in the street-facing wall of the church to perpetuate WAW's memory.

Nettie would have been twenty-two when her father passed away, but her son, Bill—named in part for her father—would have been only seventeen months old. Their feelings toward the father and the grandfather must have been conflicted. He set a stellar example as a man of God and as a proponent of the Social Gospel; he arranged a proper surname for his daughter and installed her in a barn. He was a great man—among the first Africadians to be recognized by the State—the Government of Nova Scotia and the Dominion of Canada—for his contributions to military service and public charity; but he deemed it okay for his grandchildren to grow up in a shelter for beasts.

By granting his daughter and her children a home (rent-free, I presume), WAW was doing what he could do to alleviate some of her needs, while also insisting that she care for the children that she had elected to chance to have. He wasn't a liberal father, but he was also not so atrocious as to disavow Nettie. Yes, WAW was more lenient toward Portia, but she was about to become an internationally acclaimed singer, not have to take in laundry to make ends meet.

Ultimately, Nettie transcended her circumstances: she was able to transfer from the white suds of scouring clothes to take up the black wires of telecommunications. Then, following a stint as a senior manager with the Halifax-based, federal civil service, she was appointed Commissioner of Oaths—and undertook the black ink of registering affidavits, declarations, and affirmations concerning any matter to come before a Nova Scotian court.

When Nettie passed away in August 1979, Cornwallis Street United Baptist Church was jam-packed for her funeral, with hundreds in attendance. I think they were there, partly, to honour her father and her sister, but they were also there to pay tribute to an extraordinary woman and the mother of notable children.

Being the executor for Nettie's estate, Bill Clarke came into possession of Nettie's memorabilia related to WAW and Portia, but also a set of books, quite striking for the daughter of an august minister to own. Titles included *The Prophet* (1923) by Kahlil Gibran and *The Alexandria Quartet* (1962) by Lawrence Durrell: a non-Christian in the first case and an amoral* author in the second. It was proof, again, of her non-conformist mind. She was from the Church, yes, but not of it, at least not philosophically.

There was a distance between the Whites and the Clarkes that sprang up in the 1930s, and which persisted at least into the 1980s, when White Family Reunions began to be held, on both sides of the border, in Nova Scotia and Virginia, in Ontario and in New Jersey. (Poignantly, the last time that I saw my father alive, he had come to Ottawa for the Reunion there in July 2005. As usual, I was ambivalent about attending, and had decided not to go. Then, at the last possible

---

* Durrell seems to have championed Gnosticism—a heresy—in his novels. In her diaries, Durrell's daughter, Sappho, indicates that her father sexually assaulted her.

moment for catching a timely flight from Toronto, a voice told me to throw together a suitcase and head to Ottawa. I obeyed; and then I was shocked—delighted—to walk into the Family Reunion supper at the National Arts Centre and find Bill Clarke present. I had no idea that he was in great pain from undiagnosed leukemia, and had made the long train trip to Ottawa in hopes, in part, of seeing me. I'm ashamed to note that, in accompanying him to his hotel, I walked fast—just as he had taught my brothers and I to do, and then I was surprised to turn and see him limping behind me, trying gamely to keep up.)

True: I learned more about WAW in school than I ever heard about him at home. True: I heard more at home about Portia White than I ever did hear about her father. Yet, in my mind, both were pillars of fires, glaring ardently. They are my ancestral versions of the Colossus of Rhodes (WAW) and the Aeolian Harp (Portia): practically mythical exemplars. Impossible to equal, and more marble—or sheer light itself—than flesh. But yet, still so fallible: to achieve worldly grandeur, secular glamour, and pay the price of sacrificing a portion of family feeling. Even so, their achievements were not solely individual. WAW's medals and trophies and degrees descended upon his children as spurs to accomplishment for their generation, and they did go on to achieve their own recognitions, receiving national and international acclaim. Yet, the individual and familial striving did also support communal uplift—and not just for black people. WAW's Great War leadership brought a corps of African-Canadian men to the fore, so they could return to their home communities in Halifax and Montréal, Saint John and Edmonton, Winnipeg and Windsor, Amber Valley and the Battlefords, Charlottetown and Vancouver, et cetera, and continue a pacific—but militant—struggle for *Justice* and *Equality*. Portia's career brought the Nova Scotian government to invest in classical music training for all its gifted citizens. Jack's trade unionism benefitted all workers; Bill III's democratic socialist leanings and spiritual ecumenicalism were intended also to help do away with prejudices of race and class, religion and creed. Nettie raised accomplished children, while

Lorne's folk-singing united anthems of anti-slavery and trade-union-ism, anti-war and democratic credos.

V.

On that spring evening in 1980, Gerry also said more about my own origins. She'd borne me in February 1960; but I was sickly. I landed in the Windsor hospital in April, and Gerry and her parents were respon-sibly fearful that I'd die (perhaps of pneumonia). At this point, Jean, my maternal grandmother, overruled Gerry, and called my father in Moncton, N.B. (where he had moved on January 1, 1960, to take up a new post with the railway), to tell him, "Come see your son before he's dead." Immediately, Bill Clarke came calling—on his motorcycle—all the way from Moncton to Windsor, visited me at Payzant Memorial Hospital, decided that I was his son; then wooed my mom. She accepted marriage; and, following a motorcycle-ride honeymoon in Prince Edward Island, they set up house together, in Halifax, in June 1960.

(Their wedding and honeymoon snaps display a radiant couple, sleek and chic, with all-engrossing, animated smiles. They seem happy and warm together, and, given my brothers' births, in February 1961 and June 1962, some degree of affection and romance held them fondly bonded in those first years of their matrimony.)

Reflecting on the family history, I could see that Bill Clarke was his mother's son, whether he liked the idea or not, whether he supported her "impropriety" or not. I mean, he was also a rebel, choosing to become a motorcyclist—a James Dean and Marlon Brando recreation, not quite the typical conveyance of a young Negro with enough extra cash to purchase a vehicle. After all, the machine could only be used in Nova Scotia—at best—six months of the year. It was a whimsical pur-chase. Then, he sought out an independent path as a commercial artist before putting away his paints and pencils and pastels and papers, because he could see no approved way to articulate himself in these conveyances of irrepressible vision.

Maybe that's why, when I went to meet him in early June 1983, to present him with a copy of my first book, *Saltwater Spirituals and Deeper Blues*, Bill reacted in the way that he did. I sat before his desk at the train station—and watched while he turned my book over and over in his hands, but said nothing. Nothing. I'm not sure how I extricated myself from that moment, or maybe he simply indicated that he had to get back to work. I left, but I always wondered about that encounter, about what he was feeling.

He would have just turned forty-eight (on May 20), and had likely been working for the railway for thirty years, since 1953, when he was eighteen, and his whole life was still ahead of him; when he could have—perhaps—gone to New York to paint (just as his 1959 *Diary* says that his Aunt Portia urged him to do). Instead, at twenty-five, he married Gerry, perhaps hoping that a family would give him rudder and compass, base and direction, for the next part of his life. Or did it become a trap, one thwarting his deepest desires?

We never discussed it because, shortly after, Bill left Halifax for Hamilton, ON, to take up a VIA Rail promotion. He was trying—at Pammy's urging—to wipe out all memory of his first family, my brothers and me. Maybe that's why Bill wouldn't say anything about my book: I was supposed to be "as good as dead" to him as he was moving into his Hamiltonian phase. For one thing, around the same time, I'd encountered Pammy and my half-sister (aged nine) at a Gottingen Street bus stop. Even while my half-sister said hi to me, Pammy—refusing to acknowledge me—was pulling the girl aboard the arrived bus. Clearly, there was an attempt—akin to Soviet propaganda—to airbrush the original Clarkes—wife and sons—out of existence.

Angered by his 1983 policy of trying to pretend that we had never existed, I didn't speak with—or see—Bill again for seven years—until 1990. Then a cordial relationship began that saw me visit with him and Pammy, my half-sister and her boys, when I'd visit Halifax from my work in Ottawa, my studies in Kingston, and my professorships in North Carolina, Montréal, and Toronto. Often, Bill—now a taxi driver—would run me to the airport or whisk me from there downtown to a hotel, and we'd enjoy terrific conversations about everything. Once his car broke down, and Pammy called me in Durham, N.C., to tell me that Bill was too proud to call me to ask for a loan to get his engine repaired. Naturally, I replied with a gift. After all, how many "free rides" had he afforded me? Then, whenever I received some glorious windfall of prize money, I'd tithe him a percentage.

These good relations lasted until 2000, when Gerry passed away. I invited him to her funeral, and he arrived with Pammy, which I deemed a *gauche* deed, acceptable only because she was his wife. So, I kept my counsel. However, after my beloved mom was laid to rest, Bill told me, "Now we can be a family again." Enraged that he blamed Gerry for our estrangement, I reduced contact again. I saw him occasionally 2000-2005, but still I bridled at his apparent disparagement of Gerry. Then, we encountered each other for the last time at the July 2005 White Family Reunion in Ottawa.

When he died the following month, I was—unexpectedly— devastated. It fell to me to go through his papers. I found the pix of my mom and him and his three boys, and I was thunderstruck. He had hidden away—from Pammy—the photographic evidence of his first family in a box black-marker-emblazoned, "RAILWAY." I also found a box that consisted of all my local newspaper book reviews, interviews, and articles, that he had kept assiduously, ripping them from the two Halifax dailies—not to mention all of my greeting cards and postcards to him. Most poignantly, he'd left to me his 1959 *Diary*, with the taped-on, notepad message, "For George, So He Will Understand." True: its pages unfolded to me a twenty-three-year-old and then twenty-four-year-old man, who was unsure of himself, unhappy with the railway, unsettled in his amours (though the motorcycle expanded opportunities for "comfort"—if ephemeral), but dreaming vaguely about a possible future as an artist. The young Bill was absolutely not the stern, confident—even, at times, spiteful— man who had been my father . . .

In 2007, following a poetry reading in Halifax, a mom and her adult daughter approached me to tell me that, when Bill had taxi'd them from the airport to their ritzy South End home, he'd mentioned that he had "a son who is a poet." The women confessed that, after he had left them at their door, they'd guffawed at his assertion—scoffing at the idea. To them, his comment was ridiculous. Now, they were standing before me, apologizing for their initial prejudice, and purchasing a book from me. Immediately afterward, I was compelled to write this poem:

Taxi

They were not wrong—blonde mother, blonde daughter—
To laugh. Their dark driver dazzled; he jested
Wantonly, was jauntily seductive.
Courteous, cordial, proper, politic,
He lavished wit impeccably impish,
Encyclopedia-posh, and polished—
With scholarly asides and rhymester's timing,
Prompting the ladies' yielding gaiety,
To be repaid, he could hope, *handsomely*,
With a healthy tip (that common homage).
     So when their courtly, coppery chauffeur
Claimed to have a poet-son, it seemed *cute*.
But his passengers were polite enough
To transmute their blithe doubt to nods and smiles,
To giggle privately, at homecoming,
At the audacity of their driver,
To expect *them* to credit *him*—a hack
Operator, despite his suave grammar
And stunning puns—with fathering a son
Who could credibly be crowned a *poet*.

He never knew their laughing disbelief,
Which was fair, casual, and jocular fun:
As far as they knew, men whose livelihoods
Are step-and-fetch-it stereotypes—black chaps
Delivering white ladies and luggage
Delicately to the appointed address—
Are not expected to sire any bard.
    I heard their apology for this apt
Assumption, almost tearful, but tactful,
As I taxi'd a book into their hands,
And spoke almost as graciously, graceful,
As my unparalleled father would have.

Coda

On the verge of falling in love with Molly, way back in February 1977, I accompanied my mom to Three Mile Plains, to Newport Station, to Green Street, and her mother's—my grandmother's. It was just a day-trip, but I fancied it. I skipped school that day. I preferred surely to be in Windsor Plains, my homeland, rather than in a classroom. The reason for our visit that day was mournful: while a party swirled merrily about him, Gerry's old boyfriend, So-and-So, had sat himself down in his Newport Station living room in an easy chair with a glass of beer and died, still holding onto his glass. No one'd noticed his demise until the party wound down. I think my mom wanted to revisit her childhood home to revisit some old, good memories.

Snow dusted everything; the cover wasn't deep anywhere. It was "transparent snow": the grass—brown/yellow—was still visible. I rambled about with an alder-wood cane fashioned by Dickie, the by-now quite old, iron-coloured man whom my grandmother cared for in exchange for a cut of his pension. He would've been indoors that day, even if Gerry and Jean (my grandma) had attended the funeral.

I roamed uphill, downhill, taking notes about the shared Mi'kmak/Cherokee (War of 1812-vintage) heritage of the demesne. My fingers were chilled, but still worked my pen. From maternal family info, I had a sense of our First Nations ancestry, which, I later learned, is often repressed in Africadian communities—a manifestation of anti-Indigenous racism. I wrote a poem, "i have now seen," about my Afro-Métis inheritance.

After rambling the Plains hillsides, scribbling out my poem, I went back to my Nanny's house and rummaged about a closet that held my Uncle Sock's (and likely my mom's) teachers' college books, including a copy of John Milton's *Paradise Lost* and a '60s novel set in San Francisco involving a Hippy chick who didn't mind "leaning back." The day was full of sensations—sunlit—as if the snow were birthing sunflowers.

How I loved those countryfolk who accepted who they were, who were all mixed racially/ethnically, and didn't give a damn about it; whose music dismissed the classical, favourin croonin and hollerin. I think of my Great-Uncle Charlie, who fiddled n guitar'd all up/down the Annapolis Valley. His once-wife, Mousy (birth-name Joyce), led her own Country-n-Western bands, all satin shirts and spangled this-n-that. Then there's their son—Sugar Plum Croxen—a genius of guitar—who's sired daughters in all ten provinces and one territory. Another of their sons—Larry—be a Reverend, uh-huh, with electric guitar blastin from the pulpit. I think of my cousin Kirk—a published poet and journalist and soldier. I think of Peenie and Beverley and Prim and Railway Man—sweet people—salt-o-the-earth. These be my people too; the folks for and about whom I also write and research.

Soon, Gerry and I shot back to Halifax, where I had a prom dance the next day. But before the prom, I went to a TV studio, and there, broadcast live—*via* Dartmouth Cablevision—in a brown, pin-stripe suit (my brother Bryant's)—my newborn poem, "i have now seen."*

---

* I typed up "i have now seen"—some thirty-nine years later—and offered it to *The Malahat Review* for a Special Issue on Indigenous writers. It got nixed. However, it was accepted—readily—for an exhibit of Indigenous and multicultural *objets* at Toronto's Aga Khan Museum in 2017—forty years after it was written. Super-sized, it was displayed upon a wall. Next, it got published.

i have now seen

nestled twixt warped ties of rusted train tracks,
snow, aged dingy, grey and black,
frosting loose, brown dirt and jumbled gravel,
while a stream hisses neath thin, dull ice,
and i look out over fields flecked with patches
of *grisaille* grass—
the tint of putty—
and wind, subdued, gasps
intimations of winter's seasonal assassinations . . .
under ledges of runaway clouds,
my love-hunting eyes view
stark outhouses the dirty snow frames
under a dustbowl sun.
the pothole-pocked, dirt road sprawls toward
the pine-serrated horizon,
where rough-edged hills,
lined with chicken-wire fences, sagging barns,
and derelict farms,
unfurl also.
i see rag-tag scarecrows murdered
by knifing winds, bleeding straw
in the snow-snuffed fields,
among broken wagon wheels,
the last monuments
to red-dust cowboys
who once twanged moon-June-silver-spoon tunes
to hay-ride madonnas
on rickety house steps
bordered by violently ruddy roses
and dead conches holding the ocean's roar.
this is the "now and then,"

"the future and the past":
the hollow corpse of a '57 Chevy
lays half-interred in a rambling drift,
half-smothered by the ivory quicksand.
suddenly, the shrieking banshee horn
of a rushing, steel juggernaut, boxcar hauler,
resounds and detonates across these hilly plains,
where fir trees, evergreen, point directly
to stars, visible or not,
that pinpoint where Aquarius strides
with his medicine water of galaxies gleaming,
pouring silver against indigo velvet . . .
An ancestral African seesaws his wooden rocker
in a clapboard cabin,
heated by an iron-black wood stove,
that percolates scents of cornbread and rabbit stew—
a still-life or *Home-Sweet-Home* vignette,
presenting a weeping, folk guitar
and white smoke lifting from a gnarled, mahogany pipe.
add a disordered woodpile, a dead orange tractor,
and evacuated dreams.
i have this old man's Zulu spear
(actually a Micmac cane),
and i perforate snowbanks
with the crooked, wooden point.
from now on, if i must cry,
let the tears signal *Joy*.

(Newport Station [Nova Scotia] 19 *février* mcmlxxvii)

ii.

On my bureau in my Toronto bedroom, there's a framed b&w pic, dated June '58. In it, my mom's mom, Jean Johnson, stands off to one side, dressed as if for church: she's wearing white gloves, white pumps, toting a white purse, but is standing, incongruously, on the edge of a field. Behind her, in a doorway of what could be a shack, is a dark-complected woman, looking out and slightly uphill at everyone front-and-centre in the shot: my Uncle Dave—in a lumberjack jacket, untucked open-collar shirt, dark pants, and work boots; my Uncle Sock in a sports jacket, dress pants, dress shoes, open-neck shirt, and extremely unkempt—bushy— hair (a cross between Little Richard and Don King); and my Aunt Joan, wearing a light-coloured cardigan buttoned over a flower-print, almost ankle-length dress, and suede-looking flats. Behind my aunt and uncles is a gleaming, dark-colour, late-model car, perhaps a Ford.

The snap—taken likely by my mom, somewhere in Three or Five Mile Plains, a year before she'd be pregnant with me—condenses in an instant the contradictions of my survival as an Africadian man in a society that still generates practically radioactive white-supremacist views—if with a gentler glare than the blazing Klieg lights always on display in the US. There's the *lumpenproletariat*, there's the *bourgeois*; there's the country, there's the citified; there's the suave, there's the hick; there's the sophisti- cated, there's the rough-hewn. These ways of being; they're all jumbled up, but pretty evenly, I think, in my character and in my poetics: Venezia— water, marble, light—all painterly, bumps up against Three Mile Plains— banjo, tobacco, rum—ant-hills and crab-apple trees and spirituals out a plain, wooden, white-painted church. Michelangelo and Portia White. To reach out to God *via* spirituals and to deal with the devil *via* blues. I titled one book, my selected poems, *Blues and Bliss*, to reflect this basic division in my own concerns, my own aesthetic: stained glass versus shit. And William Shakespeare be just "Billy" round them parts, where a genealo- gist is Skip, a principal is Herky, a social worker is Kishie, a teacher is Sock, and a buck-toothed, four-eyed nerd from the North End of Halifax, nick- named "Perfessor," turns out to be a prof-poet—or poet-prof—for real.

acknowledgements

Dr. Sonia Labatt, Ph.D., and Victoria University (*via* the E. J. Pratt Professorship at the University of Toronto), ferried me to most of the non-Toronto writing sites listed below (except for stops in Wolfville and Ottawa—*via* the Parliamentary Poet Laureateship; and Wells—*via* Island Mountain Arts):

Tropea & Cosenza (IT), June 1-26, 2017;

Toronto (ON), Gatineau-Hull (QC), Wolfville (NS), & Ottawa (ON), July 1-14, 2017;

Tropea (IT), June 2-9, 2018;

Windsor (ON), August 4-6, 2018;

Roissy-en-France (FR), August 14-21, 2018;

Toronto (ON), August 23-September 2, 2018;

Toronto (ON), Montréal (QC), Wells (BC), Carmel-by-the-Sea (CA), July 8-August 31, 2019;

Leamington (ON), November 2-9, 2020;

Toronto (ON), November 10-December 2, 2020;

Toronto (ON), January 3-15, 2021;

Toronto (ON), January 25-29, 2021;

Toronto (ON), March 1-9, 2021.

Toronto (ON), April 1-7, 2021.

Amanda Betts has edited my rambunctious prose beautifully, clarifying whatever I was in danger of allowing to remain distressingly obscure. She is the poet of *Enlightenment* and *Insight*, finding ways to de-clutter and simplify, so that what was ponderous becomes ponderable, what was heavy-handed becomes deft as pianists' fingers.

Similarly, Melanie Little probed every asterisk and double-checked every assertion, and repaired my grammar whenever and wherever gregarious style was yielding careless confusion. In case of nuclear war, it's good to know that she also possesses a copy of *11 Steps to Survival*.

I thank my agent, Denise Bukowski, for seeing that there was a grander story here than merely my picking up coloured markers on July 1, 1975; that there was something to be said about Coloured people surviving (even thriving versus) race prejudice.

My Aunt Joan (Mendes) and Uncle Sock (Johnson), my matrilineal cousins Plums Croxen and Sylvia Hamilton, my mom, Gerry, and my dad, Bill (and his cousin Reid White), at different times in my life, revealed to me otherwise indecipherable mysteries. My patrilineal cousins Nancy Oliver-Mackenzie, Chris White, Sheila White and Anthony Sherwood have permitted me glimpses of Portia White and her illustrious father, William Andrew White. Bessida White, of Virginia, is the keeper of the White Family genealogical records back to the 19th-century—and forward into the 21st. Toronto lawyer Dave Steeves located the Nova Scotian records of my Cherokee lineage through the Croxen clan. The Joshis of Halifax shared memories of meeting my mom in the 1960s and 1970s, when she welcomed them to Canada; similarly, Alexa McDonough told me about working for my mom and also how mischievous I was (so untrue!) as a boy. Elizabeth "Liz" Eneroth entrusted to me souvenirs related to her late-1950s friendship with my father. Catherine Verrall sent me a 1971 newspaper page featuring an interview with my mom, photos, and a discussion of her pedagogy. Due to that article, I learned—at 60 years old—that my mom had pioneered Montessori methodology for her own children and other North End

Halifax kids. I thank all the above for their observations, their memories, and their research.

Poignantly, Giovanna Riccio—herself an ineffable poet—has been the angel whispering superbly good sense in my ears every step of this otherwise lonesome, solo journey of recollection and reflection.

I have been granted one gigantic blessing, namely, my daughter, Aurélia, also a writer and artist (thus carrying on the White/Clarke "family business"). Moreover, her mother, Julie Morin, has been a consummate parent, just as she was so amicable a love and is now a dear friend. I can only pray that Aurélia will forgive my wrongs, as I forgive, at last, those of my parents, whom I continue to love dearly and whose passing I mourn *daily*.

GEORGE ELLIOTT CLARKE is an internationally renowned poet, novelist, playwright, screenwriter, librettist and scholar whose books have won him many honours, including the Portia White Prize, the Bellagio Center Fellowship, the Governor General's Literary Award, the Dartmouth Book Award for Fiction, the Dr. Martin Luther King Jr. Achievement Award, the Eric Hoffer Book Award for Poetry, and the Pierre Elliott Trudeau Fellowship Prize. His narrative poem *Whylah Falls* won the Archibald Lampman Award for Poetry and was chosen for CBC's inaugural Canada Reads competition. Born in Windsor, Nova Scotia, Clarke has taught at Duke and Harvard, and presently resides in Toronto where he teaches African-Canadian Literature at the University of Toronto. Clarke was appointed to the Order of Canada in 2008, and served as Canada's 7th Parliamentary Poet Laureate from 2016 to 2017.

a note about the type

The text of *Where Beauty Survived* has been set in Kepler, a contemporary Adobe Originals typeface designed by Robert Slimbach in the tradition of classic modern 18th century serifs. Named after the German astronomer Kepler, the typeface recalls the elegant and refined typefaces popular among Renaissance printers and typesetters. While Kepler has Oldstyle proportions, calligraphic detailing lends the typeface humanistic warmth and energy.